AF584393

Shame Shadows My Name

michela marzano

shame shadows my name

TRANSLATED FROM THE FRENCH BY GILA WALKER

GAZEBO BOOKS SUMMER HILL 2025

Gazebo Books
PO Box 375
Summer Hill
New South Wales 2130
Australia
gazebobooks.com.au

Originally written in French as *Mon nom est sans mémoire* by Michela Marzano

Italian edition: *Stirpe e vergogna* by Michela Marzano

First published in English translation by Gazebo Books, 2025

This edition published in agreement with Michela Marzano through MalaTesta Literary Agency, Milan.

National Library of Australia
Cataloguing-in-Publication Entry
Author: Michela Marzano
Shame Shadows My Name
ISBN: 978 0 6459209 4 9 (paperback)

Cover and interior design by Mountains Brown Press

Cover photograph supplied by the author

Printed and bound in Australia by Ligare Book Printers

To the memory of Arturo, my grandfather.
But also to my father, Ferruccio,
And my brother, Arturo.
To Jacques, who is always there, and to little Jacopo.
And last but not least, to Paola, my dear mother.

I never forget that the past is first of all a moving thing, like today, and that everything that lived lives still, changes, permutes, shifts, transforms, and that truth, like any good babbler, contradicts itself a hundred times a day.

Blaise Cendrars

PART ONE

Disgrace

To be ourselves we must have ourselves – possess, if need be re-possess, our life-stories. We must "recollect" ourselves, recollect the inner drama, the narrative, of ourselves.

Oliver Sacks

Michela Marzano does not exist. The birth certificate, passport, ID cards and marriage certificate all attest to the fact that the person born in Rome on 20 August 1970 is Maria Marzano.

'Why Maria?' In primary school, at the private school my parents sent me to, I had to fill out a form – a mere formality but something required by the education system to validate the years of schooling – and my father told me that I must sign 'Maria'. My parents always called me Michela, as did my friends and classmates. Even my teacher called me Michela. Yet here was my father telling me that my real name is Maria.

When I was born and my father went to register my birth, he had them record 'Maria' comma 'Michela' comma 'Rosa'. He had intended to have them write 'Maria Michela' comma 'Rosa' so that on all my official documents Michela would figure next to Maria, the name given to me in thanks to the Blessed Virgin, to whom my mother had prayed when she had trouble getting pregnant. Obviously, my grandmother Rosa was not thrilled to learn that her name only came third. 'I have had it with all the Rosas, Rosarias, Rosettas and Rosellas,' my father had said. So my mother suggested

Manuela and then my parents agreed on Michela since there were no Manuelas in my father's family, but there was a Michele, my grandmother's father, Dr Michele Campo.

The day my father went to register my birth, a friend persuaded him to put a comma between Maria and Michela, believing compound names cause problems. As a result, my real name, Michela, does not figure on any official document. The name that my parents chose for me, the one that everyone has always called me by, the one I use to sign my books and articles, the one that makes me turn around in the street if someone calls me. 'Michela?' I stop in my tracks, turn around and look who's calling me. 'Maria?' I don't stop, I continue on my way and don't even turn around. Maria? Who's that?

The only document in my possession that certifies that my name is not Maria, but rather Maria Michela, is my certificate of baptism. That is what I use when I need to pick up a registered letter addressed to Michela Marzano and avoid having to argue with the employee who would otherwise likely protest, 'How am I supposed to know you're Michela when your ID card says Maria? You do understand, don't you, that the letter could be for your mother or your sister, or even your daughter?'

But a certificate of baptism has no legal value.

For the state, I am Maria.

For the state, Michela Marzano does not exist.

'What about you, Papa, what's your name?'

I ended up signing Maria on the school document.

'Ferruccio, of course. Why are you asking me?'

'Is that your only given name?'

'My mother wanted to call me Michele too, after her father, and Arturo, like her husband, but on my identity papers, I'm only Ferruccio Marzano.'

Forty years later, rummaging through the drawers of my father's desk, I found a photocopy of a page from the baptism registry of Campi, the small town in the south of Puglia where my father was born.

It was in September 2019, barely three weeks since the birth of Jacopo, my brother Arturo's son, and I had come to visit my parents who lived in Rome. I felt the need to take stock of my life and asked myself many questions. What I needed mostly was information, to make up for my faulty memory. Jacopo's birth had unsettled me, and I felt disoriented. Why didn't I have a child? I had the impression that my twenty years in psychoanalysis had vanished into thin air.

I put the copy of my father's baptism certificate on my bed. After hesitating for a moment to look at it in detail, I immersed myself in the reading of this document with its beautiful antiquated handwriting:

> *The twenty-sixth day of the month of December, in the year 1936, the undersigned Gennaro D'Elia, parish priest of Santa Maria della Grazie, in Campi, baptised the child of Arturo Marzano,*

son of Ferruccio, and of Campo Rosetta, daughter of the late Michele, husband and wife from the aforementioned parish, born on the fourteenth day of the month of November of the year 1936 to whom was given the name of Ferruccio Michele Arturo Vittorio Benito. Godparents: Marzano Gino di Ferruccio and Malvani Virginia di Augusto.

Ferruccio Michele Arturo Vittorio Benito. I could not believe my eyes. My father is not simply named Ferruccio, as I had always thought. Aside from the first name of his maternal grandfather, Michele, and the name of his own father, Arturo, Papa also bore the names Vittorio, like the king at the time, Vittorio Emanuele III, and Benito, like the Duce.

At best I could have understood that my grandfather named his child Vittorio. I had always known that he was a monarchist deputy. I could not say that it pleased me, but I had come to accept it. But Benito? Something did not make sense. Why would my father also bear the name of the Duce? Monarchist does not mean fascist.

Aside from his sister, who called him Tuccio, everyone always called my father Ferruccio. Ferruccio, and only Ferruccio, is what is written on his ID card and his university diplomas. His students in economics at Sapienza University refer to him as Professor Ferruccio Marzano. Ferruccio is the name on his marriage certificate and on my birth certificate. It is Ferruccio everywhere, except on his original certificate of baptism. In an attempt to reassure myself, I took to thinking that it might be a mistake made by the priest at the time of the baptism. It crossed my mind to go to check the information in the Lecce archives, but the university courses I was teaching were about to begin so I had to get back to Paris. I would not have time during that visit.

A few weeks later, consulting the Lecce archives website, I learnt that it was possible to obtain a copy of my father's birth certificate by sending a simple email request to the director. All I had to do was specify the first and last name, the date and place of birth, and pay the document photocopy fee.

About ten days later, a copy of my father's birth certificate came directly to my inbox, with the subject line: *Protocol no. 3865 – Ferruccio Marzano.*

> *In the year nineteen thirty-six, on the sixteenth of November, at nine o'clock and thirty-five minutes, Arturo Marzano, age thirty-nine, Crown Prosecutor, presented himself before me, Guiseppe Guarino, at the Town Hall to report that in the house situated Via Vittorio Emanuele, at eleven o'clock and forty minutes, on the fourteenth of November, Rosa Maria Campo, his wife, gave birth to a child of the male sex whom he presented to me and to whom he gives the name of Ferruccio Michele Arturo Vittorio Benito.*

Ferruccio Michele Arturo Vittorio Benito. One after another, with no commas, exactly as it was written on the certificate of baptism. Ordinarily, this means that all these names should appear together in that order on official documents. According to Italian law, you cannot leave out any of your given names if they are not separated by a comma. So how was it that my father's names did not appear on his official papers?

'Indeed, that is bizarre,' my husband Jacques said to me that evening when I wondered aloud what could possibly have happened to my father's other given names. Did they disappear at the end of the war, with the end of fascism and the transition in 1946 from the monarchy to the republic? We were having supper and I was telling him about my discoveries. 'Why did I know nothing about this business of my father's names? What was he trying to hide? What is this mess all about?'

Nomen omen, the name is a sign, said the Romans, convinced that the name of every individual indicated their destiny. But then what was my father's destiny meant to be? And, by implication, my own?

The next day, I continued my research on the internet. Little by little, things became clear. Apparently, the civil registration was reorganised in 1954. If the expression used was 'he gives the name', one had to legally keep them all; but if, on the contrary, the expression used was 'he gives the names', then even if the name was composed of several names, the second, third, fourth and fifth names could be dropped. Strange as this distinction might have been, it allowed my father to have all his other given names miraculously disappear from his official papers, including the more-than-embarrassing name of Benito.

'So it wasn't a matter of lying,' Jacques remarked when I told him what I had learnt. 'A simple Italian-style mix-up,' he commented wryly. Jacques is a legal historian and, since his work focuses on the mafia, he knows Italian history well.

However, things were more complicated than he thought.

Let me start from the beginning.

I am a left-wing woman from a left-wing family. I have never doubted it. To be sure, my grandfather was a monarchist deputy in 1953, but that was out of fidelity to the king and the ideals of the *Risorgimento*. We had often spoken about it at home, especially because my father had wanted us to know why he, who had been a leftist since his youth, had distanced himself from the ideas of his own father. My father had been a socialist, a former economics advisor in the *Partito Socialista Italiano*, the PSI, until the disaster of Bettino Craxi, Mitterrand's friend, who was brought down by the *Mani pulite* scandal. And when my brother and I were children, he would teach us the songs of partisans.

To this day, I recall five-year-old Arturo singing *Bandiera rossa* on Piazza Balduina at the top of his lungs, and I can see my mother in a panic covering his mouth with her hand, 'Be quiet, my treasure, or we'll get beaten up.' Those were the Years of Lead and my mother was right to be frightened. The neighbourhood where we lived in Rome was one of the haunts of middle class, neo-fascist youth who would not have hesitated to beat the living daylights out of a 'leftist'. My path crossed theirs again a few years later at the private secondary school where my father sent us in an attempt to ensure that we would study harder. At Pio IX, I was the 'dirty communist', an outsider and a pain in the arse, with my jeans full of holes and my denunciations of their 'shitty fascist ideas'.

As for my brother, he was the kid who did not like football and who preferred playing with the girls. *Quér frocio de mmèrda!* Dirty faggot, was what some of his classmates called him in Roman dialect. What would they think now if they knew that the name of their beloved Benito figured on our father's birth certificate?

My father now claimed that he always knew that he was also called Benito, and that he never denied it. As far as I remembered, we never spoke of it at home.

But maybe I was the one whose memory was faulty.

Was it a family secret, or did I conveniently wipe it out of my memory to avoid having to come to terms with a burdensome past?

Jacopo's baptism was scheduled for the end of November in Pisa. To spend more time with him, I left Paris a day early. But I could not sleep over at my brother's because his house was too small and my parents were there from Rome. So I had to go to a hotel. I had been travelling so much all over Italy that I was fed up with this type of accommodation. I would find it cold, or my bed too small, or there would be too much noise, or the shutters would not close well and the sunlight would flood the room at six in the morning, and so on and so forth. In short, no matter how much melatonin and anxiolytics I took, I could not sleep well at night. But it doesn't matter, I said to myself when I arrived at the hotel. I won't be staying long. I put down my valise and hurried over to Arturo's. Who knows how much Jacopo has grown since last I saw him. The first time I took him in my arms and whispered in his ear, 'My love,' I bit my lip and corrected myself right away. 'What a love! He's so beautiful!' I clenched my fists tightly. No one noticed a thing.

I said a quick hello to my parents, washed my hands and tied my hair up. I had barely the time to take Jacopo into my arms when I heard my father protesting, 'Be careful with his head, I beg you!'

I ignored him.

Then I heard my father saying, 'The little one is crying, Arturo. You take him.'

I ignored him again.

Then my father turned to my mother, and said, 'Michela doesn't know how to handle him. Don't just stand there, do something!'

I could no longer ignore him. I felt myself suddenly thrust back in time to my adolescence when I was studying for the entrance exam to the Scuola Normale Superiore in Pisa and overheard my father one night, as I was about to go to bed, whispering to my mother, 'Okay, so she works hard, but she won't make it. She doesn't have what it takes; the others are brighter than she is.'

That night, when I got back to the hotel, I was still agitated and anxious. I took three-quarters of an anxiolytic, telephoned Jacques and complained to him for at least an hour. But it did no good. In spite of the pill and the more or less comforting words from Jacques, who had a hard time understanding what I was reproaching my father for, I simply could not calm myself down.

I fell asleep, but I kept waking up. And then I had a nightmare that prevented me from getting back to sleep at all. I am on a train and I get off, thinking I have arrived at my destination, but on the platform I realise that I am at the wrong station. I don't understand what could possibly have happened since I don't usually make mistakes like that. I lose my bearings and, after standing for a while without budging, I start walking in the station looking for directions. I don't know where I am. I don't even know anymore where I want to go. It's nighttime and there's no one in the station whom I can ask. All of a sudden, as I'm wandering through an underpass, I realise that they are announcing the train that I should be taking on platform number 8. I reach the stairs. I climb them four at a time. I trip. I get up. I fall again. And when I finally arrive at the platform, it is too late. The doors of the cars are closing, and even if I would run, run, run, the train has started and is leaving the station.

I woke up with a jolt, drenched in sweat. I could still see the image of the train disappearing on the horizon, but I already knew that it was not just a train that I had missed.

I was fifty and I was in the early stages of menopause. I was irritable, I slept little, and I suffered from hot flashes. And then there was the nearly constant fatigue, which was trying and sometimes intense. It is due to a lack of oestrogen, my gynaecologist explained to me. But I couldn't care less about her medical explanations or her replacement therapy. The problem was not weight gain or headaches or vaginal discomfort. My problem was that now it was 'too late'.

My unconscious mind was bursting at the seams. My analyst always used to tell me so when, a few years back, I would arrive in his office each week, stretch out on the couch and tell him a dream. Rare were the instances when I had to ask for his help to understand the meaning of a nightmare. My unconscious has always been an open book. So it was not hard to see that the train that was leaving the platform and disappearing into the night was a symbol for what I would never have. If I were writing fiction, I might be accused of using a trite, overly explicit image, and advised to make an effort to find a better image of loss. But this is not fiction and there's the rub! The nightmare that I had the night before Jacopo's baptism was of a train departing and leaving me behind, like my life.

Never in my childhood or adolescence had I imagined my future without a child. It went without saying that I too would become a mother. Like all my girlfriends. How could it be otherwise? At the time, there was school, of course, whole afternoons spent absorbed in books. The teacher would soon see that I was the best. All I had to do was work hard, not waste my time on clothes and the other trivialities that my mother would talk to me about – I'm not like her, Papa, I swear, I won't disappoint you, I promise. Later, there were the graduate school years at Scuola Normale Superiore in Pisa, with one exam after another until my doctorate. Then my twenty years in psychoanalysis – do you think that in the end I too will have a family, that I too will be a mother? I never stopped believing I would. All I had to do was be patient. And not rush things.

When I was little, I would often wake up screaming. It was always the same nightmare. My father was there. I was there. We were arguing. And each time I woke up screaming, 'No.' All the 'nos' that I did not succeed in saying to him during the day because my father was unmovable. He would insist and insist and insist until finally, powerless, I would say, 'Okay, you're right.' My father was the starting and end point of any discussion. It was pointless to try to contradict him. Even when he was wrong, he always had to be right. It took me twenty years of analysis to understand that things would never change and that it was up to me to stop looking for his approval, but also to tell him that he was right when he was wrong.

Two distinct lives. Separate. If I wanted to grow up and stop struggling like a fly caught in a jar, I had to mourn everything that I had waited in vain to receive from my father. I had to move on.

And so why hadn't I ignored him that afternoon? Why, when I heard him say, 'Michela doesn't know how to handle him,' did I feel boundless anger mounting inside me? And why could I no longer get back to sleep? Who had caught me once again and trapped me in a jar?

I never stopped believing that I too would be a mother.

All I had to do was be patient. And not rush things.

Before things began to rush all by themselves.

'Why Benito?' I asked my father. Instead of going straight back to Paris, I decided to accompany my parents to Rome and try to gain an understanding of this name business. 'Was it a mere fad in the 1930s? A tribute to the dictator?'

'Your grandfather was a fascist,' he replied calmly, as if it were a subject that we had discussed several times.

'Are you joking?'

'He joined the *Fasci* a few months after the end of the First World War.'

It took a few moments before I could speak again.

'And how long have you known this? I thought that grandfather was a monarchist. You never told us he was a fascist.'

My father had heard his father admit to having once been a fascist, during my grandfather's 1953 election campaign when he was running for office on the list of the Monarchist National Party. At one of his first rallies, in the Salento, some ardent monarchists attacked him vehemently, saying, 'You're not a real monarchist, Marzano!' They booed him, claiming that he was still loyal to the Duce, and shouted that he really did not care about the future of the House of Savoy. And it seems that my grandfather replied that when he returned from the front in 1919, he had been one of the early followers of Mussolini. That much was true. But a few years later, once he had become a magistrate, he had not renewed his membership in the Fascist Party. He had pledged allegiance to the king, and ever since, he had remained loyal to him.

I was flabbergasted. It was the first time that my father and I had broached the subject of my grandfather's fascism. Until then, all I had ever heard was the family legend, that he had been a monarchist, and that was that. I found myself even feeling a little guilty that I had not been more curious.

'Did he participate in the rally at the Piazza San Sepolcro in Milan on 23 March 1919, when Mussolini founded the *Fasci*?'

'Yes, I believe he was there,' my father replied laconically. 'In any case, the name of the *piazza* rings a bell,' he added, getting up. 'But what's the difference? That was back in 1919 and, as I said, your grandfather became a magistrate and he never renewed his party membership. He said so himself in 1953.'

'But that was at an election campaign rally! He was lying...'

'No, I don't think so. Why would you say that?'

'How could he have had a career as a magistrate without a Fascist Party membership card?'

'After he pledged allegiance to the king, he never renewed his membership in the National Fascist Party. That's all there is to it,' my father repeated, sounding more and more bizarre. He did not even seem to realise the implications of the fact that his father had been one of the first in Italy to espouse Mussolini's ideas!

'You do know that there were scarcely three hundred people with Mussolini at Piazza San Sepolcro that day on 23 March 1919. Three hundred jerks, Papa! Losers and misfits. Who was fascist in 1919? Hardly anyone in Italy aside from those few lost souls. Did you ever ask him for an explanation?'

My father said that he did not recall. He admitted that there were things that perhaps he never knew. He added that, at any rate, he never asked his father when exactly he joined the party. Listening to him made me think of the story of a Sicilian who, questioned by the police about an assault that took place right in front of the window of his store, told them, 'I wasn't there, and if I was there I didn't see anything, and if I saw something I don't remember.' It was a story that my father used to repeat to my brother and me again and again when we were little, a story that had enchanted us so much that it had become a constant refrain whenever something bad happened and Papa asked us who broke the vase or who spilt the bucket of water or who drew on the wall. And our answer was always, 'I wasn't there, and if I was there I didn't see anything, and if I saw something I don't remember.'

'Can you believe he never asked him a thing?' I felt the need to vent on the phone to my husband in Paris, even though he thought that writing a book about my father and my father's father was not a good idea. He did not understand exactly what I was looking to prove or to understand. 'Does it seem likely to you that my father let things go like that? Okay, I get that he was only sixteen when he attended the electoral rally where his father was accused of not being a true monarchist. But a sixteen-year-old would ask himself questions, wouldn't he? Especially if he has just learnt that his father was a fascist!'

'Right after the war was over, people seldom spoke about fascism, at least not for a few years,' Jacques commented. 'Those were the days of the Cold War.' According to Jacques, 'the defascisation of the administration and the judicial system never took place in Italy.' Fascism was not a subject of study in schools in the 1950s, and neither was it talked about in newspapers. The fear of communism was the foremost concern at the time, especially in the upper class and aristocratic circles in which my father moved, whereas Italy's belligerent recent past was repressed. 'If you do not learn to contextualise events,' Jacques warned me, 'you will find yourself making anachronistic judgements based on the moral standards of our time.'

'And what about later,' I asked him. 'Why didn't my father try later to understand how his own father could be a member of the Fascist Party?' I just can't get over it. 'A fascist from the very first hour…'

In my family's home in Campi, there was a glass case full of military medals, ribbons and stripes. I had not given it any thought for many years. I was even surprised that this memory was still alive, hidden and buried in the recesses of my mind. I used to see the case when I was a child and we would spend our summer holidays in this former convent where my father was born and grew up, the home of my grandparents, my great-grandparents and their forebears since the eighteenth century. I saw it every time my brother and I played hide and seek and I would go hide out in one of the sitting rooms – there were several of them, one after another, all in a row, with their high vaulted ceilings decorated with frescos. The glass case was hanging on a wall opposite the piano in the 'red sitting room' where family photos were also displayed.

The image came back to me and I wondered what could have become of the case. I hoped that it had not been lost when the house was emptied.

We used to go there every summer until 1977. After my grandmother died and the house was shared by both my father and his sister, we started to go less often. Eventually we stopped going to Campi at all.

Over the years, the house fell into disrepair. Then it was devastated by a fire. Some of the furniture, frames, rugs and vases were stolen. Other objects, including the books and family papers, were stored by my father in the cellar of his cousins' neighbouring home. Memory reduced to bits and pieces.

'Do you recall grandfather's military decorations?' I asked my father, who nodded. 'Any idea where they are?'

'No, I'm sorry, I haven't the slightest idea.'

'Well, let's look for them!'

No reaction.

'C'mon,' I insisted. 'I'm sure they're here in Rome somewhere in the house.'

My father sighed. He had no desire to go looking for those medals. But in the end he got out of his chair in the dining room and headed to his office. 'The display case must be here.' He opened the door of a cabinet, rummaged through his desk drawers, and lifted the cover of a chest. Nothing. Among the dozens and dozens of boxes filled with papers and odds and ends, he found nothing of interest, let alone the case with my grandfather's medals.

My mother stepped into the office and was taken aback by the disorder. When I explained to her that we were looking for grandfather's military decorations, she suggested that we check the cupboard in the hallway.

I took out the stepladder.

'Take care not to fall!' my father exclaimed as I climbed up. 'And be especially careful not to break anything!'

When I got to the top and opened the cupboard, I felt a wave of discouragement. There were so many belongings that I could not see a thing. I moved aside two porcelain vases and three coats. I took out a bag filled with old sheets. Then, finally, I saw the case, up against the wall, covered in cardboard and wrapped in silk paper. There it was. The display with my grandfather's military decorations. It was exactly where my mother told me to look.

I climbed down the stepladder, careful not to slip, went back to the dining room, put the case on the table, took off the cardboard, removed the silk paper and began to take a close look.

In actual fact, it was more of a glass frame than a display case. Instead of a picture, there was a base covered in a ruby-coloured fabric on which the medals, military buttons, ribbons and papers, and even a watch, had been sewn. It was an odd grouping. I looked fixedly at the medals in the lower part of the frame, then I shifted my gaze upward and to the left, where I saw a card, it too sewn on both sides to the fabric.

The room spun for a moment. *Squadrista*! The *squadristi* were the worst henchmen of fascism. I found myself gasping for air. Even though these words later seemed so trite to me that I wanted to erase them. Had I nothing better to say? I thought, annoyed at myself. What else could I say to describe that feeling of being sure you know something and, at the same time, not believing it, because you don't want to? No, it can't be true, it's not possible… My grandfather was a refined man, a cultivated jurist; he couldn't possibly have been a *squadrista*, one of those thugs who beat up communists with their truncheons, the *manganello*, and forced castor oil down the throats of adversaries of the regime! Fascist and *squadrista*! That was a lot to take in. I felt nauseous and about to vomit, but I swallowed my saliva. What has nausea to do with all this?

I asked my father permission to cut the thread holding the card to the material, surprised by the calmness with which I spoke. I asked my mother for scissors, even though, by then, my voice began to quiver. As did my hand when I cut the string, and my gaze when I looked at the document. Even my gaze trembled, as if my vision were blurry. I had to blink two or three times before I could see clearly again.

Now I could read!

The card bears the number 3722752, issued by the political secretary of the Fascio di Combattimento, the Fighting Band of Lecce, the 'Pasquale Leone' district group, with permission to renew National Fascist Party membership in 1942.

On the first page is information about my grandfather's military and fascist past:

Sansepolcrista = *no*; Squadrista = *yes*; March on Rome = *yes (licence no. 108702)*; 'Sciarpa littorio' = *yes*; Military decorations = *bronze medal (1917)*; War injuries and mutilations = *yes*.

On the second page, there is an identity photo of my grandfather. This photo is unlike any other I have of him. He is unrecognisable, with his furrowed eyes, a stern look, hardened features and clenched jaw.

There is the oath of allegiance to Mussolini:

In the name of God and Italy, I swear to follow the orders of Il Duce and to serve the cause of the Fascist revolution with all my might and, if necessary, with my blood.

And my grandfather's signature:

THE FASCIST *Arturo Marzano.*

I showed my father the card, pointing to THE FASCIST *Arturo Marzano.* I asked him if it made him feel as ill at ease as I was feeling, although I must say that the expression 'ill at ease' hardly conveyed – to say the least – my state of mind at that precise point in time. I was feeling devastated and furious at once. And betrayed. So my background was false from beginning to end. I grew up with the conviction of belonging to a leftist family, one of those families that transmit the noble values of equality and justice, the socialist international and the defence of the poor. Now what was left of this background?

'Doesn't this make you feel ill at ease, Papa?'

My father did not respond. Then after a long silence, he simply remarked: 'When you are finished, please put everything back in its place.' Then, 'Be careful with the cardboard, or you'll damage the medals!' And finally, 'I'm going back to my office, I still have a lot of work to do.'

'He's hiding,' my mother commented when we found ourselves alone. 'Your father never wanted to face reality. That's how it's been since I've known him.'

I paid her no heed, I wasn't even looking at her.

'What are these crosses on the left hand side?' she asked me, finally realising that it was not the right time to dwell on such matters. 'Why is the ribbon triangular and not rectangular?'

At first glance, I had not paid attention to this detail. But when I looked at it more closely, I realised that, among the military decorations sewn to the red fabric of the frame, some were Austrian or German. There was a cross with the words *vitam et sanguimen* (with life and blood) and a yellow ribbon with black stripes; a cross in commemoration of the First Balkan War in 1912 and a silver medal with the effigy of Charles I of Habsburg. What were these medals doing among my grandfather's military decorations? My first thought was that they were all related to the First World War. But again I was mistaken. Aside from the bronze medal for military valour and the cross of the 3rd Army of the Duke of Aosta, there was also a medal of the Order of the Crown and a bronze medal for the March on Rome.

'And this? What's this?' my mother asked. We both remained silent for a few moments. 'Could it be a member of Parliament card? It looks like yours, doesn't it?'

I removed it easily from its place. No need for scissors this time:

We hereby certify that the Onorevole Arturo Marzano, son of Ferruccio and of Giulia Ragusa, born in Botrugno on the 1st of January 1897, is Deputy in Parliament, card no. 590, Rome, 1st of July 1953.

My grandfather and I finally shared something, albeit sixty years apart. I too was a deputy, '*Onorevole*', although I, of course, was elected as a member of the Democratic Party and hence I was seated well on the left of the hemicycle in the Chamber of Deputies.

But right then, what we did or did not share was not the issue. The issue was of a different order entirely. My grandfather's MP card was sewn to the frame alongside his medals and his Fascist Party card, as if pride and disgrace, the card of a deputy, an elected representative, and that of a fascist and a *squadrista* were all of a piece. The sacred and the profane cut from the same cloth.

Who made this shrine to war and fascism? Who dared to place side by side the card of the Fascist Party and that of an elected representative of the republic?

For years, I had told myself that I had to come to terms with my grandfather's monarchist past. After all, monarchism seemed laughable but not scary. All the more since we used to make fun of the House of Savoy at home.

There once was a king, sitting on the sofa, who said to his maid: Tell me a story. And the maid began: There once was a king, sitting on the sofa, who said to his maid: Tell me a story. And the maid began... This was the king that I heard about when I was little: the king in the nursery rhyme that our mother recited to us. The other one was nothing but '*quel figlio di troia di nome Umberto, cognomen Savoia*', 'that son of a whore whose first name is Umberto and last name is Savoia', as my brother and I used to sing when we were children to the tune of a 1946 hymn; *vive Turai, vive Nenni*, as the socialists used to say during the referendum campaign for the Republic and against the monarchy. It was our father who taught it to us, and I was so very proud of him.

But who was my grandfather, really? And how about my father? What did he make of all this? And what about me? How was it that for fifty years I thought that fascists were always the others?

The fascists were the ones who now attacked me most virulently on social networks. The nostalgic admirers of the Duce, the true fascists, those with the Celtic cross or the Roman Eagle on their profiles along with posts by Giorgia Meloni or Matteo Salvini on the first page, those who called me a 'communist whore' and who wrote, 'SHAME! Aren't you ashamed to post a photo of the nativity scene on Christmas after having worked to destroy the family when you were in Parliament and defended marriage for all?' 'Aren't you ashamed to call yourself a believer after defending same-sex families and surrogate motherhood?' '*Onorevole*? Give me a break! You're nothing but a slut!'

This was perhaps the first time that I truly understood the meaning of the expression 'irony of history'.

My father was always calling me '*Onorevole*' in front of Promezio, the Filipino who had been doing the housework at my parents' home for several years. I had asked him several times not to do so. I had asked him to stop when I was still a deputy. 'It makes no sense, Papa', I told him, 'it's inappropriate. Why would you call me *Onorevole*?' It made even less sense after I decided to leave politics and return to what I was doing before. I don't introduce myself as a university professor either, even though that is what I do. I say Michela. Michela, that is all, and that is enough! You want to call me by my first name? That's fine with me.

I was so embarrassed when I was little and my father always found a way to slip his title of university professor into any conversation. It was still a prestigious title in Italy, but he would use it even when it made no sense.

Once we were on holiday in Alto Adige and my father wanted to take us on a trip to Austria. But the officer at the border told him that his ID card had expired and that he could not let us through. My father was astonished.

'But I'm a professor of political economics at La Sapienza in Rome!' he declared with pride.

What does that have to do with anything? I thought. Why does he keep embarrassing us like that?

The officer, unmoved, immediately replied, 'I understand, Sir, but I still cannot let you through.'

'It's a generational thing,' Jacques remarked when I told him the story. Back in the day, people were very attached to titles. But I wondered whether it was merely a generational thing for my father.

My mother had managed to convince my father to make an appointment to see a cardiologist. 'Just for a check-up, Ferruccio, you're over eighty now and it would be a good idea to do some tests, don't you think?' He dragged his feet, but gave in in the end. Before examining him, the doctor asked him his name.

'Excuse me, did you say Marzano? Like Michela Marzano?'

'Yes, she's my daughter!' my mother replied promptly. 'Do you know her?'

'I read everything she writes.'

My mother was very moved. Yes, Michela was her beloved daughter. My father, on the other hand, remained silent for a few moments. Then, looking somewhat irritated, he exclaimed: 'I write too! I'm a university professor.'

Joined the National Fascist Party (PNF) on: *15/5/1919*

In Rome, before putting the glass display with my grandfather's medals back in its place, I took pictures with my cell phone of his Fascist Party card. When I got back to Paris, I printed the photos and put them in the file where I kept newspaper articles, documents, rough drafts and notes.

I gave it considerable thought and finally decided to write this book on the story of my grandfather and my family. It was the only way to really come to terms with my past, to fit the pieces of my life puzzle together. And yet for around ten days, I would come home from the university, open the folder and just sit there without writing a thing, my eyes glued to the photos and my notes. I kept coming back to the date, 15 May 1919, the date my grandfather joined the Fascist Party. What could have led him to make this decision?

The day was about six months after the end of the war, and exactly fifty four days since Mussolini had founded his party in Milan. Driven by deep hatred toward the government and Bolshevism, Mussolini was intent on not letting the atmosphere of the war years dissipate. But when, on 23 March 1919, in a gathering in the meeting room of the Industrial and Commercial Alliance on Piazza San Sepolcro, he founded his movement, there were only a handful of people present. I could see him shout from the podium, 'We are against governmental imbecility!' As he had written in *Il Popolo d'Italia*, the newspaper he founded and headed, he went on, 'We are for the spiritual and material elevation of the Italians.'

In the course of the spring of 1919, the Italian liberal government was indeed having great difficulty containing the growing discontent of veterans of the war and meeting the expectations of the middle class, but nothing happened as Mussolini thought it would. He was convinced that he had a clear path forward, yet his party was still having a hard time gaining traction. And by 21 December 1919, in all of Italy, there were no more than 870 members, among whom was my grandfather.

Joined the PNF on: *15/5/1919*

What was he doing among that gang of desperados who supported Mussolini from the very start? I cannot stop thinking about it. What could possibly have been going through his mind? Was my grandfather rebelling against someone by joining the Fascist Party? Could anyone who was not driven by anger have let himself be blinded by the Duce's totally unhinged speeches? There was the war to consider, and the consequences and what he had lived through. But then why, out of all the war veterans, was he one of the few to become a fascist right away? Was it out of a need for social redemption? Unacknowledged contempt for his origins? A desire to lash out? Dissatisfaction? Ambition? Revenge?

I could not make up my mind and this kept me from writing. Every night, I would turn on my computer, open the file 'my story', reread what I had written, change a comma here or there, a word, an expression. Then I would look at the photos of my grandfather's Fascist Party card again and at the date that he joined the party, and I was blocked.

I did not know how to answer the questions that now plagued me. There were no letters, no photos, no diary. I had absolutely nothing. And nobody to help me out. Time seemed to have erased the slightest trace of that period. Hard as it was for me to imagine that my father had not sought answers, I had to resign myself to the idea. And although I persisted in opening the file again and again, I could not write another word.

'Invent,' Jacques told me. 'Imagine, create, tell a story.'

'It's not a novel. It's my story, the story of my family. What interests me is the truth.'

'But aren't you always maintaining that there is a huge gap between historical truth and personal truth?'

For some months, two or three years ago, I was considering writing a novel inspired by the life of Simone Touseau, the 'Shaved Woman of Chartres'. When her head was shaved on 16 August 1944, Simone was only twenty-three years old. The famous photo taken by

Robert Capa shows her with her daughter Catherine in her arms, surrounded by a crowd of men, women and children laughing, yelling and throwing rocks at her. Who was this woman, really? What became of her daughter?

I saw myself telling the story of how Simone let herself waste away little by little, between alcoholism and depression, denying until the bitter end the accusations against her. Yes, she had been the mistress of Erich Gös, the father of her daughter. Yes, she had deeply loved a German. But she was not the one who denounced her neighbours, as she had been accused of doing. I would have liked to persuade Catherine, Simone's daughter, to speak in the first person. She had decided one day to turn the page, to start all over again and never – so it seems – to tell her children the story of her mother.

I had begun the research. I had gone to the archives and even taken notes. Then, from one day to the next, I stopped everything. I realised that I did not have the right to tell this story. Even if I changed the names, in writing my own story, I would have wronged Simone and her daughter – any writer knows that in a novel you are always settling accounts with yourself. You find yourself confronting your own ghosts, projecting your own anxieties and shame. What right do we have to draw inspiration from the life of someone who was no longer there and could not give her own version of the facts and defend, if need be, her honour?

But then what right did I have to tell my grandfather's story? Where is his version of the facts? Who could defend his memory and clear his honour if his own granddaughter was sullying it and betraying him? What was I thinking when I started writing the first pages of this book? Did I think I could tell my grandfather's past in an objective way? Putting together the pieces of the puzzle as I found them and perhaps falsifying some of them according to the needs of the story – because when you write a novel, everything is permissible, isn't it? No, that was not what I wanted. Nobody had given me permission to do it. Could I give myself permission? Or did I naively think that the truth would emerge on its own, and that all I would have to do is organise the material in my possession. What exactly was I thinking?

`Joined the PNF on:` *15/5/1919*

My grandfather was one of the first to become a fascist.

15 May 1919, stamped on his Fascist Party card is proof positive of his guilt. As far as my grandfather was concerned, I could not use the excuses that many resorted to in Italy to justify the fascist past of their grandparents or uncles. At some point, they claimed, nearly everyone was obliged to become fascist, like it or not; but many of them were good people who did not subscribe at all to what Mussolini said and did; only a few violent enthusiasts were 'real', even rabid fascists, whereas the others merely conformed and adapted to the situation. And then they argued that it was never like in Germany, that you couldn't compare fascism with Nazism.

As far as my grandfather was concerned, these excuses didn't work. He was not among the mass of Italians who became fascist little by little, following others or conforming to the spirit of the times. And, even if he had been, what kind of excuses were those? Italians exonerate themselves all too readily. And in so doing they forget the resistance fighters and all those who opposed the regime and were sent into exile or imprisoned, killed or definitively crushed.

My grandfather must have been a monster.

'Monster' was the word I found when I browsed through the notes I had taken in recent months. I wrote it in red on the printed copy of the photos of his Fascist Party card. I wrote it in capital letters on the photocopy of the minutes of a parliamentary session dated 26 November 1953, when my grandfather took the floor and described the emergency laws against fascism as 'aberrant'. I wrote it in pencil several times on the pages where, by the column detailing the chronology of fascism, year after year, month after month, I noted the milestones of my grandfather's career, his promotions in the judiciary and his Order of the Crown decorations.

My grandfather must have been a monster.

But was that really what I was looking to demonstrate? When I began writing, didn't I want to take stock of my life, gain a better understanding of my father's violence and anxieties, bring his truth to light, and thereby reveal something of my own? To come to understand the pain that had gripped me since my childhood, even though every attempt I made to define its contours seem destined to fail. What obstacle were the words coming up against? What did I really know of my father and his relationship with his own father? What did I really know about the history of my family?

I knew practically nothing about my grandfather's childhood, other than the fact that he was born on 1 January 1897, in the small town of Botrugno, located in the province of Lecce, and that his father was a schoolteacher.

When I was little and my father would speak about his father's parents, he was always vague. He did not seem to be very proud of them. He preferred speaking of his mother's aristocratic background. It seemed that Ferruccio – my father's grandfather, after whom my father was named, was a self-centred, authoritarian man. When he grew old, he was abominable with his daughter Ines, my father said. Having never married, she had always lived with him, but he was never satisfied. Nothing she did was right. It seemed that he treated his youngest girl like a servant.

'And what about your grandmother? What was Giulia like?'

Over the Christmas holidays, Jacques and I went to Rome to spend a few days at my parents' and I tried to gather all the information I could.

'She died young, in 1923, more than ten years before I was born. I think that your grandfather was very close to her but no one spoke of Giulia in my home. Apparently, she was a self-effacing woman, completely subservient to her husband.'

I looked at the photo, the one hanging on the wall opposite my father's desk. My grandfather Arturo is little, maybe two or three months old. He is in his mother's arms and he looks like he is sulking. Giulia, who is seated on a wooden chair, her soft, dark hair gathered on the nape of her neck, is not smiling: her face is tense, her eyes sad, she looks preoccupied. She is wearing a small black lace cape over a light-coloured, floor-length dress with puffy sleeves. She has a ring on her left little finger and pearl earrings. Her husband standing behind her is towering over her, one hand on the back of the chair, the other holding a wooden staff. He is wearing a dark double-breasted jacket and a white shirt; his eyes are slightly narrowed and he has a long, curly moustache, in the style of King Vittorio Emanuele III.

'Why is it that no one is smiling in this photo, Papa?' My father too never smiled for photos. He simply could not do so. Even when I would try to take a picture of him with my cell phone and would call out encouragingly, but in vain, 'C'mon, Papa! Smile!'

When I got back to Paris, I felt discouraged. I began to think that I would never end up writing this book.

Then, one day, I recalled a frame full of photos of my grandfather that I had brought back with me to France a few years before. I was not quite sure why. In the apartment I used to live in, it was hanging on the wall of my office. But where was it now?

There was a box I had not opened yet, even though a whole year had gone by since my last move. That day, I finally decided to open it up. I took a pair of scissors, cut the cord, removed the lid and rummaged through it. And there was the frame with the photos of my grandfather at the bottom of the box. I had never bothered to look at it in detail. What a mistake! Every picture was annotated on the back with a wealth of information: dates, places, contexts, reasons. In this frame, I found practically all of my grandfather's history.

The first photo I concentrated on was taken in 1917. My grandfather was in uniform and had just turned twenty. *30 March, Piazza Maggiore, Bologna, waiting to be sent to the northwest front* is written by hand on the back.

Arturo is posing in an officer's uniform, his right hand on his hip; the left, along his side, is partly covered by a long woollen coat. The picture was most probably taken by his mother, I said to myself, and the image of Giulia appeared before my eyes as if my great-grandmother was right there in front of me.

Giulia simply does not understand how they can send such young men to the front, so far from their home, without any real military training. How will Arturo cope with the cold in the north, the snow and the frost? She is perfectly aware that the temperature in the mountains can dip down to minus fourteen or fifteen centigrade; the mothers of the boys who already left have told her so. In the letters they receive from the front, their sons write them about the bread that reaches them already frozen and that can't even be sliced with a knife.

Giulia is worried, but she says nothing about it to her husband. Ferruccio reads the paper every day and relentlessly rails against all those who insist on criticising the war. 'They should be ashamed of themselves! Where is their love of the Fatherland and their spirit of sacrifice? These are dark times!' And while he rants, Giulia asks herself, why is it, if he is so intent on defending the Fatherland, that he hasn't gone to the front himself? And what's with all this shouting all the time? He's going to wake up Gino!

She is in the kitchen kneading the flour and water together to make *orecchiette*, after already having prepared the sauce. Fortunately, the hail did not destroy the tomatoes in the garden this year. She thinks back again to the day Arturo left. He was so proud to serve his country and to do his duty.

'You'll see, my dear mother, that I'll lead my soldiers to victory, not to death,' he had told her right before leaving home. 'I will live up to our name, you can be sure of that!'

My great-grandmother recalls her son's last words and her eyes fill up with tears.

I was reminded of the medal of military valour that I saw in the glass display in my parents' home. I decided to send an email to a friend who is a World War I specialist and ask him where I could find information about this type of military decoration. He advised me to take a look at the official notices of nominations and promotions from 1922, which was, according to him, the year that many distinctions were attributed.

'If your grandfather was decorated for the 1914-1918 war, you should look for his name in a royal decree from that year. I'll send you a link to the site of the *Gazzetta Ufficiale del Regno d'Italia*. All the issues published between 1860 and 1946 have been digitised. You can consult them online.'

Armed with this information, it was very easy for me to find the royal decree dated 11 May 1922, and, in it, the section with the list of military decorations. On page 1086, next to my grandfather's name, I read that, in the summer of 1917, he was a second lieutenant in the 154th regiment of the infantry. He took part in the great battle of the Bainsizza, on the Karst Plateau. Between 20 and 24 August, commanding a group of riflemen and braving the danger, he went 'to different detachments, positioned at varying distances from each other, to encourage them and then lead them with fervour in an attack on the enemy's positions'.

I learnt that Luigi Cadorna, then Chief of Staff of the Italian Army, had been unyielding. The deteriorated physical condition of the troops and the low morale of the soldiers did not stop him from carrying out a great many senseless attacks on the Austro-Hungarian lines.

This he did on the Isonzo and on the Karst to gain a few meters of ground, that would be lost a short time later. And he did so again and again, like General Nivelle at the Chemin des Dames. Cadorna was set on advancing at any cost. Despite the growing number of the dead, the wounded, the missing, our soldiers were expected to mount their assaults and break though the lines on the Karst. They were expected to 'back the enemy up against a wall', as he put it at the time. They had to achieve victory no matter the cost. And Cadorna had wagered everything on the Bainsizza battle.

I turned my attention to the letters from the front, the postcards sent from military hospitals, journals kept in the trenches. I took notes nonstop, copying down whole passages of the letters in my notebooks, word for word, without even correcting the mistakes, because these mistakes too revealed something about the period, the need that everyone had to leave a trace of their despair or their fear, their courage or their desire to win this war at last. 'Mother dear,' writes Amerigo, 'the enemy tried to surprise us with barbaric means, using asphyxiating gas that turns our clothes and buttons green and stops our watches.' And Flavio writes to his sister, 'I dreamt when I was sleeping and was sad when I woke up, cause before my eyes was a scene of sacrifice.' And Francesco writes to his mother, 'Precious Mama, ask with Papa for a mass and prey that God protects me and my comrades for this day in hell and courage if we go against the barbaric enemee and I hope to have a glorius victory.'

And then there were all the mothers and wives, eyes filled with anguish, faces pale with fright, who, in the absence of letters or postcards, rushed trembling from branch to sub-branch of the offices whose job it was in each city to provide news to the families of soldiers. 'What do you mean, no news? Is he dead?' Each woman wants to understand what could have happened to her son or husband. The people working in the offices would try to reassure them: 'Signora, if he were dead, we would have been informed by the army chaplain. Don't get yourself all worked up!' 'Could he be wounded?' 'No, you needn't worry about that either. A record is kept of all those who enter or leave the hospitals.' Gida Rossi, Inspector General of the Central Office of Information for Families, writes in her memoirs about the coloured cards that were distributed to the different branches that allowed the staff to see at a glance the fate of the soldiers: dead, wounded, discharged from the hospital, missing. The employees would go through the lists: last name, first name, age, class, district… and their hearts sank at the sight of the grey cards trimmed with black – the colour of the dead. How could they give a mother the news of her son's death?

On 17 August, at six in the morning, the 3,750 Italian cannons concentrated in the Bainsizza opened fire. The soldiers of the 154th infantry regiment, taking advantage of the dam built on the Isonzo near Caporetto, took up their position to launch a vast offensive against the enemy.

I could see the scene unfolding before my eyes as if I were watching a movie. My grandfather was driven by a strong sense of pride and glory. He wanted to fight for the Fatherland. But he was also aware of the rising anxiety in the trenches, for that morning, everyone knew, would be the last attack. This was what many of them were hoping and repeating to themselves. Never mind the dreadful humidity that rose from the river at night and penetrated into their bones; never mind the rats and lice infesting the trenches and the ever-dwindling provisions. The soldiers were all worked up. All they would need is a crust of bread and a glass of wine to alleviate the nausea.

At dawn on 19 August, the shelling stopped and the infantry launched the offensive. The soldiers of the 154th infantry regiment reached the devastated village of Selo and the first line to the west of Castagnevizza. The enemy hesitated and then responded with artillery and machine gun fire. Very quickly, the situation deteriorated.

I heard my grandfather's voice. I almost felt as if I was by his side. 'Cover your faces!' he shouted. 'Your eyes, soldiers! Protect your eyes, they are shelling with gas.' My grandfather rushed from one detachment to the next, running, encouraging his comrades-in-arms, exhorting them not to yield. 'It's a matter of honour, soldiers! The day will come when we tell our children about this. Just think of the pride with which we will speak to our offspring about the Carso and the Piave!'

I was by my grandfather's side. I felt his fear but also his fervour and his desire to succeed, to put an end to this war as quickly as possible, to achieve victory and return to his home in Puglia to tell his own father, 'I did it. I succeeded. You can be proud of me at last!'

At that point, I had the feeling of a déjà vu. Was it my grandfather who sought his father's approval or was it my own father who, as a child, sought to make his father, Lieutenant Arturo, proud of him? Or was I the one who was still hoping to gain my father's recognition, and who was projecting my own fantasies on this goddamn battle?

At noon, on 20 August, the Italians tried desperately to hold onto the positions they conquered the day before. At 3 pm, they launched a new attack. For three consecutive days and nights, the soldiers struggled to advance through the tangles of barbed wire, the levelled trenches, the collapsed caves that had become graves, the demolished houses, the scattered weapons and munitions. But the enemy put up resistance just about everywhere. The Italian soldiers worked in vain to clear a path amid the cannons shooting in all directions, mortar and rifle fire, and the thousands and thousands of corpses abandoned on the battlefield. Finally, the front gave way.

The Eleventh Battle of the Isonzo, despite the capture of the Bainsizza Plateau, ended in a crushing defeat. The cost for Italy was 144,000 dead, wounded or missing. In less than a week!

In the course of just a few days, 17,000 dispatches reached the central office in Bologna dedicated to providing information to the families of soldiers, dispatches to be expedited throughout Italy, along with 1,222 telegrams sent by the mothers and wives of soldiers. The volunteers were swamped by it all. Some kept on working with heavy hearts, while others, who had lost a son or a husband, abandoned their post. Some clenched their teeth and stayed on nonetheless, even though now it all seemed absurd to them. When would this cursed war come to an end?

I turned my thoughts to wondering how we could manage today to understand what the Italians of the time had to endure.

The lyrics of an old song came to mind: *Il Piave mormorava calmo e placido al passaggio dei primi fanti il 24 maggio.*[1] This is the first line of *La Leggenda del Piave*, composed in 1918 by the Neapolitan writer Ermete Giovanni Gaeta, which immediately became one of the most famous patriotic songs of the First World War. My brother and I used to sing it when we were little. It was our father who had taught it to us and we would belt it out at the top of our lungs, especially when we came to the part that said that the foreigner will not pass: *Il Piave mormorò: non passa lo straniero.*[2] We had no idea exactly what that meant, but we sang it with gusto. Those were among the rare moments when our father would let himself go somewhat and be carried away by the patriotic spirit and the war, the sacrifice of soldiers and the victory. And then he would

[1] The Piave murmured, calm and placid, as the first soldiers passed on the 24th of May.

[2] The Piave murmured, 'The foreigner shall not pass.'

speak to us of Arturo's medal of honour. And he told us that his father was very proud to have fought for the Fatherland, despite his sorrow at the loss of so many comrades, despite the bitterness after the defeat of Caporetto, despite the disappointment at the way the veterans were treated at the end of the war.

I turned all this over in my mind.

There are things that we carry inside us that never ever disappear.

And that continue to resonate, even when we have grown up and moved to a different country.

According to my father, Arturo was wounded on the Piave during the summer of 1917 and was transported to Hungary, first to a hospital and then to a prisoner camp. I asked him if he had any letters or postcards from that period. He told me he did not, that his father did not write any, or if such letters or cards existed, he never saw them.

The second semester courses at the university had not yet begun, so I decided to pay a visit to the archives of Lecce to gain access to Arturo's military service book. I intended to take advantage of the occasion to visit my father's cousins who live in Campi and hopefully have a look in their cellar at the boxes and bags full of books and family documents that had been put there for storage when my grandparents' home was emptied. I knew I would not be able to stay long that time and counted on opening all the boxes calmly at some later date. Jacques and I planned to spend the Easter holidays in Campi.

I was the one who had taken possession of my father's house in Campi. My father, who wanted to get rid of it, had put it up for sale and the preliminary agreement was about to be signed. But, when I was elected deputy and I began coming to Italy often, I had a strong desire to reconnect with the Salento and my roots. So, I began to have the house renovated, and from 2017 on, Jacques and I would spend our holidays in the Salento.

It had never crossed my mind, however, to go look through the books and documents that my father had put away in the cellar of my cousins' neighbouring house.

When I landed at the Brindisi airport, I climbed into a taxi and asked the driver to take me to Lecce. Twenty minutes later, I was on Via Alfonso Sozy Carafa, a short distance from the historic centre of the baroque capital of the Salento, in a soulless, middle-class neighbourhood, behind the Villa Reale Garden. The archives are located in a single-storey building, a sort of blockhouse from the fascist period.

At the entrance, after showing my ID card and proof of my position at the University of Paris, I filled out a form indicating the year, month and day of my grandfather's birth. I wrote that his father's name was Ferruccio and that the municipality of his birth was Botrugno, a tiny town near Maglie, at the tip of the boot heel, opposite Albania. I handed the form to one of the librarians. He soon returned and it was like a cold shower: 'I'm sorry, Signora, there is no Arturo Marzano in the inventory of passbooks for soldiers born in 1897. Are you sure that your grandfather resided in the province of Lecce at the time of the call to arms?'

'Yes, at least, I think so,' I stammered, now hesitant.

'Well, you will have to be sure. Where did your grandfather live in 1917?'

I phoned my father. He didn't know.

But in the end, he recalled a small Italian-Hungarian dictionary that his father had given him. He still had it. And despite the mess in my parents' home, he managed to find it. I asked him to put my mother on the phone.

'Could you please take some photos of the dictionary with your cell phone and send them to me on WhatsApp?'

A few minutes later, I received three pictures of a tiny dictionary, 8 by 3 centimetres, with a red cover, though the red was now pale and faded. Inside, on the first page, right before the entry 'abbey', '*apátság*' in Hungarian, is written: 'Second lieutenant Arturo Marzano, Nagymegyer, 3 May 1918.'

Encouraged by this discovery, I dropped by to see my father's cousins and asked them to take me down to their cellar, although my plane was leaving for Paris that very afternoon. No sooner had I stepped inside the room than a wave of discouragement swept over me. The damp crates and boxes were absolutely covered in dust and dirt. Finding something would have been well-nigh impossible and I ran the risk of getting to the airport all sweaty and exhausted. Why had I never come before to sort through this stuff?

As I was about to leave the cellar, I noticed on top of a crate, a wooden box wrapped in cellophane and filled with papers. I tore off the plastic, fished around in the box and, amid newspaper cuttings from the 1920s, I glimpsed an orange envelope, with the words 'Great War' handwritten on the top.

I held my breath and opened the envelope. Inside was a green notebook. I took it out and shook off the dust. A piece of paper folded in four fell to the floor. I picked it up and read 8 January 1919. I was in shock. From what I could tell, it was the text of a brief speech that my grandfather gave that day when he was celebrating his repatriation with his friends. I opened the green notebook and read: 'Memories of my captivity in Nagymegyer (Hungary)'. Then comes the date 16 November 1917. The entry on the last page is dated 8 March 1918. And between 8 March 1918 and 8 January 1919?

I rummaged through the box looking for a second notebook but I could not find anything. 'Maybe it's somewhere else,' I said to myself before noticing the time. If I didn't want to miss my plane, I would have to hurry outside and call a taxi. I promised myself I would come back another time. 'Jacques will help me out at Eastertime,' I thought just as the right side of the box that I had just touched with my foot came undone, eaten by humidity. Tracts and manifestos from the fascist era spilled out onto the floor. What a shame I had not come here before! What a fool I had been!

At Brindisi airport, people were looking at me askance. I was waiting in line to board, when I noticed a little girl staring at my jeans. She tugged at her mother's hand and asked, 'Why is that lady so dirty?' I could feel my cheeks turning red, but I made no attempt to explain. My thoughts turned back to the journal I found in the cellar.

When I had boarded the plane, I quickly tucked my things under the seat in front of me, attached my seatbelt even more quickly and immersed myself in the reading of my grandfather's journal. I had a hard time at first deciphering his writing. Then, little by little, I began to get used to it and to differentiate without too much difficulty his 's' from his 'r' and his 'g' from his 'p'. As I read, the image of lieutenant Arturo sprang up clearly before my eyes.

16 November 1917

At dawn on 16 November – it was 4 in the morning – the sentry sounded the alarm in the trench. And it echoed throughout the line. Driven by our sense of duty, we rushed out of our straw and mud shelters. That dawn was fatal to my battalion. The Austrians, in full force, attacked on the right, after crossing the Piave, aided by the fog [...] 'Fire lads! Fire away!' I shouted with all my might. Then, in despair, I jumped out of the trench to join the firing, ready to die before surrendering [...]. I resisted valiantly with my platoon, until the Austrians surrounded us and forced us to lay down our arms. Four soldiers recognised that I was the

> officer: one of them pulled the trigger, the shot went off, but to no purpose. [...] Help me Lieutenant, help me Sir! I saw Lorenzo with blood all over his throat, pierced by a bullet. I bandaged the wound but, shortly after, he went into spasms and bled to death. Poor Lorenzo. The day before he had built the shelter for the line. [...] All around me were dead bodies, I saw one with his guts out, another with his face blasted off by machine gun fire, another with his brains all over his face [...] an Austrian struck me with his rifle and made me fall into the water, then he forced me to cross the Piave with the other prisoners [...] That night, our bed was a pile of hay. At dawn I dreamt of my mother, my father and my sisters waiting with open arms to see me during my leave, ignoring my unhappy fate...

Between November 16 and 21, my grandfather and his soldiers covered on foot a distance of about hundred kilometres on the other side of the front. They had been made prisoners and were kept from then on under the strict surveillance of the Austrians. Day after day, Arturo kept a detailed record of every time they moved. The prisoners got up at dawn, drank a cup of tea and hit the road. Sometimes, they ate a piece of bread, but it was not enough to satisfy their hunger, which quickly began to weaken them. They first travelled through the Austrian Veneto, stopping at Piavon, then at Motta di Livenza, then in Palmanova, passing through Annone

Veneto. They then walked to Slovenia, in the direction of Ljubljana, stopping first for a few days in Udine. In Ljubljana, they were transferred to a freight train that took them across Hungary. And on 29 November, they arrived exhausted and demoralised in Nagymegyer, a concentration camp located on the border between Hungary and Slovakia.

Lieutenant Marzano wrote that they woke that day at six in the morning and after listening to mass and eating breakfast, they arrived in the camp at around 11, 'full of lice, dirty and stinking'.

> Immediately we were taken to a big bathroom of sorts. We put down our personal effects and took a shower while our clothing was disinfected. We got dressed in Austrian underwear and were led to barracks filled with wooden beds and old mats. [...] At seven in the evening we ate semolina, salad without oil, an apple and 250 grams of bread. At 9 we went to bed.

I read the pages of my grandfather's journal without paying attention to the people around me or to the announcements made by the attendants. I remained absorbed in my reading even when the plane had landed and the other passengers had unbuckled their seatbelts, crowded into the aisle, opened the overhead bins and waited impatiently for the doors to open. This may well have been the very first time since I started flying that I did not jump up upon landing. I took my time instead before making up my mind to stop reading, tuck the journal into my backpack, put on my jacket and exit the plane.

> 30 November: We got up at 7 o'clock. At 8, we had breakfast: a big cup of coffee (boiled water with chicory extract) and a slice of bread, 2 centimetres thick. It's the start of a monotonous life: eat, poop and sleep. We wait for evening to come to eat and then go to sleep. Nothing to do. Indescribable boredom. The time comes for the roll call. At 7 we eat semolina, two apples and 250 grams of bread. At 9 is bedtime.

Outside the terminal, I rushed to grab a cab. This time I would not take the bus or the train from the airport to Paris. I could not wait to show Jacques the notebook and did not want to waste time. Plus, I did not want to be disturbed by people getting on and off, pushing, shoving and shouting. This time I wanted to sit in a taxi and continue to read in peace. By now, I was progressing quickly, no longer struggling with Arturo's handwriting, all the more since he often used the same words and expressions. His writing was almost as monotonous as the days he spent in Nagymegyer. The same, day after day. Nothing happens, he writes several times. Only cold and hunger haunt his daily life. 'The sun almost never comes out in Nagymegyer,' he writes on 6 December. 'It's snowing. It's freezing cold and I'm hungry as a wolf. The cold and the hunger, always together: we talked about it when we were in third grade, and here as prisoners in Nagymegyer we are experiencing it,' he writes on 11 December. The following Monday, he buys woollen socks, 'long and thick'. The following day, he sends a telegram to his parents: 'Prisoner – Nagymegyer Hungary – send me packages.' At times, Arturo plays cards. At night he thinks about his parents and his childhood.

On 14 December, someone brings up the possibility of Russia proposing terms for the war to end, which opens his 'heart to great hopes'. Arturo thinks of his Salento, his world of sunshine and fields of vines and citrus fruit. 'Who knows when the day will come when we can bid adieu to this land cursed by God and by men and go back to our land blessed by the perfume of flowers and the fertility of the earth! Who knows when the day will come when we return to our good fresh pasta!'

As soon as I got home, I showed the journal to Jacques and read some passages from it to him. He listened attentively. Then he said,

'My grandfather was also a prisoner of war. When I was little and I went to see him, he would tell me about the horrors of the trenches and of his captivity. I'll never forget it. What is the name of the concentration camp where your grandfather was held?'

'Nagymegyer.'

'I've heard that name. Wait a minute, let me check something. I have the impression that the name came up in a book that I've been reading these days.'

Jacques went to his office and returned a few minutes later with a big volume in his hand. He leafed through it and found the page he was looking for.

'Nagymegyer. Here it is! That's what I thought. It's known as the town of the dead.'

'Town of the dead?'

'Yes. Soldiers were imprisoned there in dilapidated mud-filled barracks and a great many of them died. That's why the camp in Nagymegyer was known as the town of the dead at the time.'

Only officers had the right to receive packages from their families. Many of the other Italian prisoners died of hunger, as a result not only of the allied naval blockade and the ensuing rationing but also and especially of the Italian government's neglect. Unlike the English and French prisoners of war who received food from their countries, the Italians were left to their own devices. It wasn't until August 1918 that Vittorio Emanuele Orlando, then head of the government, decided to have 500 quintals of bread and wafers sent to the detention camps. In a report from the time, Count Guido Vinci, an envoy of the Italian Red Cross in Geneva, alerted the Orlando government:

> The difference between what is happening abroad and in Italy is alarming. In France and in England, services have been set up to send 2 kilograms of bread a week for each officer and soldier [...] In Italian prisoner camps, the

> morale is as low as can be. The men are riled and on the brink of revolt: not against Austria or Germany but against their own country, aloof and thankless toward its children.

I began to have some insight into what could have been taking hold in the minds of some nationalists with regard to the failings of the liberal bourgeoisie. I was up all night. I could not stop reading my grandfather's journal. How was it that my father was not even aware of its existence? How did this precious little notebook end up in a box full of useless papers? Why had my father always told me that there was nothing but medical and law books in his cousins' cellar? And what about me? Why had I never gone to check?

When Christmas 1917 arrived, a little over a month had gone by since Arturo was made prisoner, and his morale was very low: 'Christmas Eve! The day we all await so eagerly, young and old alike. No doubt the most wonderful holiday of the year. I am feeling suddenly overwhelmed by a world of memories that wring tears from my eyes: my home, my crèche, my dear parents, my little sisters, my old grandparents, my uncles, my friends… The almond milk, the *pettole*, the *cartellate*… It hurts to spend these wonderful days imprisoned in the walls of an Austrian hellhole.'

By 31 December, things had not improved in the least. Quite the contrary, the time had come for him to appraise the year and nothing about it was good:

'A very, very cold day. I lent a soldier 10 lire. At night, I stayed in the canteen until 11 o'clock. This was how a disastrous year ended for Italy, a year full of blood, cursed by all the mothers who lost their sons on the battlefield, cursed by all! Accursed 1917!'

On 13 January 1918, Arturo fell ill. The next day, his fever went up: 'Alone, in the cold of the barracks, lying on an old mat with two dirty covers… It's better to die suddenly than to be sick!' The 15th, an Austrian doctor came to see him. He was put on a stretcher and taken to the hospital. 'I heard someone say, he's going to die! I prayed and prayed…' Some ten days later Arturo was doing a little better, he left the hospital and his life went back to what it was before. The weather conditions were all he noted in February in his journal: cold, snow, wind, fog, rain. On 1 March, he received a package: bread, needle and thread, linen, buttons, soap, and he replied by telegram: 'Package arrived – Send me some pasta and sauces.'

The notebook ended on 8 March with a laconic entry: 'Very cold day'. I have no way of knowing if he really tried to escape, as he said he intended to do. Nor if he succeeded in convincing the other Italian officers to follow him. Many of them feared being sent to the Fortress of Komárno; others simply didn't have the courage to try…

The war ended on 4 November 1918. The morning of 2 November 1918, the *Corriere della Sera* announced that the enemies were overpowered by the Italian army. The next day, General Badoglio, General Scipioni, Colonel Gazzano, Captain Maravigli, and Major Accissi meet with members of Parliament and held talks into the night to set the precise terms of the armistice. 'Austria capitulated', was the headline of the *Corriere della Sera*, announcing the news of the victory.

But it was not until the end of December that Arturo was able to come back home. Proud of the heroism of his soldiers and the blood shed for the beloved Fatherland, he willingly accepted the delays in the general demobilisation. 'I too want to go back home as soon as possible,' he told those who were protesting against the foot-dragging of the government. 'But the means of transportation must first serve for the raw materials and the food that the country needs! The provinces invaded, pillaged, robbed and starved by the barbaric enemy now need all the help they can get,' he repeated with conviction. 'Now is the time to think of Fiume and of Dalmatia. I'm sure our king will find a solution!'

On 8 January 1919, he organised a toast to celebrate the repatriation.

> At dawn on 3 November we heard the echo of the bells of Sangiusto ringing and sounding the call to celebrate. This echo told us that all Italy was celebrating. It told us of the salvation of our loved ones; it told us that we were free; it told us that the Austrian eagle had been crushed by the

> valour of our soldiers. [...] My thoughts then flew to our ancestral olive trees. [...] Let's drink to our health, my friends! And let's make a toast to the health of our soldiers who demonstrated their heroism and bravery. And finally let's drink to the health of our king who, with energy and serenity, accomplished the destinies of Italy. A toast to Trieste, to Trento and to Fiume. Long live Italy! Long live the king! Long live the army!

My grandfather never spoke to his wife or his children about the war years or the months he spent in the 'town of the dead'. Some people need to talk all the time about what they lived through in order to survive; others clam up, refuse to talk, all they want is to forget. Even if some things you never forget, they stay inside you, and one day or another they resurface. Wasn't that what happened to my grandfather, a few years later, when he was elected deputy of the Monarchist National Party and that in the course of discussions in a committee, in speaking of the war, he went overboard?

Among the most important documents that I collected in recent weeks were the minutes of parliamentary proceedings. No one could alter those records or make them disappear. And they could be consulted online. They are objective, faithful transcriptions of the words pronounced during the meetings and the most significant gestures. And that was precisely where I saw the war and its demons resurface, in the transcription of my grandfather's words during a meeting in the 1950s.

It was 18 April 1956 and the deputies were discussing a bill on the celebration of the tenth anniversary of the liberation, with the publication and distribution in schools of a volume dedicated to the Resistance. Some deputies protested. They maintained that the history of Italy should be analysed in a homogeneous manner, without giving more attention to some events rather than others. They asserted that it was preposterous to concentrate so much attention on events related to the Resistance. Others, on the contrary, cited the writings of historian Luigi Salvatorelli. They argued that the young people needed to learn what it means to reclaim lost freedom and how many sacrifices doing so had cost. That is when the *Onorevole* De Totto, member of the Italian Social Movement, a neo-fascist party that drew inspiration more and more overtly from the ideas of the Republic of Salò, spoke up: 'How can anyone give credit to Salvatorelli, who insults the veterans of the First World War by writing that they were people who were accustomed to a life of violence and adventure?'

It seemed that De Totto's remarks were booed. It also seemed that he then decided to walk out of the meeting. At least, that was what I read in the minutes of the parliamentary session, just before the exact transcription of my grandfather's intervention. Indeed, it was former Lieutenant Marzano who took the floor after De Totto to speak about what he had lived through forty years before: 'I must admit that I have not read what Salvatorelli wrote. But I would very much like to see the person who wrote that the soldiers of the 1914-1918 War were accustomed to violence and adventure. Salvatorelli, we left school to fight in the trenches of the Karst and the Piave for the purpose of defending the Fatherland; not out of violence, since violence was not taught to us by our professors, but out of love for the Fatherland and in a spirit of patriotism.'

The minutes mention applause from some deputies and gestures of disdain from others. It states that the *Onorevole* Marzano pounded his fist on the table and that the president of the committee called him to order. It notes that, like De Totto shortly before, Marzano too walked out of the meeting.

'Brothers, what was the point of fighting? For whom did we shed our blood on the Carso and the Piave? I agree that love for the Fatherland should now replace hatred toward our vanquished enemy, but what is our government doing in the meantime?'

Arturo felt inflamed. He was living in Venice and had not yet been discharged. But from time to time, he would take a few days' leave to go to Rome for an exam. He still had a few left before getting his master's degree in law. It was in the capital that he met Giuseppe Bottai, the director of the journal *Roma Futurista*. And that on 15 May 1919, he took part in the creation of the Roman section of the Fascist Party.

'Liberals and Socialists are nothing but a load of bumbling idiots,' he went on while one of his companions refilled his glass with wine. When he was slightly drunk, Lieutenant Marzano would get heated and rant: 'My dear comrades, the future is Mussolini's fascism!'

A few officers listened to him with interest. Others ignored him and continued playing cards.

'Forget about politics, Marzano!' Alberto said to him.

Alberto couldn't wait to be discharged and go home to Bologna. His wife wrote him that little Luisa was growing up nicely. When would he be able to embrace her and resume his former life again?

'But what about the promises they made to us? And what about our comrades who fell on the Piave? It is our duty to fight for them!' My grandfather did not want to return to civilian life as if nothing had happened.

'What does this Mussolini say, Arturo?' asked Vittorio who fought with my grandfather on the Isonzo.

One evening, on 21 August 1917, Arturo saved his life. Having tripped over a rock while running and sprained his ankle, Vittorio was lying there helplessly under fire from enemy lines, and my grandfather, instead of finding shelter from the hail of bullets and grenades, helped him up, heaved him on his back, and lugged him to the trenches, right before a grenade exploded exactly in the place Vittorio had fallen.

'Mussolini is on our side. Look! Read what he wrote!' He took out a cutting from the newspaper. 'It's an article published in his newspaper on 16 January, an article that Mussolini dedicated to us: "To those who are returning!"' He showed the article to his comrades, pointed to a few passages that he underlined and started to read out loud. 'For three years we have been appealing to the men in the government: *Signori*, go generously and spontaneously to meet those who will be returning from the trenches. Do not be afraid of bold ideas! Demonstrate greatness in your words and especially in your deeds, for the times, the needs and the hopes are great!'

'How rhetorical, Arturo! It's truly insufferable.'

'Patience, Alberto, hear me out,' Arturo said. 'The veterans are returning. And they don't even have the aesthetic and spiritual satisfaction of seeing themselves greeted triumphantly, as they deserve, for these soldiers literally demolished one of the most powerful armies in the world...'

'That's true!' Vittorio interrupted him. 'I like this Mussolini.'

'C'mon Vittorio, try at least to keep your feet on the ground!' Alberto was exasperated. 'There is nothing concrete there. They're just words. Words, words, words...'

'That's where you're mistaken, Alberto! Mussolini has proposed concrete measures. He cites France as an example, where an indemnity of about 250 lire is being provided to all soldiers, and he has demanded that our government do the same. I agree with him completely. The time has come to revamp the hierarchies! We have to act; we owe it to our Fatherland! Haven't you heard what all the veterans of Veneto are saying?'

Alberto sighed. He stopped attending these meetings of veterans. All he wanted was to go back home. How many times did he have to repeat the same thing?

My grandfather kept at him: 'So you'd rather see other people decide for you? All those bourgeois who couldn't care less about us? Not to mention what is rearing its ugly head in Russia. Are you aware of the communist danger? We cannot not respond to the provocations and violence of the communists!'

I had another nightmare last night. I woke up with a jolt and reached up to touch my head and my hair. I dreamt that I had lost all my hair. Well, not exactly lost it, but that it had been cut very, very short, as if someone had shaved my head. For a few moments, I was absolutely paralysed. It took me a while to realise that it was only a dream. And even then, I still could not calm down.

I got up and went to the living room. I drank a glass of water; I lit a cigarette. I was finally beginning to simmer down. Then I thought of Simone Touseau and the other shaved women and my heart sank.

What was my subconscious trying to tell me? Why this nightmare now? Whom had I betrayed? Whom was I betraying? My grandfather? My father? Myself?

Fortunately, I have no children, I said to myself as I stubbed out my cigarette and opened the window; I had no desire to hear Jacques's objections when he would get up and see that I was already smoking. How could I have taken care of a child when I had not even felt capable of taking care of myself? What could I have told a child who would have seen me in this state? That Mama is sad and does not know why? That Mama is crying, but it is not very serious, my treasure, it will pass, I swear, it's really nothing?

All of a sudden, I recall what my friend Claudia said the last time she came to Paris for her work, and we went out for dinner together. We had not spent time together, just the two of us, without husbands or children, since the days in Pisa at the Scuola Normale Superiore. I spoke to her about Jacopo's birth and the book I was writing. I told her that the birth of my nephew had been very unsettling for me. That it forced me to face my family's past. I asked her what had finally convinced her to have a child when she had always as a university student said that she did not want to be a mother, that it did not interest her, that that was not what truly mattered in life to her.

'I made up my mind because I felt the duty to transmit some of the trust and love that I had received,' she replied.

I looked at her dumbfounded.

'But what happens if you haven't received trust and love? What do you transmit to a child then?

'A time comes when you have to get a grip on yourself, Michela! You can't spend your life complaining.'

'But what if you lack the basis? What if the foundations are simply not there? If life continues to betray you? What is there to get a grip on, my dear Claudia?'

`March on Rome` = *yes (licence no. 108702).*

On 28 October 1922, the *squadristi* began to converge on Rome, undeterred by the blockades that the regular armed forces set up in Orte and the resistance in Civitavecchia of the Marxist and anarchist *Arditi* battalions. And my grandfather was there. When I tried to talk to my father about it, he seemed sceptical. He did not understand how that could have been possible. At the time, Arturo was already a magistrate, wasn't he?

But my grandfather was there. Even though, as we now know, the 28 October march on Rome was initially a bluff by Mussolini, who did not come to Rome until 30 October. He took a train from Milan, travelling in a sleeping car, and went directly to see the king, who had refused to sign the state of emergency decree proposed by the head of the government, Luigi Facta. Vittorio Emanuele III could have held his ground, but he decided instead to entrust the Duce with the responsibility of forming a new government. And, on 31 October, while squadrons of Blackshirts marched past the Quirinal, he saluted them with Mussolini from the balcony of the palace.

My grandfather was there. I know that many

people went out of their way to obtain this goddamn certificate once fascism had come to power. How many bogus 'March on Rome' certificates are there? Such proofs were bought and sold among the high-ranking members of the regime, and some people still have them on display in their homes! Never would I have imagined that I would count one day among those who could boast having one.

`March on Rome` = *yes (licence no. 108702).*

Arturo was a member of the Fascist Party's San Cesario section, where he had moved when he left Rome and his comrades and friends Fabbri, De Martino and Patrignani, and he knew all about the *Marcia*. I discovered that he asked for a leave from the Crown Prosecutor in Lecce, that he arrived in Rome a few days before 28 October and that he participated in punitive expeditions in Trastevere and in the Trionfale district, and even took part in the assault on the socialist newspaper *L'Avanti*'s printing press!

My grandfather was there and I simply couldn't get over it. Especially when I reread the speech that Mussolini gave in the Chamber on 16 November of that year: 'I could have carried our victory much further, and I refused to do so. I imposed limits upon my action.' What were you thinking the next day when you read the Duce's words in the newspaper? That he was right? That he indeed imposed limits on himself and that there was absolutely nothing illegal about his action? What about the destroyed newspaper press? And the molested activists? 'With 300,000 young men, armed to the teeth, ready for anything and almost mystically prompted to obey any order of mine, I could have punished all those who have slandered and thrown mud at fascism,' Mussolini continued. Were you also convinced that it was legitimate to punish the opponents of fascism? 'I could have made this deaf and grey chamber a bivouac of maniples,' he went on, encouraged by the applause from the right. Modigliani cried from the tribune: 'Long live Parliament!' But the word was laughable at the time. No one believed in the Parliament anymore. They shushed him on the right and Mussolini resumed his speech: 'I could have bolted the Parliament and formed a government exclusively of fascists; I could have done so, but I did not wish to do so, at least not then.' Naturally, *at least not at that moment.*

`March on Rome` = *yes (licence no. 108702).*

No matter how hard I tried, I simply could not understand how my grandfather could have endorsed an end to democracy. How could he have accepted Mussolini's demand for full powers from the Parliament? 'Without full powers you know perfectly well that not a lira – not a lira, I say – would be saved'? Did he truly believe that a politician could not achieve anything without wielding full powers? And what about freedom, grandfather? When you fought on the front, weren't you fighting for freedom too?

In his famous essay *The March on Rome and Its Surroundings,* initially published in France in 1933,

Emilio Lussu, deputy from 1921 to 1924, an opponent of Mussolini from the start, and one of the great witnesses to the rise of fascism in Italy, gives a detailed description of the November 16 session. In this text, Lussu recounts with great insight the seizure of power by the fascists. When I reread his account of the session and the reactions of some of the deputies during Mussolini's speech, I had an uncanny sense of déjà vu. It took me back a few years to when I was a deputy in Parliament. The tribunes would fill up when important measures were being discussed, and some of the deputies behaved in ways that struck me as being just like the behaviour described by Lussu. Fortunately, the times were not as tragic, but I would wager that, had they been, alas, it would not have changed a thing. The same misbehaviour, the same improprieties. Some whistled, other shouted, to prevent a member from speaking, and the ushers would regularly have to empty the public tribunes. One day, I took the floor during a discussion on the bill on end-of-life issues to defend the right of terminally-ill patients to stop treatments, including artificial nutrition and hydration. And someone from the tribune yelled: 'Murderer! What freedom are you defending, Marzano? The freedom to die?'

`March on Rome` = *yes (licence no. 108702).*

My grandfather was there! And it made no damn difference to me if he was so in good faith, believing the Duce's words when he explained that the fascist violence was trivial compared to the violence of the

Bolsheviks in the years 1919-1920. He was there, and, in the end, there was no excuse. I could not find even one for the father of my father. I could not, I would not, it would not be right. All I felt was shame.

'Shame makes no sense,' my father would say when I was little and I told him I was feeling ashamed. 'When you haven't done anything wrong, there's no reason to feel shame. Did you do something wrong?'

For years, I thought that my shame was the product of my desire for perfection, and that this desire for perfection was, in turn, the result of my fear of not being able to live up to my expectations. Now I wondered if that reasoning held water, or whether, for years, my mistake was not understanding that shame was in fact the real starting point.

Now I had the feeling that it is passed on from generation to generation. That we drink it from mother's breasts and breath it in our father's arms. It is a disturbing legacy that we have to face, one day or another. Even if the truth risks eluding us. And most of the time, no one will know what really happened.

I tried to think back to the first time I felt shame. I had just turned three when my brother was born, and I was jealous. I remember lying to the babysitter – yes, I lied to her; I remember it distinctly – I told her that I was fine, that I didn't need her, that she could go take care of the baby. So, she went off to his room to put him to sleep and, as soon as I was alone, I grabbed a pair of scissors and cut my hair. When the babysitter came back, I felt ashamed. But that was just the beginning. Later I stopped eating. I didn't feel like it. I wasn't hungry; meat disgusted me. I chewed the meat into a ball, held it in a corner of my mouth and waited. When would the babysitter go away to look after my little brother? And as soon as she had her back turned, I spit it all out in the trash. I was ashamed, but I couldn't change the fact that I hated my little brother. Yes, I hated him, even though he had done nothing to deserve it. He was just a little baby, but I was little too, wasn't I?

My second memory of feeling shame was also when I was three years old. I was in a city park with my mother and my brother. He was still in the stroller, but I could go play. 'Why don't you go play on the slide,' my mother insisted. She saw that for some time I had been staring at the slide but did not move. There were lots of children on it, and I was ashamed. I don't know why, I don't know about what, but it was as if I was paralysed. I remembered nothing after that. At least not until I woke up in the arms of my mother who was running to the car. In the interim, it seems, I had climbed up the slide and fallen off it, dislocating my collarbone and losing consciousness. What really happened? Did I slip? Did someone push me? Did I lose my balance? Did I jump? All that I remember is the shame.

I did remember, on the other hand, everything that

happened a few years later. I was six and I was taking part in a treasure hunt for children organised in the mountains. There was a boy, Daniele, who was a little older than I was and whom I liked a lot. A few children had been randomly chosen to form teams, but no one wanted me on their team. I was ashamed. At some point, someone remarked to Daniele that I'd been left out and that he could take me with him. And he replied: 'No, not her! She's dumb.' Maybe when he said this, he didn't realise that I was right there by his side. But I was and I heard him. Why did he think I was dumb? Why did he say that in front of everyone? What had I done? What had I said? Admittedly, whenever I saw him, I would turn red, I never knew what to say, I'd feel confused and ashamed. But why did he think I was dumb?

When I sat for the competitive entrance exam to the Scuola Normale Superiore and there were only three of us in all of Italy to be admitted in philosophy, the first thing I thought of was the word 'dumb' that Daniele had used in speaking of me. His contempt and my shame. Right before murmuring, 'I'm not dumb, you poor fool! I hate you; I hate you and all the other boys in the world …'

PART TWO

The Sin

No one has the right to execute an order that involves a criminal act. In our life, there is a boundary beyond which we no longer have the right to participate [...] This is the foundation of all ethics; this is the foundation of all law.

Fritz Bauer

At the beginning of 1924, my grandfather left Rome and moved back to Puglia. He was appointed *pretore*, a monocratic judge, as they say in Italy to designate a single judge, in a small town in the heart of the Gargano massif. Today, the small city of San Nicandro Garganico, which towers over the Adriatic Sea in the distance, seems quite tame. But at the time, the modest capital of the Gargano had an incendiary reputation. It was one of the cities that was the most troubled by conflicts between peasants and landowners, and some leading trade unionists, such as the brothers Giuseppe and Domenico Fioritto, lived there. Above all, it was seen as a den of anti-fascist socialists, communists and anarchists. When my grandfather arrived there, he found a derelict courtroom and a worrisome number of crimes and misdemeanours awaiting judgement.

The year 1924 was a dramatic year for Italy. After the anticipated dissolution of the Chamber of Deputies on 25 January, there were an increasing number of violent acts and assaults by fascists throughout the country. Knowing that the regime was not yet definitively established, the *squadristi* carried out 'punitive expeditions' against all those they considered enemies of the regime. For a yes or for a no, they attacked people with their truncheons; they threw their adversaries to the ground, beat them up, and forced them to drink castor oil. *Manganello et olio di ricino*: that was the recipe of the *squadristi* for what they called the 'purge of subversives'. More fear than harm, say the nostalgic admirers of the Duce today. But sometimes, the harm caused by these punitive expeditions was all too real.

On 28 February, in Reggio Emilia, Antonio Piccinini, a militant trade unionist and a candidate for the Parliament, was brutally murdered. That night, a group of Blackshirts gained entry into his house using bogus Socialist Party cards. They abducted him and took him to one of their homes, where he was subjected to the worst torture. They stripped him naked, hung him by his arms on a butcher's hook, and cut open his stomach with a knife before finishing him off with a pistol, four shots at point-blank range. On 16 March, it was Antonio Corgiola's turn in Milan, during the attack on the headquarters of the *Arditi*. Gangs of *squadristi* roamed the country in their trucks, spreading violence and terror, and the elections of 6 April took place in a very oppressive climate. This was particularly the case in Abruzzo, Campania, Calabria and Puglia. Mussolini's national list, which brought fascists together with some liberals, such as the famous Orlando, won a resounding victory.

At the very first meeting of the new Parliament, several deputies protested against the violence and the many attacks on democracy that tarnished the electoral campaign. On 30 May, in a highly charged atmosphere, deputy Giacomo Matteotti, the secretary of the Socialist Party, took the floor to denounce the lack of freedom and the machinations that marked the elections and he demanded that they be annulled. On 10 June, when he was scheduled to take the floor again to speak up about the financial scandal involving the Duce's brother, Matteotti was abducted by the Blackshirts.

Italy was going through a crucial moment in its history. Everyone held their breath wondering what would be the fate of the head of the opposition. Two months later, on 16 August, his body was found in the environs of Rome. The country was in a state of shock and highly divided: The partisans of the regime were in doubt or kept quiet, while the rest of the Italians were torn between fear, dismay and disapproval. Some thought this affair would put an end to the fascist experiment.

Even before Matteotti's body was found, my grandfather was worried. In San Nicandro, the political leaders on the left were quick to mobilise their militants to protest against the abduction of the Socialist Party secretary. The victim's fate was still unknown, but the socialists, knowing that the peasants were upset, thought that fascism could be swept away by the shockwave that the kidnapping of the socialist leader caused.

Judge Marzano decided to react decisively. He summoned the marshal of the Carabinieri and instructed him to put an end to the unrest and to the hostile demonstrations against the regime. He knew that certain youth gangs no longer hesitated to occupy the city streets and squares and shout calls to insurrection. The landowners were worried. Some of them had even been exposed to threats right in front of their homes. He therefore gave the order to arrest anyone inciting insurrection.

On 2 August, the marshal of the Carabinieri caught a group of young peasants on the Torre Miletto road, near the San Nicandro convent. They were on their way home after a day of working in the fields, and were singing *Bandiera Rossa*. Thus, they were deemed to be caught in the act of inciting insurrection. The marshal arrested all of the young people and immediately brought them before Judge Marzano, who decided to try them on the spot and, to make an example of them, sentenced them to the maximum penalty prescribed by law.

My grandfather was the first magistrate in Italy to sentence teenagers and young adults, fifteen to twenty-five years old, to several months in prison for the mere fact of having sung *Bandiera Rossa*. This decision was meant to serve as a warning. In the new fascist Italy, no one should be allowed to defy the regime. In his judgement, Arturo described *Bandiera Rossa* as an 'insurrectional cry' that could only cause public unrest and disturb the peace. 'This song tends to elicit an adverse reaction in people's souls and foster class hatred. In the tense present-day political climate, it can lead to bloody uprisings,' he wrote, concluding, 'Likewise, if the Communist Party or Socialist Party were in power, songs like *Giovinezza*, the fascist hymn, would be considered calls to insurrection.'

Ten days later, Judge Marzano received a letter from the secretary of the Fascist Party of San Nicandro, Antonio Gabrieli, congratulating him for his 'energetic', 'very effective' and 'intrepid' judgement, which confirmed, wrote the fascist leader to Judge Marzano, the latter's 'true spirit as a *squadrista* and fascist from the very first hour'.

After this infamous exploit in Gargano, Arturo was transferred to the south of Puglia, near where his father lived, in a rich county town of the Salento located some fifteen kilometres from the baroque city of Lecce.

He was very happy to be appointed judge in Campi, a small prosperous city, reputed in the region as much for its vineyards and olive groves as for its culture and tobacco manufacturing. A real engine of the Salento economy, tobacco manufacturing provided a livelihood to tens of thousands of factory workers in the winter months. And in Campi, there were two big factories, one owned by the Reale family of Lecce and run by the parents of Carmelo Bene, and the second owned by the family of the city's mayor, Don Giuseppe Guarino.

When my grandfather arrived in Campi, he did not know a single person. He had a few weeks before him to find his bearings and get in touch with the mayors of the cantons in his judicial district. Before taking up his post, he wanted to get a feel for the region and an idea of the problems with which he might be confronted as well as the social and political climate in the Salento.

There was talk of strikes and of coalitions of tobacco workers. These *tabacchine* were known to be hotheaded, and the fascists considered them an easy prey for socialist and communist propaganda. Their working conditions were among the roughest of the time. But they found the courage to unite in fragile unions that were in the crosshairs of the *squadristi*. The situation was therefore different than in Gargano, but it was no less tense. In this old civilisation of Magna Graecia, in this Salento steeped in ancient memories and culture, in this 'land of remorse', the women were the ones to lead the dance more than the men. It would not take long for Arturo to realise this.

'It seems that the mayor is comrade Starace's brother-in-law,' Arturo, intrigued, said to himself that morning, on his way to city hall to meet Don Giuseppe Guarino. 'If it's true, that is quite promising,' he thought as he proudly climbed the steps. Like Arturo, Starace was a fascist of the very first hour. But whereas Arturo chose to pursue his studies and enter the judiciary, Starace went on to become one of the party's high-ranking officials.

As soon as he took up his post, the new judge received letters with words of welcome from all the mayors of the surrounding area, from Novoli, Cellino San Marco, Salice and Squinzano. They had been looking forward to his arrival. Major Francesco Orlandini, marshal of San Pietro Vernotico, sent him a particularly warm telegram: 'honoured to have the opportunity to shake hands with you soon – ready for the closest and most fruitful cooperation.' As for Giuseppe Guarino, Mayor of Campi, he immediately invited the new judge to city hall, delighted to meet the man who had condemned the communists who sang.

Before stepping into the office, Arturo took a deep breath and made an effort to smile. He was eager to focus his thoughts and find the right words to introduce himself to Guarino.

'Ah, Honourable Judge Marzano, please come in, come in!' The major was seated on the far end of a huge office with two windows overlooking the collegial church of Santa Maria della Grazia. 'How delighted I am to meet you. The news of your resolve has made its way all the way here. Your reputation as an upright magistrate has preceded you!'

Arturo thanked him, with a show of slightly feigned humility.

'Rest assured, your honour,' Guarino continued, 'you'll have no trouble here. The people in this region are not interested in political fighting. Most fortunately. Rome is far away, and polemics at the higher echelons of the state are ever farther. Here the people need bread and work. They don't care about the rest.'

Arturo expressed relief to hear that this was so. But he nonetheless ventured to ask a few questions. 'What about the tobacco factory workers? What's the situation there? They say that some of them are highly politicised, that they regularly instigate protests and strikes… It seems that some workers in Trepussi even decided to take to the streets.'

The mayor paused for a moment. Then he replied: 'Just rumours, Marzano. Here no one complains. On the contrary! When people have the chance to work, they thank the heavens and are grateful for their fate. I invite you to come visit our factory. You'll see with your own eyes the good spirit that prevails among our *tabacchine*.'

'With great pleasure,' Arturo replied as he helped himself to a small marzipan cake from the silver plate on the desk. 'These are excellent. They remind me of my childhood.' The two men looked at each other. From the very first glance, the mayor of Campi and the new judge had understood each other perfectly.

In Campi, the Guarinos' tobacco factory still exists. It was converted by Don Giuseppe's son into a museum of sorts, displaying sieves, funnels, spinning wheels, mortars, weights, measures, copper pots, clay vases and baskets. It is not far from my grandparents' house.

Last summer, Jacques and I visited it. A 'discover your local heritage day' had been organised by the municipality and the residents of Campi had been invited on a tour of the former tobacco factory. Intrigued, Jacques and I joined the tour and followed a guide who explained how the work proceeded. He told the group about the big party that was thrown every year in celebration of the completion of activity at the beginning of spring, attended by the employees and the owners. Some workers would be busy around the coal-fired barbecues, while others would help Maria, Don Giuseppe's wife, get the big table in the garden ready; some would prepare eggplant parmigiana, others the beignets with aromatic herbs that are the specialty of the Salento.

'For these celebrations, my father spared no expense,' Tonino, the son of the former mayor of Campi, told me when I went over to say hello at the end of the tour.

'I'm Ferruccio Marzano's daughter. Do you remember him?' I asked.

'Yes, of course, the son of Arturo!' He squinted to get a better look at me. 'How is he? I haven't seen him for a long time. He doesn't come this way anymore?'

'You're right. He doesn't come often,' I said, raising my voice somewhat. Tonino was now very old and didn't hear very well.

'Did you know that my father and your grandfather were very close?' he asked.

I replied yes. Although only a few months prior, I had known nothing about their relationship. Just as I had ignored the fact that my grandfather had been a fascist, like Guarino's father, and that, for the tobacco employees, the work in the factories had been a nightmare. But maybe in Campi, there are some things that were forgotten all too quickly. Or else they were granted very little importance in an effort to smooth the edges of the past. 'Everyone in the town knows the fountain of Don Giuseppe and calls it that; why erase history?' the communist mayor said in 2017, when a journalist asked him how the municipal council could have dedicated a *piazza* in Campi to the former fascist mayor. Guarino was mayor of the city during the darkest period of fascism. And he was the brother-in-law of Achille Starace, the secretary of the Fascist Party, and one of the most loyal supporters of the Duce. 'My father was never a diehard fascist,' Tonino nevertheless declared on the same occasion, adding that, fascist or not, it was precisely during the period when his father was the mayor that running water was brought to Campi. Not before and not after: 'It was on

3 November 1928, and the crowds filled the piazza to applaud my father who was inaugurating the fountain. It was the first time that they had seen water gushing freely! For centuries, people had had to go look for it and draw it from wells.' Then, returning to his father's purported fascism, he maintained: 'I never heard my father exalting such thinking, and I very rarely saw him wearing the black shirt, except on occasions when he was forced to do so by a higher-ranking official.'

No, history cannot be simply erased. Campi's former mayor was right. It was indeed at the time of fascism that the good people of Campi had access to running water for the first time. But to dedicate a *piazza* to a fascist mayor of his native city is a symbolic gesture, exactly as it was symbolic, after the defeat of fascism, to rename 'Corso Starace' as 'Corso Italia'.

That was what I was thinking as I left the tobacco factory and approached the *Largo Fontana di Don Pippi*, and sat with Jacques on a wrought iron bench next to the small fountain. How was it that no one mentioned the suffering of Cosima, Michelina, Maria, Concetta, Oronza, Rosaria, and all the other tobacco workers whose professional cards Tonino had jealously kept?

During the visit to the former factory, much was said about the smell that pervaded the streets of the city in summer when the tobacco leaves were drying in the sun. In every alley and every yard, the women, seated on the stoops of their homes or on the ground, threaded the tobacco leaves before attaching them to the *tiraletti*, the wooden frames that were then leaned against the walls. In the evening, they took the frames inside their homes to protect the tobacco from the humidity. I too have a vague memory of the *tiraletti*. When I was little, leaves of tobacco were still dried in the sun in the backyards, and I would approach the frames set against the wall and breath in the bitter smell of tobacco. Sometimes I would brush my hand against a leaf and, at the mere touch of my fingers, it would crumble to pieces.

The guide commented that every year, Donna Maria, Giuseppe Guarino's wife, took souvenir photos with a plate camera. Someone praised the patience and the meticulous care with which Tonino collected documents and objects belonging to his family over the years. But not one person even furtively mentioned the living and working conditions of the tobacco workers, the songs that they sang at dusk when returning home, worn out and dead on their feet, the revolts between 1925 and 1926, the arrests in 1927, and the massacre in 1935 in Tricase, when the police of the fascist state opened fire on women demonstrating. About seventy women were wounded and five of them died on the street.

Where did these fragments of reality go? Who remembers the fatigue and the lack of sleep of these tobacco workers, when the wooden crates of dried tobacco leaves arrived at the factory and the women would get up at dawn, walk kilometres across the countryside, arrive at work already exhausted, and then, from dawn to dusk, for a paltry wage, select the tobacco leaves, arrange them in sheaves, press them, put them in rooms overheated by the fire of furnaces whose temperature they controlled with their bare hands, all in deathlike silence?

Fimmene fimmene ca sciatu allu tabaccu, ne sciate doi e ne turnati quattro, sang the women on their way home after work: 'Women, women, you leave for the tobacco factory on two and come back on four.' Devastated by fatigue and pain (there were no breaks, not even to eat) and under the inflexible gaze of the *mestre*, they barely managed to swallow the crust of bread that they had hidden in the pocket of their overalls. These *fimmene* seem to have left no trace in Campi, at least they did not crop up in the discussions in which Jacques and I took part in the former tobacco factory of the Guarinos, or in the book that Tonino wrote about his family, *Legami di sangue, famiglie e vicende all'ombra di Achille Starace*, which I bought a few days after the visit.

Since Tonino's father and my grandfather were friends, maybe I would be able to glean some additional information on Arturo's past was what I was thinking when I started to leaf through the book. But I was quickly disillusioned. It was a purely sanitised version of history: Donna Maria always took care of her workers; during the lunch break, they snacked on the *friselle* and the pickled eggplant that were on the house; his uncle Achille Starace, the Duce's right arm, was a man whom time ultimately proved right, and so on *ad nauseam*.

In Campi, my grandfather found lodgings with the Perrone family on Umberto Street. He worked hard. Busy with civil, penal and administrative procedures, he spent his time in court. But whenever he had the chance, when he'd finished examining a case, writing a sentence or having discussions with the lawyers, he strolled through the streets of the city, with his gloves and his walking stick. My father stressed this story of his father's gloves and cane. He did not know exactly when his parents met, but he said that when Arturo walked through the streets of Campi, the girls from the upper class would stop to watch him, intrigued, interested, even after he finally chose my grandmother Rosa out of them all.

'My mother was very, very beautiful,' my father said. 'She was the loveliest of them all,' he insisted when he saw the perplexed look on my face. For in some of the photographs I found of my grandmother, she is not pretty at all. She wears dark clothes buttoned up to her chin and looks annoyed and strict. She does not seem particularly well kempt either. Later, I discovered the portrait of a young lady inside an oval frame surrounded by a Pompeian red and gold border on an arch in the living room of the home of my father's cousins. She has loose hair and is wearing a dress with a décolleté. She seems to be flying, like an angel. She holds a crown of roses in her hands, her dress is ochre and her gracious face is turned upward. My father's cousin told me that it was my grandmother and that the painter had fallen in love with her. 'She was very beautiful,' she added, and the painter, when he was asked to decorate the walls and arches of the house, asked that she sit for him.

But let us return to my grandfather strolling through the streets of Campi with his gloves and his walking stick. One evening at the end of March 1925, in front of the entrance gate facing Via Umberto I, he happened upon my grandmother. Rosa Campo had just turned twenty-six and her mother was intent on her marrying, but not just anyone. She had her mind set on the young Licci, a very good catch who was courting Rosa.

'What are you waiting for, Rosa? Do you want to be an old maid? At your age, I already had three children. When are you going to make up your mind?'

Rosa had no interest in Licci. In fact, there wasn't a young man in Campi who interested her. She had known all of them for years and was bored whenever she went to a party. But when she met Arturo, something intrigued her. She knew right away that he was the new judge – her friend Ninuzza, who had met Arturo at the city hall, had already spoken to her of him on several occasions. She said that Judge Marzano was friendly but never unduly familiar.

Instead of closing the gate quickly, as she would usually do with a stranger, Rosa stood there on the threshold, rooted to the spot. Arturo came up to her and introduced himself. He was perfectly aware that she was Rosa Campo, that her family was one of the most prominent in Campi, and that her mother, Donna Giuseppina, 'had the stink under her nose', as the expression goes in Italy, meaning that she was snobby and haughty. For her daughter, she wanted a noble match and she had already driven away many suitors.

Rosa felt the heat rising to her face and could not muster an answer to her mother, who was asking her from afar why she hadn't come in yet. She made a face, by way of an apology. And he smiled at her.

Rosa apparently fell in love with Arturo right away and quickly decided they would be engaged, but her mother categorically refused to see her daughter marrying this man. He was a judge, to be sure, but not an aristocrat. And not even from a good bourgeois family. Giuseppina apparently opposed this marriage with all her might and, even after the wedding, she refused to welcome her son-in-law into the family.

A widow from the age of thirty-seven, Giuseppina had single-handedly raised Angelo, Vincenzo and Rosa, and had managed the family properties inherited from her mother, the Marquise of Prato. Her father, Carmelo, was also from a noble Neapolitan family. His grandfather had bought and renovated the house on Via Vittorio Emanuele, a former convent built during the Renaissance.

In the part of the house my father had inherited and now mine, the old convent's structure was still clearly visible: the solid wood and wrought iron porch, the courtyard onto which all the main rooms opened, the suite of reception rooms, the high rib-vaulted ceilings of exposed stone, the backyard with its ancient well, and, beyond that, the garden and terraces offering a view of the polychrome dome of the Chiesa Madre and the church of Santa Maria delle Grazie. Now that I had it restored, you could see the frescoes, the decorations in Lecce stone and even the Malvani family coat of arms: an azure and fess gules charged with four fleur-de-lys surmounted by a gold star.

'C'mon, Mama, I beg you, please let me go!'

On 26 July 1926, a big celebration was organised in Campi in honour of Achille Starace. Rosa was all dressed to go. She had one of those fashionable high-waisted dresses adorned with glass beads made especially for her by the best dressmaker in town. Her cousin was wearing a similar model the day of her birthday; she had it made in Lecce from a model that had come straight from the capital.

'I don't believe it is fitting for you to go out this evening in town. Neither your cousin Virginia nor your cousin Maria will be going and, for my part, I haven't the slightest intention to step foot out of the house. This man, this Starace, is a social climber. *Ci ete? Ce bole?* He does not interest us at all!'

After having visited the construction site of

the Puglia aqueduct, the leader of the Fascist Party decided to profit from the occasion to see some of the towns in his native Salento. And that night, in Campi, his brother-in-law decided to grant him honorary citizenship. Arturo had asked Rosa to accompany him to the ceremony. 'Prefect Murri will be there along with Crown Prosecutor Orsini Ducas and Baron Bacile di Castiglione,' he announced some weeks before the celebration. 'It is an excellent occasion for us to officially announce our engagement, don't you think, Rosetta? We will be very well received. Comrade Starace knows exactly who I am. He knows that in March, I too was in Rome with the other judges who paid tribute to the Duce. Do you recall? I showed you the photo. The one where I am standing next to Mussolini: He is in the centre, majestic and imposing, with his arms crossed, and I am right there beside him on his left.'

'Virginia and Maria are still very young, Mama. And after all, I'm not going to be loitering in the streets. I only want to go with Arturo to the reception that will be held at town hall after the ceremony. Everyone will be there, Mama. Why not me?'

'I don't like this judge, Rosa! How many times must I tell you? He's a social climber. All that interests him is your dowry, your properties and your titles of nobility. Forget this man. Listen to your mother who loves you. You still have time to change your mind. Why don't you take an interest in somebody from Campi, whose family and origins we know?'

After primary school, Giuseppina had chosen not to pursue her studies.

'What do you need beside reading, writing, and arithmetic?' she'd reply to anyone who asked why she decided not to continue her education. 'You get married, you have children and you take care of your family. What else do you need? After all, I know everything I need to know to manage a household and oversee the work of the staff!'

She had a strong character, confessed my father, who grew up by his grandmother's side. She was never satisfied. The domestics never lived up to her expectations: Lucia did not know how to make the sauce, Concetta was sloppy with the housework, the cheeses that the peasants brought them on Christmas and Easter were of poor quality. 'Who do these *cafuni 'mbrujuni* think they are?' Nothing and no one was ever good enough. Except, of course, for her eldest son, my father's uncle Nino. She readily forgave him for everything, especially after her husband's death: his gambling losses, his hidden or official mistresses, his superficiality and his cynicism.

'I'm going out, Mama. I'll see you tomorrow morning.'

Rosa had inherited her mother's character and was not about to give in. She had decided to go to the celebration with Arturo, and she would go come what may. It was pointless to argue with her, pointless to invoke the Madonna and Saint Pompilio, pointless to make a fuss.

'If your father were still alive today, you wouldn't behave this way. He would put you in your place, you impudent girl.'

And Rosa would retort, 'Don't let your son influence you with this dowry business! Nino would do better to think about how much he spends on his card games and his mistresses instead of getting in my way. Pay no attention to his caprices, Mama!'

According to my father, my mother was capricious. And so was my brother, who resembled her. And when I did not obey him, and things subsequently went awry, I was obliged to say he was right.

Capriciousness and *joie de vivre* were one and the same in my father's eyes. 'Ah, this *joie de vivre*,' he would say with a drawn out, hollow sounding 'ahhh', dripping with contempt, if my brother and I would start laughing during lunch or dinner. Something had fallen, or my mother had said or done something, any pretext would do. When you're young, and sometimes even when you're grown up, you can burst into laughter over nothing. But my father considered that laughing or joking meant taking things superficially. And taking things superficially was proof of an inability to give depth to existence.

'In life, things don't happen by themselves,' my father always said. 'You have to force them to happen and to force them to happen requires rigour, perseverance and order.' The exact opposite of what he thought my mother embodied.

When he met my mother, my father fell madly in love with her. She was breathtakingly beautiful. When I looked at pictures of her, she reminded me of Italian actresses from the 1960s. I even convinced myself that they were happy in the first years of their marriage. But gradually over time things turned sour, and my father got it into his head that my mother was responsible for all his failures and woes.

'Do you like this dress?' my mother asked her husband one day.

At the beginning of their marriage, my parents were by no means well off. For years my mother had bought nothing. She had made do with what she had, making sacrifices and trying her best to show her husband that she was not a frivolous woman.

'I hope you never wear it,' he replied icily.

His disdain was such that, having by chance witnessed this scene, I ran to lock myself in my bedroom and held my doll in my arms to console her and tell her not to cry.

When I told this story to Jacques, he was speechless. 'But what did your father mean by what he said? I don't understand.'

The problem is that I too never understood the exact meaning of those words, and I never accepted the attitude that my father had toward his wife. As if the mere fact of having bought a dress was proof of guilt. In what sense? And why?

'Don't tell me what I should or shouldn't do! I'm the one who decides, I'm the man. I will never allow you to push me around. That will never happen! Do you understand? Never!'

This happened a few years ago. I was in Rome, at

my parents' and I heard screaming from the kitchen. I rushed out of my bedroom.

My father's face was all red and he kept on screaming. My mother was all white.

'Papa, stop! You should be ashamed of yourself! Do you realise what you're saying?'

By now, I was the one who couldn't calm down. My parents had been married over fifty years and I had witnessed so many scenes like this from the time I was a little girl.

'That's enough! I've had enough of your delusions of omnipotence!'

'Do you think you know how your mother was when I met her? And everything that I've had to do to make sure she didn't destroy you and your brother's life, like her mother destroyed hers and her husband's?'

Just as everything seemed to be going well – engagement, career, renown and honours – someone tried to undermine my grandfather. In November 1926, an anonymous complaint was sent to Cavaliere Leoni, the crown prosecutor in Lecce.

The petition reads as follows: 'Marzano has lost his ability to make objective judgements; he does not preside over the court in a fitting manner; he is often absent; he applies sentences incorrectly; he neglects his work.'

The prosecutor in Lecce, who disliked the young upstarts who had begun for several years to take over the courts in the Salento, leapt on the occasion and, in January 1927, he had Arturo transferred to Vico del Gargano, a small judicial district in the province of Foggia, a several-hour drive from Campi.

But Cavaliere Leoni had moved too hastily and his intentions miscarried. Arturo was not the kind of man to let himself be sanctioned without fighting back. After the initial embarrassment and questions about what had happened and what exactly he had been accused of, he decided to file a complaint with the public prosecutor in Bari, requesting that he be subjected to an official investigation. 'These boors have no idea who they are dealing with!' Arturo told himself. 'What riffraff! Are they aware that in March I was in Rome with other comrades to pay tribute in person to the Duce? Are they aware that I was at his side and that Mussolini looked me straight in the eye and shook my hand?'

In Campi, Arturo Marzano's engagement to Rosa Campa had given rise to gossip and malicious talk. It seemed that the anonymous complaint sent to the prosecutor in Lecce had been motivated by jealousy.

In the Malvani family, news of Arturo's transfer was not well received. Donna Giuseppina took advantage of the situation to try to persuade Rosa to break up with Arturo. 'Cancel your engagement, Rosetta! An end must be put to all thing gossip; our family has always been respected and held above others!'

The anonymous accusers did not however realise what they were up against. They underestimated not only Rosa's stubbornness but also Arturo's curriculum vitae, for he could boast of being a good magistrate and also a faithful devotee of the regime from its earliest days.

Of this, Arturo hastened to remind the public prosecutor of Bari, who was the superior of the prosecutor of Lecce, and he immediately took up the matter. In December 1927, less than a year after my grandfather's transfer to Vico del Gargano, the investigative committee working with the court of appeals in Bari issued its unanimous opinion: Judge Marzano enjoys widespread esteem and all the best citizens of Campi are unhappy about the prospect of his departure from the area; instead of being persecuted, he deserves to be encouraged.

Arturo was promoted deputy crown prosecutor to the court of Lecce. Cavaliere Leoni was removed from his post in Lecce and transferred to Potenza.

For my grandfather, it was a victory. For Rosa, who could resume her life as a lady surround by domestics and under the vigilant and benevolent eye of her mother, it was a great relief.

On 2 June 1927, at 10.15 am, Arturo went to the town hall and announced to the mayor his and Rosa Campo's intention to get married. He took several weeks off to personally take care of marriage preparations. He wanted things to go quickly, and for the civil and religious ceremonies to be celebrated before the end of the year. Rosa stayed at home that day, despite the fact that her presence was required for the mayor to publish the banns. But this publication is precisely what was problematical for Rosa and her family.

'What need is there to let the whole world know that Rosa and Arturo decided to get married?' Rosa's mother Giuseppina asked. And when Don Giuseppe explained to her that it was standard procedure, she replied: 'For others it may be, but not for us. We are not like the others.'

When I looked at the register of marriage notices from 1927, it irked me to see that the entry for Marzano-Campo was crossed out. A note indicated that the future bride did not show up and that the notice would not be displayed on the door of the town hall. What was the source of this obsession with always doing things differently? And then, in reading the registers of Campi from 1927, I discovered something else. On 10 October 1927, the very day of the wedding, Rosa did not leave her home. The mayor received a medical certificate attesting that Signorina Campo was unable to go to the town hall to celebrate her marriage due to a nervous depression. The mayor took it upon himself to go in person to the Campo family home. And there, in the former convent, he married my grandparents.

'Papa, did you know that grandmother refused to go to the town hall for the wedding?'

'What's that?'

'Well, she had a medical certificate sent to the mayor so that the wedding could be held in her home.'

'That strikes me as odd.'

'It certainly is! But it is written on the marriage certificate. What do you think this business of a nervous depression was all about? Did your mother suffer from mood swings?'

My father didn't know much of anything. He didn't even know before I told him that a civil wedding had been held on 10 October 1927. He had only ever heard about the religious ceremony at Santa Maria delle Grazie, when his mother, fatherless since the age of twelve, was escorted to the altar by Carmelo, his grandfather. He knew that all the aristocratic families in Campi came to the gathering at their place, that it was a magnificent celebration, that they had danced, and that his grandmother had worked on the buffet preparations for weeks.

'And what about your mother's nervous depression?' I insisted.

This business about the medical certificate vexed me even more than the annulment of the wedding banns. What need would there be to invent mood disorders? Rules are rules, aren't they? Or did my grandmother actually suffer from such a disorder? Once again, where was the truth?

'A rule is a rule and it must be respected,' my father would always say when my brother or I would ask him to make an exception. My father could never tolerate what he called 'the atavistic southern Italian tendency to try to find ways to get around rules'. Even though he was born in the Salento, he always complained about the laziness of people in the south, and their mania with taking their time and procrastinating. My father thought that such a mentality had to be changed. As an upstanding socialist, he thought that progress and culture had to be brought to the south. He was always very fond of his native region, but at bottom he had only contempt for the attachment to old traditions, the homemade pasta, the tomato sauce that took days on end to prepare, all the habits that seem outdated to him. He had studied in Harvard and Cambridge, had become a neo-Keynesian economist, an intellectual, a progressive. To his mind, everything that did not go well in our family was my mother's fault. She had remained provincial and had never managed to break free from southern customs. He, on the other hand, had emancipated himself from traditions, had lived in America and in England. For dinner he wanted to eat soup and cheddar cheese and not the good old *orecchiette con le cime di rape.*

'They thought of themselves as different from others,' said my mother, who after years of keeping quiet, was refusing to be silent anymore. 'They always felt above everything and everybody and they tailored rules to their liking.'

Nowadays, my mother was speaking up, protesting, sometimes even screaming.

'After more than fifty years of hearing that I did not understand anything and that he was the one who knew what to do… Now I know that your father is the one who never understood a thing about life!'

'A rule is a rule,' my father would always say. But then why did his own mother not go to the town hall like everyone else? Now I found myself being the one to argue the value of rules. After having heard my father praise them for so long, now I was the one who was unwilling to tolerate subterfuge, lies and deception. I cannot stomach people who think they are smarter than other people and who are ready to profit from the good faith of others. As Jacques says, I am sometimes uncompromising. Always too hard on myself and on others. More royalist than the king.

I had only one photograph of Arturo and Rosa's wedding, without a date or annotations. It belonged to my father's cousins. They gave it to me the last time I went to their place. It was taken to the courtyard of my grandparents' home: I recognised the big side doors and steps of the terrace stairway, and I also recognised the wrought iron balustrade. A century later, practically nothing had changed, only the pavement was different: At the time, there was a very lovely pavement of *chianche*, the stone of Lecce. Who had the awful idea of replacing them with those horrible concrete slabs I discovered there when I was a child?

Arturo and Rosa are in the second row. Five children in the front row make it impossible to see the bride's wedding gown. Only the upper part of Rosa's dress is visible along with the veil that surrounds her head and covers her face, secured to her forehead by a cord. Unlike Arturo, who is extremely serious, my grandmother is smiling politely. Yet Arturo's face has delicate features while Rosa's is plump, almost bloated. She looks incredibly like her own mother, who poses by her side, all dressed in black with a crown of short hair and bangs, and heavy features. Not beautiful in the least. I told Jacques that I found my grandmother's wedding dress rather shabby. He replied that I'm exaggerating: 'That's what it was like at the time!'

But when I searched on the internet for photographs of wedding dresses in the late 1920s, they did not look anything like Rosa's. No lace, no tassels, no broaches, no diadems on the picture of my grandmother. And then there's that coarse cord around her head and, instead of a string of pearls around her neck, she is wearing only a white scarf.

Arturo decided to take his wife to Venice for their honeymoon, but first they made a stop in Bologna. That is where Vincenzo, Rosa's brother, had studied medicine and still lived and worked. Rosa so wanted to visit the city that her brother had spoken to her about so often. Arturo's memories of Bologna were linked to the war and he would have rather avoided the city, but in the end, he gave in. He also gave in when his wife insisted on going to see Vincenzo, who was working at the Bazzano medical centre. Arturo detested diseases. He would shudder at the mention of tuberculosis; anything that concerned the human body made him anxious, and also he and Vincenzo didn't get on. My grandmother's brother was a liberal anti-fascist and no supporter of the regime. Yet Arturo gave in again and again, even when his wife asked him to go with her to Elena Venturoli, a dressmaker with a shop on Via Saragozza. Vincenzo had told her that Bologna's nobility went to her to have their dresses made.

A postcard dated 16 October 1927, sent to my father's cousins' mother, shows Arturo and Rosa on Bologna's Piazza Grande. Surrounded by pigeons, the newlyweds stare at the camera. They seem not to know whether they should stay still in front of the camera, despite the pigeon that landed on Arturo's arm, or wave away the pigeons at the risk of exasperating the photographer. I found the postcard with the wedding picture that I got from my father's cousins. With the photo and the postcard, there was also a bill signed by Elena Venturoli.

When Arturo saw Rosetta's eyes light up at the sight of the window display, he decided to give his young wife a dress. Rosetta chose the model and fabric. But when the package from Elena Venturoli arrived in Vico del Gargano, where they had rented a small flat while waiting for the Bari court of appeal to pronounce judgement on the accusations against Arturo, she flew into a rage and wrote a letter to the dressmaker. '*Ce bbete 'stu nastru cafunescu?*' Did she show her husband the gold trim on the waist and sleeves and complain to him? 'Look at this ribbon! Isn't it vulgar looking?' Arturo did not agree. He liked the dress a lot and didn't think it was vulgar looking. On the contrary. He thought it was dainty and elegant. But when Rosetta got an idea into her head, there was no reasoning with her. She raised her voice, started to scream and then began complaining that she had a headache and stayed in bed for days with her eyes closed.

On 23 November 1927, Elena Venturoli replied to my grandmother. In addition to the bill for 431.50 lire for the dress and the sky-blue velvet cape, the dress's silk lining, the buttons and the buckles, the box and the delivery, there was a brief letter filled with grammatical and syntactical mistakes but extremely clear:

Dear Signora, I am sorry that you do not like the dress and you want to remove the gold finish around the waist, the reflection of gold takes on the shade of the velvet and makes the dress look so fancy and high-class and not crass at all! Believe you me Signora that this is not to my taste only [...] and the more you wear it the more you will like it because my models are stylish for one, two, even three years [...] If you want to send me back the trim on the neck and the sleeves, go ahead, but I tell you that when you are dressed like this, you do not look crass at all, you look distinguished and fashionable.

'It's *cafonesco*!' my father used to say. Even though it was a little like the *joie de vivre* business: I could never really get a handle on it. Who decided what was distinguished and what was vulgar? Who established the criteria? My father regarded nearly everything that others did as vulgar, hence *cafonesco*. Home-made pasta and fresh ricotta, nail polish and mini skirts. It was vulgar to cook all day long, like my mother did when she had people over for dinner at home; it was vulgar to go window shopping on Saturday afternoons when I was a teenager and my mother suggested that I go out with her…

Pretentious and snobby! A bit like me, alas, for I get miffed at garish colours or excessively high heels. And I told Jacques that it seemed vulgar to me to wear all those jewels: 'Don't you think she looks like the Virgin of Loreto?'

On 15 January 1928, Arturo was transferred to the court of Lecce. On 21 June, he was appointed deputy public prosecutor there. On 11 February, he was transferred to Brindisi, where he remained until 4 December 1933, when he was transferred to Rome. On 17 April 1930, at the instigation of Mussolini and the Minister of Justice, he was named knight of the Order of the Crown of Italy.

I wanted to understand what exactly my grandfather said or did to earn this title and also to get ahead in his career as he did, but I had neither photos nor letters from the period. What did Arturo do in Rome in 1933? How long did he stay there? Did his wife go with him or did she stay in Puglia? When Rosaria, his eldest child, was born in September 1934, was he with my grandmother or was he still in Rome? Why didn't he pursue a career as a minister? It should not have been hard for a fascist of the very first hour?

'The judiciary was independent,' my father said when I asked him if he knew something about those years. 'It was a separate branch,' he insisted with the tone of someone who knows what he's saying.

Had he forgotten that in Italy the independence

of judges from the executive and legislative powers was not established until 1948? At the beginning of the twentieth century, all the judges were under the oversight of the Minister of Justice, a situation that certainly did not improve with the advent of fascism. Quite the opposite. As Minister Alfredo Rocco repeated with pride: 'The judiciary is being invaded by the spirit of fascism much more rapidly than the other branches of government.'

'At the time, crown prosecutors depended directly on the Minister of Justice; they were even subordinate to prefects, Papa!' I couldn't let my father get away with speaking nonsense. 'At any rate, by 1932, being a member of the Fascist Party had become mandatory to be admitted to the judiciary. And only those who could prove that they were good fascists had the possibility of advancing in their careers.'

'Everything in the state, nothing outside the state, nothing against the state.' Mussolini's formulation sums up the totalitarian spirit of fascism: synthesis and unity of all values. The Fascist State was to dominate every aspect of the lives of Italian people. Any public official acting against government guidelines was dismissed. All parties, aside from the Fascist Party (PNF), were dissolved. Anti-fascists were sentenced to internal exile in the far corners of Italy and freedom of expression vanished. New prefects loyal to the regime were nominated and a court dedicated to the 'defence of the state' was established.

By 1928, to be hired for any position whatsoever, you had to be registered on the lists of job applicants in your region of residence and priority was given to members of the PNF.

By February 1929, teachers had to swear allegiance to Mussolini in order to continue teaching.

By 1930, academy rectors and university presidents had to have been members of the PNF for at least five years in order to keep their positions. That same year, in the Alto Adige, an Italianisation campaign was launched: all names – of people, cities and entities – had to be translated into Italian.

By 1931, even university professors – normally unaffiliated and independent – were obliged to swear allegiance to fascism.

That same year, Achille Starace, the mayor of Campi's brother-in-law, became secretary of the PNF. When the *Gazzetta des Messogiorno* announced it on 8 December 1931, they described Starace as an 'energetic' and 'tenacious' man, a 'descendant from an ancient lineage' and someone 'firm in his convictions'. It was now his responsibility to 'reach the people', 'keep them from weakening' and 'keep them more and more watchful'.

In Campi, Donna Maria and Giuseppe Guarino organised a big reception. Arturo and Rosetta were invited to the party, but Arturo was detained in Brindisi. He had a very important hearing at the court the following day and couldn't get away. 'Unable to come – we share in your joy – hearty congratulations – warmest regards – Arturo and Rosetta.'

Giuseppe read the telegram to his wife who smiled with pride: 'We will have the opportunity to celebrate with them at Christmas. I know you get on well with Arturo, Pippi. Achille also esteems him greatly, for being rigorous, dynamic, driven and bold.'

'*Qui giace Starace vestito d'orbace – in pace rapacious, in guerra fugace – a letto pugnace, requiscat in pace.*' My father taught me the refrain, which was in fact an epitaph that began to circulate in Bologna immediately after the fall of fascism, and perhaps even before. Starace was loathed by students, even during the fascist period. He had the reputation of being a magnificent fool. My father had picked up the refrain, even if his version went as follows: '*Qui giace Starace, di niente capace, di tutto rapace.*' This variation left out the reference to Starace's sexual exploits and the 'rest in peace' in Latin. Maybe that was how he learnt it from his uncle, his mother's brother, who lived in Bologna and who, unlike his brother-in-law, did not like the fascists at all. Every time the topic of fascism came up at home, my father would always trot out this refrain. He would recite it and burst out laughing, and my brother and I would laugh too. We also thought of Starace as a clown. 'A ludicrous character, that Starace was,' my father added, turning serious again. 'A pathetic man. Can you imagine that he decreed that men could no longer wear top hats, that the Nativity scene was fascist but the Christmas tree was not, and that tea was fascist, unlike coffee? In a word, a real idiot. The years of fascism were terrible for Italy, my children. Don't ever forget it!'

Fascism had been a nightmare. And that was that!

I was proud of my father.

When I was a child, I did not understand what my father meant when he said that my mother had destroyed my life and my brother's life. I did not understand it, but I put my trust in him, not in my mother. He was my model. And for years, my greatest fear was that I would become like my mother.

I think back to the birthdays that my mother organised when my brother and I were little. She always prepared everything herself. We never had the kind of appetisers and delicacies from a caterer that were served at my friends' parties and that I longed so much to have. How lucky they were! We had a lot of things, but all of them were homemade: the ricotta and spinach shortcrust pastry pie; the brioche with mortadella and cheese; the cake with custard and chocolate cream.

'Mama, I don't like the liqueur that you put in the cake.'

'What liqueur?'

'The bright pink one; it's spicy.'

'It's not a liqueur, my treasure, it's Alkermes, and the recipe for this custard cake calls for it. That's how it's prepared. It's written in my grandmother's recipe notebook.'

I think back to my clothes for school. Everything I wore, the sweaters, the shirts, the dresses, were all made by hand. My mother knitted, sewed and embroidered. The smocks, the buttonholes, the epaulettes, the sleeves, the designs on the front…

'I found a model with little swirls. Look how pretty it is, Pumpkin,' she would say.

But I hated the sweaters and the dresses that my mother made. I wanted to buy them, like all the other girls did. Why did I have to be different?

I wanted to be like the others and I felt like a pauper. Everything in our home was fixed up and patched up: the buttons on my father's jeans and his socks; the reinforcements on the elbows of worn sweaters and pieces sewn over holes on the knees of pants. Tape, scissors, needle, thread, glue. My mother spent a crazy amount of time recycling, tidying up, reusing. Nothing was thrown out; nothing was wasted. I didn't understand why she always said that there wasn't enough money. Why wasn't there? Papa taught in university. She was the one who didn't work. She was the one who didn't earn money. It was her fault.

When my mother started teaching art education in middle school, my brother and I were already in primary school. Even though she was teaching, she was the one who came to pick us up, who helped us with our homework, who did the shopping, the housekeeping and the cooking. She took care of everything. And as soon as my father came home, the shouting and screaming began.

'Your father would walk around the house making sure that everything was in order, and he always found something wrong. I was terrified,' my mother was willing to tell me now.

But at the time, I had no idea. In those days, I thought that she was the hysterical one. Why wasn't she like Paola's mother? I would wonder about this, seeing how my girlfriends' mothers were always well-kempt, always elegant, always had their hair perfectly in place. Why does she wear that awful blue eyeshadow that she bought on sale in the supermarket? And at the beach in the summer, why does she use olive oil mixed with sea water instead of suntan lotion?

I will never be like her. My model was my father, not her.

Why were things like that? No doubt, I will never know. Did it start when my mother had surgery for a herniated disc and I was left alone for several weeks? I was only a year and a half old. Did I feel abandoned? Or did abandonment have nothing to do with it and would I always have thought my father was right? Was it just in my genes, in my blood, in my lineage? Or did that have nothing to do with it either, and that was just how things were, period?

I wanted my father to see me, to listen to me, to be proud of me, to say those words to me. 'I'm proud of you.' Plainly. That's all. He never said them. Or is it that I did not recall him doing so? Every time I tried to put together the pieces of my family's puzzle, I fell into a maze of mirrors and my reflection came back to me refracted into multiple images. It was not only the past that was eluding me. It was my own identity.

Of those days of being alone when I was a year and a half old, I have no memories. I was too little. Nevertheless, I am sure I felt alone and abandoned. That's how I see it, and that's how I relive it whenever my mother tells me the reaction I had when she came back home. Why didn't anyone take me to see her in the hospital? Why didn't my mother say anything to me when she put me to bed the night before she was admitted? Why did she simply disappear without giving me any explanation?

It seems that when my mother came back home with a cast from her pelvis to her neck, I would not go near her. I didn't run to her; I didn't try to throw myself into her arms. I stayed there, motionless, hidden in the corner of the corridor.

'Give me the little one,' my mother said. 'If I sit down and someone picks her up, I can hold her.'

I had no recollection. It was my mother who told this to me. But when she said that, once I was in her arms, I did not want to let go of her, I have no trouble whatsoever believing her. As I did when she told me that that night, when she put me to bed and tried to leave the room, I started to cry and she decided to stay with me until I fell asleep. But my father intervened and locked her in another room, and I continued crying for hours. Sooner or later, I was going to stop crying and calm down, my father argued.

'Do you want her to start having bad habits? Don't you want to teach her that there are rules in life and that rules must be respected? Do you want her to be a spoilt child? Are you out to destroy her?'

When I was little, I didn't want to grow up to be like my mother. She was not sure of herself; she didn't know how to behave in public and had a *petit bourgeois* mentality. That's what my father always said and I accepted what he said, even though I had no idea what having a *petit bourgeois* mentality meant. I heeded my father's advice, even when it was nonsense: Don't drink during meals or you'll gain weight; don't take acetaminophen for a fever, it's a natural reaction of the organism.

What was I looking for from my father? But maybe the problem was the question itself. Maybe I needed to stop asking it, to put it aside and suspend judgement. Any answer would be partial at best. And perhaps more damaging than useful. Why try to grasp the truth as if there were only one?

My father was born in Campi on 14 November 1936. When Lucia knocked on the door of my grandfather's office to announce that the '*signurinu*' was doing well, that he was sound in body and mind and that Donna Rosetta was waiting for him in the bedroom, Arturo found it hard to contain his emotion. Can a fascist, I wondered, feel moved? I thought back to how my father often said that my grandfather was a sensitive man. I thought back especially to what my mother said. She had known Arturo when he could not even speak anymore, and yet when he saw her for the first time, he was extremely moved. He had understood that she was his son's fiancée and he had cried. It is possible to imagine that my grandfather had a hard time containing his emotion when Lucia announced the birth of his son. Aren't we all a bundle of contradictions? Can't we be hard on ourselves and on others and yet feel moved when something touches us deep inside, something that throws the meaning of our lives into question, that confirms our childish fears or our old hopes?

Arturo returned to live in Campi in 1934, just before my father's sister Rosaria was born. For seven long years, my grandmother could not get pregnant. That may be the reason that my grandmother was not overly concerned when the doctor told my mother that she would not have children right away, that there was an obstruction in her fallopian tube and she'd have to take certain treatments and be patient. My grandmother simply advised her to go for spa treatments. Then finally, Our Lady of the Rosary graced her with a child and a daughter was born. At first, Arturo did not take the news that it was a girl well. He would have wanted a boy, since men are the ones who ensure the family posterity, who pass on the name of the family. Then he was consoled at the thought that, since Rosetta had become pregnant once, it could happen again.

Ferruccio's baptism was celebrated on 26 December 1936, at Santa Maria delle Grazie, and then again that very night, in the company of Giuseppe Guarino and his wife, the Prato family and the Malvani, Magi and Tocci cousins. In the afternoon, during preparations for the reception, a telegram came from Achille Starace expressing his very best wishes for happiness. Arturo rushed to the kitchen, took his wife in his arms and said, 'Look, Rosetta, read this! I told you that the news would reach Rome!'

I did not have a photo of the baptism, neither of Ferruccio nor of his parents. And no trace of Starace's message. The one and only thing I had to hold on to was a brief discussion between Giuseppina and Arturo that my father spoke to me about, and which he knew because it was the source of much laughter in the family for many years. It seemed that, once the religious ceremony was over, Giuseppina was furious at the priest.

I decided to tell the story exactly as my father described it to me, to invent nothing and to stick to his memory. I decided to open a small window on that day in December and to close it immediately thereafter. The day of my father's baptism is only a piece of the puzzle that I was trying to put together, a touch of colour on a fresco that, from 1936 onward, was painted only in black and white. The scene was more or less as follows.

'*Ci ete stu Pirandello? Ca c'entrava quiddu cu lu piccinnu?* Who is this Pirandello? And what does he have to do with my little one? I'm going to give that quack of a priest a piece of my mind tomorrow! Did he forget whom he was dealing with?' Giuseppina was beside herself when she left the church. The complaining started as soon as she stepped out of Santa Maria delle Grazie and continued the whole way home: She was protesting as she descended the steps of the church, as they walked along Via Vittorio Emanuele; she was still moaning in front of the porch of the house as she rummaged through her purse for the keys. During the sermon, Don Gennaro spoke of nothing but Pirandello and of his recent disappearance. '*Ci ete stu Pirandello?*' she repeated with insistence, glaring at her son-in-law and getting more and more riled up.

'C'mon, Giuseppina. Calm down!' Arturo smiled. 'Luigi Pirandello is one of the giants of our country! He even won the Nobel Prize two years ago.'

'So what!? What does he have to do with Ferruccio?'

'He died a few days ago, and Don Gennaro simply wanted to pay tribute to him. Speaking of him at Ferruccio's baptism was a way of celebrating the arrival of the little one.'

'I'm not so sure about that… But if you think so.'

'You'll see that our Ferruccio will do great things when he grows up. A great destiny awaits him.'

'But…'

'Now that's enough! Stop making a fuss!'

End of scene.

My father could not stop laughing when he told this story.

'There are things Grandmother really didn't understand,' he said. 'Poor thing. How could she have known who Pirandello was? She had no education, she never read a book. All she knew was the opera.'

The first photograph of my father dates to 30 January 1937. Ferruccio is in his father's arms. Arturo is seen in profile looking at his son. The baby is wrapped in an embroidered white cotton sheet and is wearing a bonnet, white as well. On the photo is written: 'My Ferruccio (and his father) at two months and sixteen days.'

'Who wrote this on the photograph, Papa?' My father had pulled out an album of photos during the Christmas holidays.

'It's my father's handwriting,' he replied after examining it for a few seconds. 'He was the one in our family who was obsessed with photos.'

My father started flipping through the album and added that Arturo was very attached to them and wanted to make sure that he and his sister would have a trace of those distant days when they were older.

'This one with my mother is very lovely, don't you think?' he murmured, pointing to the picture of his mother standing in the garden next to the stone well holding him in her arms. On this photo too there's an inscription: 'Rosetta and my Ferruccio, 28-8-1937.'

'Excuse me, Papa, but when did grandfather find the time to attend to the photos? Wasn't he crown prosecutor at the time? Why didn't mother take care of the photos?'

'Because he took care of everything!'

Ten years had passed since Rosetta and Arturo were married. And not a day went by without Rosetta thanking God for this unexpected gift. Arturo always knew how to behave and what to say. Arturo managed to stand up to her mother. Angelo, her brother, may have played it smart, but Arturo didn't let him get away with things.

Of course, her husband would lose his temper at times. When he did, he would lock himself in his office and hours went by before he decided he was ready to speak to anyone. Of course, it was not easy to leave Campi after the marriage and follow Arturo to Vico del Gargano. And it was not easy at all to stay at home by herself when her husband was transferred to Rome. But little by little it all worked out: The Virgin Mary was good to her and Arturo came back home. Now they were together again and Ferruccio was born. She had no reason to worry or be afraid anymore. Everything worked out. Arturo was crown prosecutor at the juvenile court of Lecce and the prefect of Lecce had even appointed him to be a member of the provincial committee of surveillance of newspapers. There was only one thing that Rosetta could not understand. Why does her husband keep telling her he wants to make a career for himself? What kind of career would he still like to have?

'Orderly, precise, attentive.'

My father repeated this mantra to my brother again and again. It was an obsession with him. As if it made any sense to torment a six- or seven-year-old with this business of order, precision and attention.

My father had two states of mind: When he was calm, he would make up rhymes and limericks which, seen today out of context, could even suggest a measure of levity; when he was tense and nervous, he would threaten, scream and use his hands.

Se vuoi bere da bagordo, aspettar devi il raccordo. This rhyme (*bagordo*, literally 'revelry', and *raccordo*, 'ring road') loosely translates as, 'if you want to drink your fill, you'll have to wait until the ring road'.

Let me clarify the context. It was August and we were driving from Campi to Rome. Between eight and ten hours in a car with no air conditioning. That wasn't the problem. No one had any back in those days. The problem was that my brother and I were not allowed to drink during the entire drive. My father would not budge an inch: Otherwise, you'll have to go to the bathroom and I'll have to stop, do you understand? And he only stopped to get gas, otherwise we drove straight without a break, eating the sandwiches my mother prepared for us and one glass of water, at most.

'I'm thirsty,' protested my brother, who never let himself be intimidated by our father's orders.

I too was thirsty but I didn't say a thing. My father's 'no' was categorical. And one day when we were nearing Rome but were still on the highway and my brother repeated that he wanted something to drink, my father made up this rhyme about wanting to drink our fill and being able to do so when we reached the ring road. From there to the house, it took half an hour at most and so, even if we really had to go, we could hold it in and not make him waste time at a rest area on the road.

E chiesero a Ferruccio il bambino dov'è? Sta rompendo le scatole cattivello com'è.[1] The original version was a Christmas poem: *E chiesero a Giuseppe il bambino dov'è, e caddero in ginocchio davanti al Re dei Re.*[2] In a moment of light-heartedness, my father had adapted the words of these religious verses to suit my brother, at least in his mind, while maintaining the rhyme. He was always very proud of his rhymes. And this one was quite funny. It was a crying shame when it later became a source of torment. It was a crying shame when there was nothing at all to laugh about. When, on the pretext of Arturo's being a 'naughty boy', Papa would take him into his office, lock the door, and do his homework with him, a wooden spoon in his hand. My brother

[1] And they asked Ferruccio, Where is the child? He's being a little troublemaker, causing mischief as usual.

[2] And they asked Joseph, Where is the child? And they fell to their knees before the King of Kings.

would scream and cry and that evening at the dinner table there would be black and blues on his arms, legs and sometimes even on his face.

My father was persuaded that his son needed to be corrected, put back on the right path, straightened out. Unlike me, who from the time of my birth had immediately slept through the night, Arturo slept little and was always agitated. Unlike me, who already concentrated on my homework in primary school and never moved from my chair, he wanted to play and have a good time as well; for him, it was out of the question to sit for hours at his desk. And so what?

'Strike a balance within yourself,' my father would constantly shout at my brother at the top of his lungs. As if the little child could have understood what it meant to strike balance within him. How easy is it to strike a balance inside yourself? Even when you grow up, it is not something you can achieve and, what's more, you learn that such a thing does not exist, that no one is really well-balanced, that everyone is groping and trying to find their way as best they can. But this my father did not understand, he did not even try, and he was extremely brutal with Arturo. Everything Arturo did was wrong: He was agitated in school; his classmates made fun of him; he did not want to play Foosball; he loved playing with Barbie dolls…

'Be self-reliant; learn to find solutions to problems by yourselves.'

After circling the neighbourhood several times looking for a parking space, my father would always leave the car in any old place: on the sidewalk, obstructing the pedestrian crossings, double parked. He would turn on the hazard lights and get out, telling my brother and me, who were little at the time, that he would be right back.

'And what if someone wants to get out and we're blocking them?' we'd ask him every time he'd double park the car.

'You'll tell them to wait,' he would reply with the same lack of consideration.

'And what if they're in a hurry and they get angry?'

'You'll tell them to be patient and that I'll be right back.'

'And what if …'

'That's enough! You're grown up now; figure it out for yourselves!'

And it always ended the same way. My father would take forever to come back. Someone would come and want simply to get out of their parking space, we would tell him that our father will be back very soon, the person would wait a few minutes, then begin to look at his watch and come to ask if we had the keys. And since, despite our entreaties, our father never left the keys with us, the person would either call the police or get into our car, release the handbrake and push the car until he could pull his car out of his parking space.

And invariably when my father returned, he would make a scene and scream.

'You're useless, worse than your mother! You'll never amount to anything!'

It was the same story every time. My brother would start laughing and I was so ashamed that I wished the earth would swallow me up.

My grandfather was named Commander of the Crown at the end of 1937. It was the king who nominated him, *motu proprio*, and not on the recommendation of the Duce or the Minister of Justice. But, nevertheless, I could not help cringing. The date was not innocent. By late 1937, the first decrees on the 'defence of race' had already appeared: To fight against 'mixed blood practices', a directive prohibited 'relations of a conjugal type between white men and black women'. The fascist regime had taken a clear racist turn.

Jacques told me again not to fall into the anachronistic trap.

'It was a marginal issue at the time,' he said.

But it wasn't marginal for me. At the time, fascism was not only the hope of misguided young people who felt they had been sacrificed by the liberal bourgeoisie. Fascism was a well-established regime that played into the hands of big business and which was becoming racist.

How could my grandfather accept this without protest? For this is precisely the problem with this nomination! And the fact that it was the king that nominated him commander, *motu propio*, and not a ranking member of the fascist regime, does not constitute by any means an attenuating circumstance.

It would be absurd even to think it does. If Arturo had done nothing more than manifest his disagreement with these decrees concerning race, he would never have been appointed commander.

'The same applied to many people at the time,' Jacques objected.

But that made no difference to me. Accepting the idea that certain races needed to be defended at the detriment of others was an outrage. Plain and simple.

'Race is a feeling, not a reality,' Mussolini had said in 1932 to the German writer Emil Ludwig.

Between 1929 and 1932, the Duce and the writer of Jewish origin met on several occasions at the Palazzo di Venezia. In these conversations, they disagreed, even violently at times, about fascism and Nazism, which was not yet in power in Germany but was beginning, with its frightening theories of race, to take centre stage in the political debate.

'Nothing will ever make me believe that biologically pure races can be shown to exist today,' Mussolini had said to Ludwig at the time, assuring him that Italy would never adopt the mad notions advocated by the new Nazi party. 'National pride has no need of the delirium of race,' the Duce had added. 'Italians of Jewish birth have shown themselves to be good citizens, and they fought bravely in the war.'

The conversations between Mussolini and Ludwig were published in 1932 by Hoepli Editore and were immediately circulated throughout the country. How was it that by 1937 the Duce had changed his mind completely? Why did he decide to adopt racial laws against Jews in 1938?

It was on 14 July 1938 that the evening edition of *Il Giornale d'Italia* published the 'Manifesto of Race'. It seems that Mussolini boasted several times that he had written it himself. 'The Jews do not belong to the Italian race,' point 9 of the manifesto declares. The Jewish population 'is made up of non-European racial elements differing absolutely from the elements from which the Italians originated'. The manifesto was thereafter published on 5 August in the first issue of the journal *La Difesa della razza*, founded by the Il Duce himself to popularise the principle and politics of fascist racism, and directed by Telesio Interlandi with the help of Giorgio Almirante, the future secretary of the Italian Social Movement (MSI), a neo-fascist party. Signed by a dozen scientists, the manifesto was accompanied this time by a few explanatory sentences: 'It is high time that Italians declare themselves forthrightly to be racists. All of the policies that have been conducted by the regime in Italy until now are underpinned by racism. The concept of race is present very often in the Duce's speeches. The question of racism in Italy has to be treated from a purely biological, not philosophical or religious, standpoint. The concept of racism in Italy must be essentially Italian and Aryan-Nordic in outlook.'

There were people after the war who claimed that the Duce did not really believe in these ideas about race and that he instituted anti-Semitic legislation to please his friend Hitler. But nothing is less certain. Within a few months, an increasing number of laws, guidelines and decrees were adopted, touching every aspect of the professional and private lives of Italians, and marginalising and discriminating against the Jews. A national census was conducted. The citizenships for Jews granted after 1919 were all revoked and it was prohibited for 'foreigners of Jewish race to reside in Italy, Libya and all the possessions of the Aegean Sea.' Jews were not allowed to teach and no Jewish child could enrol in a public school.

Nearly a hundred university professors lost their jobs, along with 200 lecturers, 133 associate lecturers, 279 secondary school teachers, 100 primary school teachers, 400 employees of the public sector and 150 servicemen. In addition, 200 university students, 1,000 high school students and 4,400 primary school pupils were forced to stop their studies.

Injustice became the rule, including in the very body charged with the administration of justice that is the judiciary.

Lawyers and magistrates, regardless of their position or rank, knew this perfectly well. But nearly no one reacted or expressed disagreement. The same was true when on 5 December 1938, the Minister of Justice, Arrigo Solmi, launched a competition for 214 positions as justice auditors, requiring that candidates not only provide a certificate proving their membership in the Fascist Party, but also a declaration of 'not belonging to the Jewish race'. Neither did anyone protest when Solmi demanded a similar declaration from all magistrates already in office to verify the 'racial purity' of everyone in the judiciary.

On the basis of the information provided, the Minister of Justice dismissed fourteen Jewish magistrates and forced four judges, who bravely refused to comply with his orders to present a declaration certifying that they were not Jewish, to sign a request for early retirement.

The surname, given name and title of every purged magistrate appeared in the official gazettes of the ministry, which were distributed to all the courts.

My grandfather knew about this and he kept silent.

Every magistrate had access to these bulletins. Anyone in a position of responsibility was aware of what was happening. And even if none of the purged magistrates worked in Lecce, Brindisi or Bari, my grandfather could not have ignored the purges that were taking place. Jacques could talk of 'anachronism' from here to doomsday; I could not accept it.

Arturo knew. And, like the others, he kept silent.

My conscience was clear. That was what I said to myself, even though I could hardly say that I was feeling okay, at bottom. But I needed to hold onto something because, otherwise, everything risked coming undone: my unshakeable certainty of having always been on the right side of history, my small angelic world, my father's good leftist conscience, the possibility of looking at myself in the mirror without shame.

My conscience was clear. That was what I kept repeating to myself. At home, we always spoke of the Shoah, even though we used the term 'holocaust' at the time, and it was only later when I arrived in France that I understood that the extermination of the Jews was not an 'inevitable sacrifice' as the word 'holocaust' denotes; it was a drama, a tragedy, a catastrophe, which is the literal meaning of the word 'shoah'.

At home, we always spoke about it. I was barely eight when we watched the TV series *Holocaust*, a year after having watched *Roots*. Between seven and eight years old, I learnt that white people had reduced black people to slavery and that the Nazis had wanted to exterminate the Jews. I learnt how far human cruelty and madness could go and understood that human beings are not only capable of committing irreparable crimes, but that they also sought absurd justifications for the unacceptable.

My father insisted that my brother and I watch *Roots* and *Holocaust*.

'They have to know what happened, Paola!' he told my perplexed mother.

'They're still so young. Are you sure that it's a good idea to show them these programmes?'

'Children have to grow up with an awareness of evil and suffering,' he replied. 'Otherwise, how will they know the difference between good and evil when they are older?'

My conscience was clear. After having watched *Holocaust*, I read *The Diary of Anne Frank*, Primo Levi's *If This is a Man*, Vittorini's *Conversations in Sicily*, and Bassani's *The Garden of Finzi-Continis*. In my room, I became an anti-fascist, a member of the Resistance, a socialist. Italy's history was dark under fascism, but my father taught me to be on the side of the left and of the Resistance. I was on the right side of history, and I would always live up to the ideals of my father and my family. Needing reassurance, I continued to repeat this to myself today.

But was my family always on the 'right side'? Was my conscience truly clear? Or was I only trying to seek forgiveness for a dark past, a past shared by so many Italians?

Forgiveness, like love, is not 'because', writes Jankélévitch, but rather a matter of 'even though': 'The being who is loved and the misdeed that is forgiven, indeed, are not strictly speaking the reason for forgiveness and for love; they are much more the anti-reason and even sometimes insanity.' So why then was I stubbornly insisting on looking for explanations? Why couldn't I simply accept the idea that my family's past was as dark as that of Italy?

'The few Jews living in Otranto were perfectly well integrated for decades and not at all distinguishable from other Italians. They continued to live peaceably and engage in their usual activities,' writes Tonino Guarino, the son of the mayor of Campi, in the book that he wrote about his family and in which my grandfather's name is mentioned. 'The wealthy Masraghi and Petrachi families, even though they were known to be Jewish, were not affected in the least. They had always been close to the Staraces and they continued to be so,' writes the nephew of the Fascist Party's secretary general. Just before adding, in speaking of his uncle: 'Achille never brought up the subject at home, and furthermore it did not concern the Salento. The only thing that changed in the region was the indication *Aryan race* mentioned on ID documents, to which the population gave no importance, in contrast to what happened in other regions of Italy.'

Unbelievable! I said to myself as I hurled the book to the floor. For goodness' sake, how could anyone write this kind of thing in our day? I was furious. And what about the publisher? They let that pass without a word?

In the 1930s, few Italian Jews resided in Puglia. That much was true. The infamous statistics compiled by the fascists bear this out. Puglia counted 94 Jews, which was very little in comparison with, for example, the 11,789 living in Latium or the 3,460 living in Venice. But what was also true was that the campaign for the defence of racial laws was extremely violent in Puglia. As it was also true that the echo given to Starace's propaganda 'against all forms of pity' was striking. Without forgetting the persecution of Jewish families in Lecce, Maglie and Glatone. A case in point was the purge of Lieutenant Colonel Mosè Cohen, obliterating in a single stroke the fact that he was a decorated veteran. Another was the fate of the Agranati family that had a tobacco factory franchise and were deported to the concentration camp in Lacedonia immediately after Italy entered the war.

History cannot be obliterated, the mayor of Campi said in 2017, when he was asked how he could have dedicated a public square to Don Giuseppe Guarino, the former fascist mayor, Starace's brother-in-law. But how then have some fragments of history in Campi been obliterated, seemingly forever? Why these double standards?

'I wasn't there, and if I was there, I didn't see anything, and if I saw something I don't remember.' Inadmissible. The 'delirium of race' that Italy, according to Mussolini, had no need for, claimed many victims, even in the south of Italy. And having been good citizens or having fought courageously on the battlefields made no difference. The mere fact of being Jewish was, even in Puglia, a mark of disgrace and of infamy.

'I wasn't there, and if I was there, I didn't see anything, and if I saw something I don't remember.' Unacceptable. Because in point of fact, the people of the Salento were actually there. Not only Achille Starace, who signed the racial laws, or Tonino Guarino, who had the gall to write that his uncle never discussed the subject at home, as if the simple fact of not speaking about it could negate its existence. But also my grandfather, who was crown prosecutor and hence custodian of the laws and their application, and all those who lived there, and who, with the mention of *Aryan race* on their ID cards, thought they could demonstrate their purity and integrity.

Everyone knew and everyone collaborated with the fascist regime.

I picked up Tonino's book and reread the passage. 'The Jews living in Otranto were not at all distinguishable from other Italians.' What does that mean? Were they distinguishable elsewhere? 'The only thing that changed in the region was the indication *Aryan race* mentioned on ID documents, to which the population gave no importance.' What does that mean? They label you and you don't react? Does being Aryan and not Jewish make you feel better? And what if it was the opposite? What if you had been 'Jewish'? Would you have been ashamed? Would you have had to lie and hide?

When you do not confront the past, it acts on you.

When you delude yourself into thinking that it is gone, it resurfaces.

It catches up with you sooner or later. And you will have to pay your dues.

And my dues? What were they? I was beginning to piece together all my discoveries, and I found myself confronted with a heritage that was very different and much weightier than I had imagined. To be sure, there was nothing particularly dramatic or exceptional in this heritage: It was shared by many families of dignitaries who actively participated in the fascist experience. But for a woman of the left who had always been convinced of being on the right side of history, it was a bit much. I would have liked to rid myself of it. But how could I? I could not deny its existence. I was the one who undertook this journey back in time and I would now have to see it through to the end. But how could I come to terms with my past when it was overwhelming me?

I was exhausted by everything that was resurfacing. The very thought of leaving my place, going to the university and giving my courses made me nervous. That was how it was for days. And when I came home at night, my head was ready to explode. I didn't clean, I didn't shop, I didn't do anything practical. And given that Jacques had always relied on me until now for such things, everything seemed to be coming apart at the seams.

I kept waking at night plagued by doubts and anxieties. My sleep was one nightmare after another. Most of my dreams vanished without a trace in the morning, without leaving me even an image or a word to hold onto. And when by chance a nightmare persisted and haunted me, it was even worse. What was the appeal of remembering a dream if I could not interpret it?

We are not trees. Our roots do not determine us. But the family heritage is something we all carry with us. We are the fruit of a history transmitted from generation to generation, which persists and lives in each of us and which shapes us – even when many of our memories are inaccessible – influences our way of being and doing, and deposits sediments in our language, in our singular way of naming things.

'Well, are you going to tell me what you dreamt?' Jacques had had enough of seeing me sulking since I woke up.

I relented in the end and told him about it, even though I was ashamed.

'It was horrifying! I dreamt I was at the doctor's. I had to have some tests done and a patch needed to be chosen to put on my back. The doctor hesitated, saying he wasn't sure what patch to use. You have to match the colour of the skin, he said. If you don't match the polymorphism of the DNA, the body will reject it. I see that your complexion is dark. Do you have African origins?'

'What do you mean?' Jacques asked me.

'What do I know? That was exactly the question that I asked the doctor in my dream, but he didn't answer me and he consulted my mother. Then he invited me into his office again and told me: "Your mother is Caucasian, no doubt about it. But I can't use a Caucasian patch on you because your mother is not your mother." Can you imagine that, Jacques?'

'Come now. Calm down. It's only a dream.'

'Wait, I haven't finished. The end was horrible! After telling me that my mother wasn't my mother, the doctor added, "I'm sorry to break it to you like this, it may seem harsh, but sooner or later you'll have to accept the facts: You are not of the same race as your mother." That's what he said. In exactly those words, I swear! He said I wasn't of the same race as my mother!'

We were on holidays at the seaside. It was August. My brother must have been thirteen, fourteen at most, so I would have been sixteen or seventeen. My father set a curfew at 11:45, with a quarter of an hour grace period, not a minute more. 'What a drag!' I would say to myself every night when I looked at my watch and saw that I had to head home while the others could stay out and enjoy themselves. Yet I stuck scrupulously to the rules, knowing my father made no allowances. When my mother pointed out to him that we were the only ones who had to come home so early, he told her to shut up: 'I make the rules around here. How many times do I have to repeat that to you?'

One night, it was already past midnight and my father began yelling, 'Where's your brother?'

'I don't know. We weren't together.'

'How come?'

'We have different friends and I haven't the slightest idea where he is.'

My father was furious. I could sense that he was about to do something stupid.

'Calm down, Papa. Please!'

'I will not calm down one bit!'

I had an oppressive feeling in my chest, as if something was weighing it down and keeping me from breathing. I couldn't take the screaming; I couldn't take it anymore.

'Where is your son?' My father went into my mother's bedroom. She'd gone to bed, knowing full well that it was pointless to try to reason with her husband when he was angry. 'Get out of bed and go find him!' my father shouted. 'Right this minute!' He sounded like he was out of his mind.

My mother got up. Without saying a word, she got dressed. She was about to leave the house when I stopped her. 'Mama is not going anywhere!' Now, I was the one who was screaming. Even louder than my father. 'Leave her alone! What does she have to do with this?' I was trembling. 'I hate you!'

Just then Arturo walked in. He took in the scene and started laughing. It was his way of protecting himself, I knew that. This had been his reaction since he was a little boy, whenever there was a problem or an argument. But this time, it was too much for me. I couldn't take my father humiliating my mother because of his antics. So, I threw myself at him, 'Where the hell have you been? Do you see how late it is?' My brother kept on laughing. 'Asshole!' I blurted out, and I slapped him. He stayed there without moving, used to being slapped around.

Every time I think of this incident, I feel sick to my stomach. My brother was still very young. And instead of defending him, I lashed out at him. Instead of rebelling against my father and against his oppressive authority, I demanded that my brother adapt to it, like I did. 'A collaborator,' I say to myself every time I think of it. What would I have done in the fascist period?

It's hard to describe exactly what the atmosphere was like at home when I was a child. For a long time, Jacques would tell me that he could not understand what had kept me from rebelling against my father.

'He's not a monster,' he would say. 'He's unbearable and a pain in the neck, to be sure, and he never listens, but that's a bit like all fathers, isn't it?'

His father also screamed at times, and fought with his mother, but it wasn't his problem. It didn't stop him from living his life and concentrating on his own affairs.

But in my case, no one in our family could concentrate on their own affairs. It was a bit as if we were living in an aquarium, or better yet, in a prison with no doors or windows. My father was everywhere, supervising everything, like in Bentham's panopticon. There was a time when I hoped with all my heart that my mother would find the courage to take my brother and me and leave him.

'Why do you stay with him, Mama,' I'd ask her.

But she stayed and she said nothing. And I looked down on her for it.

Later she told me that she had wanted to leave him but that he threatened her, 'If you leave, you will never see your children again.'

'And you believed him, Mama?'

'Of course I did. He would have done it. He would have succeeded in convincing everyone that I was the crazy one and that it was best for the children. Can you imagine everything I had to endure when you were kids?'

During my first years of psychoanalysis, I hated my mother. I hated her for not being the model I would have wanted. I hated her for not defending my brother and me against our father. I hated her because I wanted a mother who was sure of herself, a mother I could rely on. She did everything she could to be perfect, so that my father would appreciate her, and she would be loved by her children, but she failed on all fronts: My father humiliated her, my brother didn't obey her, and I could not stand looking at her defeated face.

'Can you even imagine everything I had to endure when I found myself head of the family at the age of twenty-one?' my papa would say when I asked him why he was always so stressed and why he treated my mother so badly.

'Can you even imagine everything I had to endure when you were kids?' my mother would say when I started reproaching her for not having defended us.

The destructive power of secrets and silences.

At least as destructive as the power of the words that my father would fling like stones against my mother and her family.

'What are you saying, Papa! Please, that's enough. Enough, enough, enough…' I would put my hands over my ears so I couldn't hear him. I would go to my room, close the door and read, my hands still pressed against my ears. While on the other side of the door my father screamed, 'diseased blood', 'cursed race'.

'No, they were not Jews on my mother's side,' I replied to my analyst the first time this business of 'race' came up in our sessions. What do the Jews have to do with it? I thought. My analyst is making no sense.

'Race'. I have no idea how many times I heard my father pronounce that word. Along with 'cursed', 'vile', 'diseased'. He would say it when he argued with my mother and lost control. He would hurl it at my brother when Arturo came home from school with a note from his teacher or a bad mark or when he didn't want to do his homework. Or when he was disobedient. My father couldn't stand not being obeyed. It was inconceivable to him that my mother, my brother or I would not immediately carry out to the letter everything he told us to do.

One day, he came to pick Arturo and me up from school. We stopped in front of a stationery store on the way home. My brother was seven and his teacher had asked him to get different colour pens: a blue one for dictation, a black one for addition and subtraction, a red one for rules of grammar, and a green one for multiplication and division.

'Make sure you take a package of medium-point Bic, don't take the fine-point pens!' my father instructed him. 'They don't write well, the ink doesn't come out, you have to press down hard on the paper and then you end up making holes in your notebook!'

And when my brother came out with a package of twenty fine-point Bic – obviously he hadn't obeyed – all hell broke loose: screams, slaps, curses, cursed race... And all this because of some blasted fine-point pens.

'Race'. And when it wasn't 'race', it was 'blood'. It was 'diseased' or 'contaminated'.

When my father lost it, he would lash out at my mother and her family, the source of all his woes and an example not to be followed. He was not going to allow his son to become a failure. Over his dead body.

In the afternoon, he would lock himself up with Arturo in his office: my brother at the desk, my father seated next to him, with a book in one hand and a wooden spoon in the other. 'Stop yawning and concentrate!' my father would yell as soon as my brother looked away from his notebook. 'What that hell is that?' he would comment when he read his essays. 'Read it out loud!' he'd shout. All the while, Arturo was learning to create a parallel world: Physically he was there, but in his mind he was elsewhere. He was learning to invent, to create, to escape into his overflowing imagination.

'Race'. The word is vile. Why did my father keep bringing it up? Where did this obsession come from? How did 'race' make its way into the vocabulary of a socialist academic in the 1970s?

I took to biting my nails. I couldn't keep from pulling my hair out. I was hungry all the time. I tried to control myself, not wanting to become a 'repulsive fat cow', as my father used to say about overweight women. But I was always hungry when I was a teenager. I could have done nothing but eat all the time. Then I began dieting and rebelling, like my brother, hurting myself in the process. I would give in to the hunger and then have to make myself vomit. Only then did things go back to normal and I felt calm again.

What I needed to vomit, more than the food, was the anger.

A thousand times I asked my father for explanations. But every time he would accuse my mother and my mother's mother of being at the origin of everything that was wrong.

'Your grandmother was a wretched woman.'

'Why do you say that, Papa,' I asked, not understanding what he was trying to tell me.

'She was meddlesome and a gossip. And instead of taking care of your mother, she'd go play canasta, and her fool of a husband let her.'

Yet, still today, I don't understand the connection between my grandmother, my brother, being a failure and the 'cursed race'.

What did my father fear? What was he so afraid of?

The facts: My mother's mother would often play canasta with her friends. They would take turns hosting these get-togethers. They'd have tea and pastries and play cards. When I was little, I once went with my grandmother to one of her friend's houses. I liked all the red, yellow, green and white chips. 'How do you play with these chips, Grandmother? Is it like a construction game?'

My grandmother played canasta, like lots of women of her age at the time who didn't work. After finishing the housekeeping, they would go spend the afternoon with friends, talking, taking walks or playing cards.

And so what?

'But your mother didn't read either, Papa, did she? She never learnt a foreign language and never did volunteer charity work, as far as I know.' But when I pointed this out to my father, he got angry. 'How can you speak of your grandmother that way? You should be ashamed of yourself!' he snapped. 'She devoted herself body and soul to her husband. She never played cards, and she wasn't spoilt like your mother's mother! With a husband who never knew how to impose his will...'

More facts: My mother's father adored his wife. He pampered her and never protested when she'd go off in the afternoon to play canasta with her friends. And what reason would he have had to complain? They had built a harmonious relationship. My grandmother took care of everything and then afterwards, in the afternoon, she would be with her friends. And so what? Where's the problem, Papa? Should she have stayed at home? Should she have been at her husband's beck and call around the clock? My grandfather also had his quirks. I remember one day how vexed he was because the meat was overcooked to his taste. He refused to eat it. Then he went on and on about the overcooked meat for hours. A relationship between a couple is a give-and-take, isn't it, Papa?

Some facts again: My mother was a neglected child. She recognises this herself. When she was little, she was often sent to her grandmother's; sometimes she didn't even sleep at her parent's. She never understood why and she is still pained by this today. She told me that one day she asked her mother for explanations, but her mother didn't know what to say. Maybe my grandmother was a superficial, somewhat frivolous woman. And so what? What absurd logic allowed my father to use things against his wife that she had confided in him when they first met? Strong with the weak and weak with the strong. Is that the lesson, Papa?

What are you so afraid of? What terrorised you when you saw that your son did not want to be like you, that you were a negative model for him and that the manliness that you showed off nauseated him? What were you afraid of when Mama sought some freedom and independence? Why was that threatening to you?
Giuseppina Malvani, my father's grandmother, was widowed at the age of thirty-seven. Her daughter Rosetta, my grandmother, was not a young widow like

her mother, but at the age of sixty she too found herself alone, with a hemiplegic husband in a wheelchair.

The men in my father's family died or took ill. Or, like his uncle, they didn't marry, but they squandered their wealth on gambling and women. It was the women in the family who survived and took charge. Meek in appearance, they were the ones who laid down the law. Maybe that explains my father's fears?

But when I tried to speak to him about it, he clammed up.

He clammed up and wouldn't speak to me anymore.

Il Diritto razzista, 'Racist rights'. This is the name of a political and legal journal published in Italy starting in 1939 and entirely devoted to racial topics.

The first thing that came to my mind when I read the title of the journal is the contradiction of terms between *diritto* and *razzista*, 'rights' and 'racist'. The expression 'racist rights' strikes me as an oxymoron. But it was not, alas, in the times of the Duce. It was racial supremacy that underpinned the very principle of fascist law, not equality.

For a long time, I thought that the word 'race' should be removed from our constitution. All human beings share 99.9 % of their DNA. Keeping this term seemed to be pure madness to my mind. But as I delved into the racism of the 1930s, I gradually began to change my mind. We all belong to the same race. There is no doubt about it. But racists exist, have always existed, and unfortunately, always will. The word 'race' has to be kept in our constitution as a permanent signal, a way of giving an ethical and judicial force to the historical condemnation of racial laws and the Shoah. As the Deputy Laconi argued in the discussion held on the formulation of article 3 of the Italian Constitution, this term is needed so as not to forget that well-defined racial principles were used as a political instrument and that they 'provided a criterion of discrimination between Italians consigned to categories of the damned and the chosen'.

The first issue of *Il Diritto razzista*, edited by the *squadrista* Stefano Cutelli, appeared in May 1939. Unlike the journal *La Difesa della razza*, which was a pure organ of propaganda without standing, *Il Diritto razzista* had serious pretensions, with support from a scientific committee made up of eminent jurists, such as Santi Romano and Antonio Azara.

In one of the texts published in the first issue, we read that 'The Fascist State rejects, even with respect to the race factor, the democratic postulate of the clear equality of all legal subjects.' The author was Michel La Torre, a State Councillor. I could have chosen any other article or author; it wouldn't have mattered. The gist is always the same. The authors may have different ways of putting it but, at bottom, they are merely restating the same deplorable ideas. 'And it could not be otherwise,' La Torre continues, 'since equality between unequal persons is as unjust as inequality between those who share the same condition.'

I copied the sentence word for word. I mulled it over, making an effort to see the meaning in the absurdity of these assertions. Then, gradually, I understood that La

Torre was dressing the old Aristotelian principle in a fascist sauce: that 'equals should be treated equally and unequals unequally'. This is not in itself absurd. On the contrary, it is even useful when it comes to distributive justice, that is to say, the distribution of goods, services or resources according to the economic and social situation of the recipients. It is unfortunate that La Torre applied this inequality to human beings – as Aristotle had done in his day – ignoring (or forgetting) that in terms of dignity, value and rights, all human beings are equal and must be treated as equals. It is especially unfortunate that the principle 'equals should be treated equally and unequals unequally' is still being cited absurdly today as the principle governing civil rights. I recalled that, when the law on same-sex marriage was being discussed in the Italian Parliament in 2016, some homophobic members of Parliament actually cited Aristotle.

'Why should homosexual people have the same rights as heterosexuals?' a deputy from Matteo Salvini's party asked after the end of my speech. 'They are different, or aren't they, Marzano? Explain it to this assembly, explain it to the citizens who are listening to us at this very moment from their homes! Cause if they are different, then they are not equal, and if they are not equal, then why would they also had the right to marry like heterosexual couples do?'

History is a cycle that repeats itself. *Corsi et ricorsi*, as the Italian philosopher Gianbattista Vico said. In 2016, Deputy Marzano spoke words that the Deputy

Marzano of 1953 would have found abhorrent and condemned.

'The growth of the Italian population is important because there is strength in numbers, but we must also make sure that the Italian nation keeps its purity by refraining from encounters with inferior races to avoid being contaminated by their blood.' I read this passage from La Torre's article again during Easter in 2020 at a time when the term 'contamination' had become part of our everyday language. For weeks, the world had been paralysed by the COVID-19 pandemic and language itself was changing as a result: shelter-in-place, self-isolation, fear, pain, anger and powerlessness. Then there were all the rules of social distancing: no more handshakes, hugs, or kisses, but now we had elbow bumps, masks, disinfectants and other Personal Protective Equipment, Zoom conferences and working from home.

In the midst of a pandemic, to read about the superiority of one race over another is particularly grotesque. We were hearing, however, that in many countries the elderly were no longer being admitted to intensive care units because there was not enough room for everyone and a selection had to be made. The discriminating criterion in this case was age rather than skin colour, ethnicity or religion. Is that any better? Is it the same? Is it worse? When I would have to explain ethical principles to my students, I could tell them that during the COVID-19 crisis we witnessed the triumph of utilitarianism. I would no longer have to rely on thought experiments to bring home the meaning of a moral dilemma: Whom do we save? And whom do we let die?

For years, I used John Harris's *The Survival Lottery* to explain the paradoxes of utilitarianism to my students. The English philosopher starts from the observation that there are very long waiting lists today to benefit from an organ transplant. Thousands of people wait their turn to get a heart, a kidney or a liver and they will perhaps die before getting the transplant due to a shortage of human organs, which need to be removed when the heart is still beating and the donor is brain dead. So, Harris, in the name of maximising the common good, proposes to select a person by lottery who will have all their organs removed, so that by sacrificing one single person, several others can be saved. By and large, my students are dumbfounded by the idea. 'How is it possible?' they ask me, disturbed. I wonder how they will react when I speak to them of the shortage of places in intensive care units during the pandemic? Will they still think it unjust to sacrifice old people to save the young? And that the value of human life is the same, regardless of skin colour, religious belief, professional skills, gender, nationality and age?

The past is never past. We only delude ourselves into thinking that some things will never happen again. History always catches us unprepared.

If we cannot come to grips with our past, and do so profoundly, it will end up devouring us. It will drive us to repeat the same mistakes. It will force our hand and reveal our cruelty.

Last night was awful. I had such an absurd nightmare, I couldn't interpret it, even after hours of trying. This time, my unconscious played a bad trick on me. I couldn't figure out what it was trying to tell me. There must be a significance. A trace, a threat, a sign. But try as I may to piece together the images, they all run amuck in my head.

I knew that when I awoke it was 4.50 am. Jacques got up to go to the bathroom and when he returned, he took me in his arms and said: 'You were crying.'

I knew that there was a man in my dream and that he was shouting 'dirty whore' to his daughter. 'Where are you going dressed like that?' seeing her wearing a mini skirt. But was the man who was screaming really her father?

I knew that I stood by watching the scene helplessly – but was I merely watching or was I the whore? – and I was terrorised.

I knew that I heard a voice asking for help, before disappearing, swallowed up by the sewers. It was the voice of a baby who was sucked into the water draining, but how did it get there? Why was no one saving it? Who was this baby?

Despite all my efforts to fit together the pieces of the puzzle, no picture emerged. Something was always missing that kept an image from taking shape.

Or else the pieces of the puzzle were all there already, but I could not or would not put them together.

I listed the key words: man, violence, whore, terror, baby, death. I read them again and again, but nothing came to mind. All I heard was the sound of my heart beating. What was this nightmare? Was it related to my book or to the pandemic?

When French President Macron declared a state of emergency, he said we were at war. On 18 March, when I saw images from the region of Bergamo of an army truck filled with dead bodies, I thought, 'It's happening.' With burial chambers and crematoria saturated, the coffins had to be transported to Ferrara, Bologna, Modena and Padua, with no one to leave a wreath of flowers. These people were dying without a goodbye and without an 'I love you'.

The lyrics of a song that Barbara wrote about her father dying without a goodbye, without an 'I love you' came to mind and my eyes filled with tears.

Madame soyez au rendez-vous
Vingt-cinq rue de la Grange au loup
Faites vite il y a peu d'espoir
il a demandé à vous voir [...]
Il voulait avant de mourir
se réchauffer à mon sourire
mais il mourut à la nuit même
sans un adieu sans un 'je t'aime'[1]

[1] 'Madam, please be there at the meeting / 25 Rue de la Grange au Loup / Hurry, there's little hope / he asked to see you.' / [...] He wanted, before dying / to find warmth in my smile / but he passed away that very night / without a farewell, without an 'I love you'.

What if my father were to die now? What if I couldn't get back to Rome and hold him one more time in my arms, even though the last time we saw each other, I told him I hated him again?

It takes time to find the right words to describe what it means not to be able to say goodbye to a mother or a father. And to remember things that were done and things that were not, promises that were broken and those that were never made, stolen caresses and those that were rejects. Memories – yes, memories forever and always – with which you have to try to live, even when they don't add up at all.

I couldn't work anymore. It was as if I were in a stationary space and time, deprived of words. I'm always saying that words help bring order to the world and contain suffering, and here I was drowning in disorder. Right when I was in the process of piecing together the years of fascism and the disaster of the Second World War, I found myself groping blindly in the chaos of an epidemic that disrupted the framework that I had painfully begun to define.

On 14 April 1939, the secretary of the Fascist Party of Lecce asked my grandfather to sit on the federal committee of discipline. It is mentioned in a small article that I found looking through the online archives of the journal *Gazzetta del Mezzogiorno*. I was trying to reconstruct the timeline of my grandfather's career between 1939 and the end of the Second World War, but very little was available on the internet.

I had planned to go to the Central State Archives in Rome where the personal files of judges between 1860 and 1970 are kept. I was hoping to be able to consult my grandfather's. I had bought plane tickets, told my parents I was coming, and organised my university schedule for that purpose. I had made arrangements for everything. Planned for everything. Except for the pandemic. And the impossibility of going anywhere. And the powerlessness.

Obsessively, I typed on the keyboard of my Mac the words: Arturo, Marzano, prosecutor, crown, Lecce, 1939, 1940, 1941, 1942, 1943. But apart from official decrees and a few mentions in the newspapers of the day, I found nothing. What's more, when I searched online for my grandfather's name, my brother's came up, since he was named Arturo after our father's father. Every occurrence of my brother's name on the Web relates to the history of Italian Jews who emigrated to Israel between 1920 and 1940, or else to Zionism and the Israeli-Palestinian conflict, or yet again to equal opportunity and to gender studies. These are his areas of research. I stopped on one page of Google search results. Like a twist of fate, there is a link to my brother's most recent book available on Amazon, *Onde fasciste, la propaganda araba di Radio Bai (1934-43)*, and, immediately below it, another to the historical website of the Chamber of Deputies: *Arturo Marzano (1897-1976), Second Legislature, National Monarchist Party.* I wondered, a bad twist of fate or the nemesis of history? Or both? I continued the search but found nothing else. One question consumed me. When would I be able to go back to Italy?

I decided to shift my attention to what I already had in my possession.

In 1938, the statutes of the Fascist Party were modified to ban from the party 'Italian citizens who, in accordance with the provisions of the law, are considered to belong to the Jewish race'. The statutes also state that the members of the federal committee of discipline – and hence my grandfather along with the five other members of the committee of Lecce – were among the high-ranking members of the party with the power, starting in 1939, to 'deplore', 'suspend', 'remove' or 'expel' whoever was accused of violating the 'party's political or moral discipline'.

That same year, Arturo participated regularly in the meetings of the committee for the *confino* of the province of Lecce, with the prefect Petragnani. The purpose of this committee was to decide who were opponents of the regime and who should be sent into internal exile, confined, as Carlo Levi describes in *Cristo si è fermato a Eboli* (*Christ Stopped at Eboli*), in an isolated region of the country. Arturo was entrusted with this wretched task and showed himself to be ready and willing. He even received high praise for his zeal and his competence from the prefect of Lecce. Clearly, he was fully a part of this fascist world that I had learnt to fear and loathe. There was no need for me to invent a thing, or even to interpret the events. In 1938 and 1939, the ties between Arturo and the Fascist Party were very close. This is a fact. What was there for me to add?

The horrors of our present are always interacting with our own personal history. When you have been through a catastrophe, the catastrophe never disappears, just as the past never dies. Every week I would go to my analyst's office, lie down on the couch and try to get a handle on my life, and each time I would say to her, 'Everything is falling apart.' But everything was not falling apart right at that moment; it had all fallen apart a long time before.

The unconscious has no sense of time. Everything that has ever happened is always present. And we find ourselves completely stuck when it all comes tumbling down.

The loss, for some, is irreparable. How devastating it must be not to be able to say goodbye to a loved one, not to be able to bury them. How unbearable to see one's dreams, projects and hopes go up in smoke. Even the spring is cruel today. The sun is shining in a cloudless sky, but for whom is this damned sun shining? And what about the church bells? *For whom the bells toll*, wrote Hemingway. It was wartime, there were trenches and bloodshed everywhere, and there were the bells, the slow, repeated chiming of the bells.

I thought of this as I opened my office window and looked out at a small patch of blue sky, and my mind went to something I had read as a child somewhere – I couldn't recall where – that was said to have been written on the walls of Auschwitz: *I believe in the light even when I'm submerged in darkness; I believe in God even when he is silent.* These lines came to be etched in my heart, but with anguish in my eyes and an exclamation point on my lips: How could one believe in the light and in God before dying?

When Mussolini appeared on the balcony of the Palazzo di Venezia on 10 June 1940, at exactly 6 pm, and announced his declaration of war against Great Britain and France, my grandfather was in Campi.

He had not gone to the courthouse that Monday morning. He had stayed at home to work and now that he had finished his work and he could join the rest of the family, he had no desire to hear his mother-in-law grumbling or to play with little Ferruccio. Arturo had other things on his mind. He was preoccupied and tense, and he feared the worst. There had been talk of imminent war in Italy for days. The victory of the Germans was so abrupt and so overwhelming, and France was about to fall. Arturo stayed in his office and when Lucia, on the insistence of his wife, came to propose a cup of tea, he sent her away. He did not want to be disturbed. Not by anyone. How many times must he repeat himself? He sat on the red armchair by his desk, turned on the radio and adjusted the volume. When he heard the Duce begin to speak, he held his breath.

Images of that evening are available online from the archives of the Institut Luce. Mussolini's speech lasts no more than a few minutes. I watched the video once. Then I watched it again, dwelling this time not only on the Duce's words but also on the crowds flooding the squares of Italy to listen to his voice broadcast over loudspeakers by the national radio. At times, I paused the video and took notes. Then I started it again.

'Duce! Duce! Duce! Duce!' the crowd screams as Mussolini appears on the balcony. He raises his arm in a salute. 'Duce! Duce! Duce! Duce!' the hordes shout again and again. Mussolini leans on the parapet, listening with a satisfied look to the popular euphoria, and he raises his right arm again. 'Duce! Duce! Duce! Duce!' Mussolini makes a sign and the crowd falls silent. Then he begins speaking, his arms on his hips, in a ridiculous pose: 'Fighters of land, sea and air, Blackshirts of the revolution and of the legions, men and women of Italy, of the empire, and of the Kingdom of Albania, listen!'

Long pause. The crowd cheers again, 'Duce! Duce! Duce! Duce!' Mussolini ignores them and continues: 'The hour destined by fate is sounding for us. The hour of irrevocable decision has come.'

In the video I was watching, you can see the packed piazzas in Florence, Forli, Naples, Bologna and Bari, the same celebratory atmosphere everywhere. 'A declaration of war already has been handed to the Ambassadors of Great Britain and France.'

Each word is punctuated, emphasised, underscored: 'Several decades of recent history may be summarised in these words: Phrases, promises, threats of blackmail [...] If today we have decided to take the risks and sacrifices of war, it is because the honour, interests, and future firmly impose it.'

At times, Mussolini stops, excelling as he did in controlling the crowd's reactions.

'There is only one order. It is categorical and obligatory for everyone. It already wings over and enflames hearts from the Alps to the Indian Ocean: Conquer!'

The dictator pauses.

The people start shouting again, applauding, cheering the Duce, their saviour, their hope. Did they have no idea of the tragedy awaiting them?

'And we will conquer in order, finally, to give a new world of peace with justice to Italy, to Europe and to the universe. Italian people, rush to arms (Yes!) and show your tenacity, your courage, your valour.'

'Yes!'

Mussolini salutes and walks inside. The crowd, hysterical, explodes with joy.

What was my grandfather's reaction that day? Did he too explode with joy? Or did he realise the folly of it all and the inevitable tragedy that was looming? Italy was not ready to go to war. Many senior-ranking fascists were well aware of this.

Obviously, I will never know for sure what my grandfather felt. The piece of the puzzle of that afternoon of 10 June 1940 is missing. But by now I knew my grandfather's mindset like the palm of my hand. I could guess his gestures and emotions and I knew that for him it was not at all a time for joy.

Ever since the war had broken out, Arturo had been following the events closely. At first, in 1939, he had been relieved when Mussolini had declared Italy's non-belligerence. He had agreed entirely with Vittorio Emanuele III when the king spoke of the 'still too weak military machine', and expressed doubts about Italy's entering the war. Until the last moment, my grandfather had hoped that this war would not take place.

But the Duce had spoken. And my grandfather submitted, once again. In all likelihood, he said to himself that Mussolini was right. Clearly, Germany will win. It's only a matter of weeks, maybe even days. And Italy cannot allow itself not to be at the armistice talks and not to benefit from the victory. No one wants a repetition of what happened in 1919. Who can forget that? Surely not a veteran of the First World War. This time, the victory will not be spoilt. Mussolini was right. How could it be otherwise. Italy has to enter the war too.

No joy. But no recrimination either. '*Credere, Obbedire, Combattere.*' Believe, Obey, Fight. The fascist slogan was by then second nature to Arturo. What's more, he had always believed in the Duce. And he had always obeyed.

A few days later, Arturo received the order to go to Bologna to serve as a substitute military attorney. He set off immediately. When he arrived in Bologna, he wrote to Rosetta to reassure her.

> The trip went well; Bologna is very beautiful; I had coffee with Vincenzino; I reported to the command of the VIth Corps and met the major with whom I'll be working. In the evening, I went back to the hotel early and fell asleep almost immediately. Please promise me, Rosetta, that you won't worry too much!

My grandmother answered him right away.

> You have left a great emptiness. We're feeling alone and discouraged. Who knows how long you'll be away! Ferruccio is inconsolable, he's always asking for news of his papa, and when I put him to sleep and you're not there and I tell him to send you a kiss, he starts crying and doesn't stop.

Arturo wrote to Rosetta every day, telling her about his daily life and his boredom.

> The VIth Corps hasn't been mobilised yet and there's very little work; tell Ferruccio and Rosaria that a little bird has told me that they've been naughty and if they continue, I won't bring them anything when I come home; tell them that their father blesses them every morning and every evening and sends them kisses, and that he's far away to serve the supreme ideal of our Fatherland. Tell this especially to Ferruccio, my little darling, so that he will learn to love his Fatherland!

Every day, his wife answered him, with words of advice or of complaint: Don't change your habits too much; be careful not to overeat, especially in the evening, because you're not used to it; don't go to bed late and don't smoke; I worry if you do and I get migraines…

When the seventy-fifth anniversary of the liberation of Italy was celebrated on 25 April 2020, it was the first anniversary that I felt my conscience was not clear. I too would have liked to post with pride on social networks #Iremainfree because I believe in freedom. I always have. So why shouldn't I write it, why shouldn't I also sing *Bella ciao* from my balcony, #bellaciaosonbalconies, since that year we could not take to the streets to do so. But now it was hard for me. I felt dispirited. I knew now that my background was very different from that of the grandchildren and relatives of Resistance fighters. Unlike them, I had nothing to feel proud about.

It was easy to talk about 25 April 1945 in hindsight, seventy-five years later. But where were your parents and grandparents? Were they really members of the Resistance or did they switch sides at the last minute? Now they were being lumped together, as if all things were equivalent. People, it seems, were fed up with talk of the right and the left; they'd had their fill of ideologies. I was in Parliament the day when Matteo Renzi, the leader of the Democratic Party, preached change in the following terms: "The question now is no longer to pit the left against the right, but rather movement against immobility.' And they were all there, applauding and cheering, just to get a seat or a promotion. Isn't that a form of collaboration too? Where is the resistance, my dear companions?

Maybe I was becoming bitter. Probably as result of the isolation. Or the fear of not being able to go back to Italy for quite some time. The Italian Embassy in Paris's website announced in no uncertain terms that, although the borders were not closed, you had to have a serious reason to travel there. Family or professional reasons could qualify but not a very deep nostalgia for the country. And yet I missed Italy. I yearned to listen and speak my mother tongue, the only one in which I feel truly myself. Wasn't that a serious enough reason?

I was not born into the Resistance. I did not have that luck. But my resistance is active every day, in my opposition to conformism and to monolithic thinking. I think in my own way.

Resistance is not found in genes or in nature. It is a choice, a decision, the conviction that, without freedom, we are dead even before dying.

I pay the price of my past, of my grandfather's wrongs, but my choice is clear. I too am in resistance. And I draw on the courage of those who have learnt to resist the adversity of life, because courage also involves confronting our misfortunes and working through them, gritting our teeth and moving forward.

PART THREE

Amnesia

Strip a writer to the buff, point to the scars, and he'll tell you the story of each small one. From the big ones you get novels, not amnesia. A little talent is a nice thing to have if you want to be a writer, but the only real requirement is that ability to remember the story of every scar.

Stephen King, *Misery*

'When did you first hear about the Holocaust, Papa?'

There must be a reason my father insisted so much that my brother and I watch *Holocaust* when we were young. At least I would think there was. At the time, many parents did not allow their children to watch the TV miniseries because they felt it was better for little children not to know about certain things.

'When I was in America, during the festival of Pesach, American students used to invite foreigners who were at the university to join them for lunch. I know it was some time in the spring, I can't recall exactly when, that talk at the table was entirely devoted to the Shoah. I admit that I didn't know much about it.'

'And?'

'It was a shock. I had never heard about the concentration camps and the gas chambers. Yes, I assure you!' he added, seeing the look in my eyes. 'It may be hard to believe today, but until that day, I had never heard about it.'

The year was 1962. Barely a year had gone by since the end of the trial in Jerusalem of Eichmann, who had been captured in Argentina by Mossad agents. In Israel, the trial was broadcast live on the radio. Televised images reached the rest of the world a few days later.

In spite of the interest stirred by the first Russian space mission, the one that sent Yuri Gagarin into orbit, and the worsening crisis in Cuba, the Eichmann trial remained the media event of 1961. Millions of people discovered the horrors of the extermination camps which, even in Israel, had been underestimated until then. In the immediate aftermath of World War II and the Nuremberg trials, people had stopped talking about Nazism and fascism. As if the chapter were closed.

'Did you discuss the Eichmann trial?'

'I don't remember. But, afterwards, when I went to England, I know we did. I followed the whole story. Do you remember Duccio? When you were little, we used to see each other every summer, he and his family. He was Jewish. There were a lot of Jews studying economics at Churchill College in Cambridge. I've already told you the story of Eva, Ursula Hirchmann's daughter, right?'

'Yes, Papa, you've told me that story a thousand times! But let's get back to Eichmann. What did you do when you came back to Italy? Didn't you feel a bit ashamed that you came from a fascist family that had participated in the Shoah in one way or another? Did you try to understand your father's past better?' After all, Mussolini was Hitler's ally, and he passed the anti-Semitic laws in 1938.

Silence. But it just doesn't make sense. It was the 1960s. My father discovered the tragedy of the Shoah, talked about it with his friends, was captivated by

Zionism and then returned to Italy and acted as if nothing had happened?

To be sure, things in Italy in the 1960s were not like in America or Israel. Even in Germany, after more than ten years of collective amnesia, the national reckoning with Nazism was just beginning, little by little. In 1963, two years after the Jerusalem trial, what was called the 'second Auschwitz trial' opened in Frankfurt, thanks to the determination of the Hessian district attorney, Fritz Bauer. In Italy, at the time, nothing was moving. But my father divided his time between Italy and England. What could have prevented him from taking an interest in his own father's past?

A friend of mine told me about the novel by Géraldine Schwarz, *Those Who Forget*, in which she tells the secret story of her family. Schwarz, who is about my age, decided to explore her family's past and the way it intersected with the history of Germany. Her father never directly addressed the question of the connections between his parents and the Nazi regime. 'What good would it do?' he would say when she put the question to him. He had his suspicions, but he never tried to find out whether or not they were true. *What good would it do?* Was that what my father told himself in the 1960s after he came back from Harvard and Cambridge?

Jacques chided me, claimed I was on a slippery slope, falling into a trap. But he was wrong. Granted, the anti-Jewish laws of 1938 did not propose to exterminate the Jews in the way the German 'final solution' did.

However, these laws were informed by a completely biological racist approach. Granted, when Mussolini learned of the existence of the gas chambers in 1942, he was shocked, according to Raoul Hilberg. But he maintained nonetheless his military and ideological alliance with Nazi Germany. Then, in November 1943, Fascist Italy decreed the seizure of Jewish property, followed by the arrest and internment of Jews. This is proof that the laws of 1938 were the first steps in the extermination of the Jews. All the more so, given that the persecution of the Jews in Italy was neither sudden nor imposed by Hitler, as Renzo De Felice and George Mosse claimed. It was perfectly in line with the heritage of the Italian colonial experience. When, in 1936, the Duce went to war against 'miscegenation' in the colonies and claimed that 'mixed race people' were a biological attack on the integrity of the race, racism was already present. First the Blacks, then the Jews.

Italians do not want to face this chapter in their history. They continue to see themselves as nice people who have never exhibited the brutality of the *furia francese*, the Carolingian cavalrymen, or the plunderers of the Italian army, no less the rage of the Nazi soldiers. '*Italiani, brava gente.*' But it's a cliché! The truth is quite different. Jacques was wrong.

But maybe I too was wrong in focusing solely on my father's denial. After all, what had I done for almost fifty years? My grandfather was a monarchist deputy, and I had seen a picture at my father's cousins' house of him standing next to King Umberto II, and I never doubted this family legend. So, wasn't I too complicit in this amnesia?

Suddenly, I realised that blaming my father was merely a way of justifying myself: The famous glass case with my grandfather's medals hung on the wall in the red living room of the Campi house, and when I played hide-and-seek with my brother as a child, I would pass right under it, just like I used to pass by the photos of Arturo in a military uniform, wearing the beret with the golden eagle perched on the fasces.

So, what conclusions could I draw?

List of excuses: We stopped going to Campi in the late 1970s, after the death of my grandparents; when we started studying the fascist period in school, the situation at home was tense and I was completely obsessed with the idea of leaving; when I got to the Scuola Normale Superiore in Pisa, I began to suffer from anorexia; after my doctorate, I moved to Paris.

I have a passion for lists: lists of clothes to wash, lists of things to buy, lists of articles to write, lists of books to read. I have a fixation on drawing up such lists; somehow lining things up one after the other, day by day, sometimes even hour by hour, reassures me. I grew up surrounded by successions of very strict rules and schedules that had to be rigorously respected. I don't know what it means not to have schedules, and when something does not go as planned, I lose it. There is a file titled 'things to do' on my desktop, which I update every week, highlighting the most urgent tasks in red, less important ones in green, and those that I could perhaps postpone in yellow, even though every time I use yellow I feel on edge and have trouble breathing. When I try to take a very deep breath, I sometimes make an awkward movement and get a crick in my neck that leads to cervical, dorsal and lumbar pain. I am always in pain somewhere, no matter how many patches I use. The pain never goes away. The other day, a friend told me that it was probably because I am so 'wired' that my vertebrae, my muscles and my tendons give way. I strain so hard that sooner or later I end up cracking. Sometimes I say to myself that my life would have been altogether different if I had been less stressed by the schedules and rules that my father imposed on us. And nothing gets on my nerves more than hearing people complain about not having had enough boundaries when they were young.

But I found myself here digressing.

I was hiding behind my lists and my obsessions with order and avoiding the real issues.

I was avoiding in particular looking for the lowest common denominator of the excuses I just listed, even though the strategy is always one and the same, including right now: namely, escape.

Ever since I was a little girl, I had never stopped running away.

I ran away from my past and my father.

I ran away from my country and my mother tongue.

And now I was also running away from my guilt.

When I was elected deputy in Parliament and decided to move into the house in Campi, the idea was precisely to return to the place where it all began. Even though the first time I went back there with the architect, I was flooded with childhood memories and the fear of drowning in them invaded me. Every time I entered a room I was overwhelmed by an image or a reminiscence. An image from the end of summer, when we would be leaving and my father would close the porch gate, and my grandmother would hold on to the handle and kiss it because she did not want to leave. The memory of my aunt giving us cakes, putting them on a plate and counting them, bringing her face close to the table and adjusting her glasses with thick lenses to see better. Once I took advantage of a moment of distraction to grab one, and when she counted the cakes again, she had to add another. The recollection of Grandmother's cold forehead exposed in the coffin in the living room. I had gone over to see her and had touched her skin, which was so cold that I took fright.

When the renovation work was done, my father came to visit his old home. I was so proud of myself that I wanted to shout, 'Did you see what I accomplished, Papa? You see? It wasn't impossible.' But I didn't shout. I didn't say a thing. What would have been the point? To humiliate him? To show him that I had succeeded in order to stress the fact that he hadn't? And what exactly was I proud of?

I had restored the family home, to be sure. But was that enough to repair the history of those who had once lived there?

All the more since, the first summer I spent in Campi, I did not even bother to take a look at the boxes and crates stored in the cellar of my father's cousins. I had just cleaned out my husband's mother's house. I wasn't about to start again with my grandfather's things, was I? I said to myself that it could wait. Why spoil my holidays?

I found excuses for myself and felt reassured.

Escaping. Once again.

I still wasn't ready. And it was only Jacopo's birth that really obliged me to stop running. There was no turning away. Why hadn't I had children? If my brother, who is gay, had one, why not me?

For weeks I had been obsessing about that heap of files and documents that I glimpsed in early January, piled up in the basement of my father's cousins' house, and I was fuming at myself. I had planned to spend a few weeks in Campi after the end of the second semester classes, before the beginning of exams. But here I was still stuck in Paris. The pandemic had dashed my plans. And now, I was furious with myself. How much time had I lost!

I was stupid, superficial, foolish.

'Let time take its course,' my mother used to say when I was little and in a hurry.

I hated when she said this, and now, all of a sudden, for the first time perhaps, I could perceive a different meaning. To come to an understanding of certain things, you have to let time do its work, you have to let things settle.

The time of memory is never linear.

There are things that we look at, but do not see. Despite the traces they leave.

My mother told me that my father was behaving irresponsibly. Now that the stay-at-home orders had been relaxed, he wanted Giorgio, the young man who had been helping him use his computer in recent years, to start coming over again, even though the virus was still spreading, and my father was over eighty.

'I'm worried about Giorgio bringing the virus into the house,' my mother explained. The preceding months, alone with my father at home, were extremely hard on her. 'Please, Michela, talk to him; you're the only one your father listens to a little!'

So, I called him. Even though my father does not listen to me. Not in the least. On the contrary, because he is sneaky, and also smart, he always manages to find a way to do or say something that changes the nature of the game. I told him for the umpteenth time that he had to be careful not to bring strangers into the house, considering his age, and, out of the blue, he switched to another subject.

'I found something that belonged to your grandfather. Are you interested?' My father knew perfectly well what my answer would be. But he paused, waiting for me to give him the confirmation he knew was coming. 'Of course I'm interested, Papa!

What is it?'

'It's a book. And on the first page, there's a note that I think is of great importance for you. But I'm not telling you any more about it until you convince your mother to let Giorgio come over.'

There was my father. Doing his usual. Even now that he was over eighty. He would try anything to get his way.

'If you get sick, you're the one who'll suffer, not me!'

'I'll think about it.'

'Good, think it over! In the meantime, can you tell me the title of the book you found and what the note says, please!'

'It's a novel by Arthur Koestler titled *Darkness at Noon*.'

Published in English in 1941 and translated into Italian a few years later, the novel tells the story of a high-ranking Soviet party official who, accused of counter-revolutionary activity, is arrested in the middle of the night, put in prison, found guilty and sentenced to death. On the first page of the book, my grandfather wrote with his typical obsessive attention to detail: 'Arturo Marzano, Attorney, Law Office, Campi Salentina-Lecce, 8 February 1949.'

I left my grandfather in October 1944, acting as military crown prosecutor. I found him again in February 1949, working as an attorney. Why was he no longer a magistrate? What happened? Was it his choice to move into private practice to make more money? Although, he had no need for it, given that his wife's family had quite enough. And I knew he was very attached to his profession as a judge. It would not have been like him to leave the magistracy of his own free will.

I asked my father, but he had no recollections in that regard. All he knew was that, at the end of 1949, his father participated as a member of the public prosecutor's office in a famous trial against a group of communists accused of having organised a massacre in Ginosa, a small town near the port of Taranto, and that all the accused were acquitted. So, by the end of 1949, Arturo was a magistrate again. But what about before?

I did an internet search but found nothing. I needed access to my grandfather's personal file. I couldn't do without it anymore.

The reading rooms of the Central State Archives *(Archivi Centrali di Stato)* had reopened to the public. All I had to do was hop over to Rome. I could surely find the time to do so before the start of the second session of exams.

But there was a hitch: As a precautionary measure, they were not accepting more than ten people per day, and you had to make a reservation in advance online. When I tried to do so, I discovered that there were no available spots before the end of July.

'What's to prevent you from getting around the problem and submitting an archive request by correspondence?' Jacques asked me.

Two days after sending an email to the head of the archives, I received an extremely detailed answer from her. She told me that she had looked over the lists of magistrates compiled by the archivists and found my grandfather's name in a section of the catalogue that was only accessible to the staff of the archives. Arturo Marzano's file was in envelope number 619. If I were interested, I could write to the director of the reading room and request an electronic copy of it.

'You see,' Jacques remarked, 'you should never put too much store in stereotypes.'

But my husband was wrong. This woman was but an admirable exception to the stereotypes about the Italian administration that were, alas, soon to be borne out. The director of the reading room answered me nonchalantly after a week, asking me to transmit, 'to whom it may concern' and duly completed, a request for admission to the telematic consultation. I *duly* filled out the form, which asked me, in addition to the usual personal information, to specify the year I obtained my doctorate, which research laboratory I was working in, and to supply a list of my main publications related to the dossier I was seeking to consult. I indicated that I had not yet published anything in relation to this dossier, and that my research involved reconstructing the life of my grandfather. This answer must not have pleased the reading room director, since he did not reply to my email. I wrote him again to say that I needed the dossier in question for a future publication, and I crossed my fingers. About ten days later, I received the following email: 'Your request has been registered. Due to the large number of requests, we are unable to grant yours at this time. We will process your request as soon as possible. As soon as possible, we…'

Receiving this reply brought to mind what my math teacher used to say when he had completed the proof of a theorem on the black board. He would turn to us with a smile and declare, 'There you are! This completes the proof.' And so it was that the archivist's reply was proof positive of all the worst stereotypes about the Italian administration's inefficiency, slowness and laziness.

I then decided to write to Stefano, my historian friend who is very familiar with the Central State Archives, and I asked him for help. I told him everything, explained the problem to him, and he began pulling some strings. A few days later, he told me that he had personally contacted the director of the reading room. 'Now, everything should move smoothly,' he reassured me. 'Someone will be writing or calling you shortly. You'll see, everything will be resolved quickly.'

And indeed, the next day I got a call from an archivist, but the problem was not resolved. He informed me that my grandfather's dossier had been identified, but that it was not possible to copy it because it was much too voluminous. He added that this was rather unusual for a magistrate. Generally speaking, their dossiers did not contain much. This one had too many documents for them to provide me with a complete copy.

'So, what are my options?'

'Well, I can try to reserve a spot for you around 23 or 24 July. Does that work?'

'Farò, farai, faremo,' my father would always say when he asked my brother or me to do something we didn't want to do, and we would reply: 'Tomorrow, Papa!' 'I will do, you will do, we will do,' he'd quip. Just before coming out with his other refrain, this time directly in dialect: *'Quiddu c'à fare crai, fallu osce.'* Don't put off to tomorrow what you can do today. Anticipate. Organise. Predict. Always anticipate; otherwise, there's bound to be trouble. This principle of anti-procrastination would be reiterated in various ways: 'time waits for no one'; 'nothing ventured, nothing gained'; 'fortune favours the bold'. Whatever the expression, the idea was always the same: Time passes inexorably; he who waits loses his chance.

I grew up with this sword of Damocles over my head, taking to heart everything my father said, even though he himself never heeded his own principles. On the contrary. In his life, he was always delaying, postponing, procrastinating.

But I internalised the anti-procrastination rule. I even reinforced it to the point that, for me, anything that is not done right away will never be done.

Right away or never: two sides of the same coin; the Manichaean thinking in which I have always been trapped, in spite of all my efforts to stop thinking in terms of dualities – all or nothing, true or false, good or bad, black or white. In the end, in spite of my twenty years of psychoanalysis, I continue to function like a computer: 0-1. I am split.

Splitting. Freud spoke of *Spaltung* to designate the processes of division that characterise the psychic functioning of someone who undergoes a trauma. But what trauma did I undergo?

I hadn't a clue. Most probably, I would never know what happened during my childhood. And, in the end, it didn't really matter. Often there is no precise point in time and no specific event at the root of suffering. Often the problem is related to the emotional instability of the individual's environment, or to the constant repetition of a painful experience. Invisibility and transparency. Accompanied by a deep wound.

Psychologists explain that, for a child, nothing is worse than ambivalent parents, who are present at times and disappear at others, who respond at times with affection and at others with brutality. From idealisation to contempt, from love to hate; and suddenly everything becomes dark. How does one avoid falling into the abyss, when one has grown up subjected to contradictory injunctions? Do what I say and not what I do. Listen to me, but don't follow my example.

'I'd love to attend a performance of Verdi's *Rigoletto* at the San Carlo in Naples. It's my dream.'

My father repeated this for years, singing, '*Cortigiani, vil razza dannata, per qual prezzo vendeste il mio bene?*'[1] and it made me heartsick. Poor Rigoletto, poor father! He sang: '*A voi nulla per l'oro sconviene, ma mia figlia è impagabil tesor!*'[2] He sang and sang. But while dreaming of being able one day to attend *Rigoletto* at the San Carlo or even at the Baths of Caracalla, he never actually tried to go. Even though the Baths of Caracalla were only half an hour from the house. Was it hard to book tickets? Not in the least. Why then did he never allow himself to go?

I want to, but I can't. And when I can, I don't want to anymore.

The main thing was never to give himself the chance to be happy.

Enjoying life was a sin. Wasn't that what my father always reproached my mother and my brother for? Their shameful *joie de vivre*?

[1] 'Courtiers, vile damned race, for what price did you sell my beloved?'

[2] 'For you, nothing is forbidden for gold, but my daughter is a priceless treasure!'

On 25 July 1943, Mussolini was arrested as he was leaving the Grand Council of Fascism, and King Vittorio Emanuele III made an announcement on the radio that he should have made twenty years earlier, at the time of the March on Rome: 'In this solemn hour of grave anxiety which is descending on the fate of our Fatherland, everybody must take up his post. No recriminations can be allowed.' Marshal Pietro Badoglio was appointed by the king to replace the Duce, who in the meantime had been imprisoned in a location kept secret.

On 2 August, the PNF was abolished, the term 'Fascist' was removed from the name of every organisation or institution, and it was decided to remove the image of the *fasci littori* from the soldiers' uniforms, as well as from government stamps and letterheads.

On 8 September, Marshal Badoglio announced that he had signed the armistice with the Anglo-Americans and, at dawn on 9 September, Badoglio fled Rome with the king and some representatives of the government, and took refuge in Brindisi, an ancient port of Puglia that had already passed under the authority of the Anglo-Americans.

Italy found itself divided in two. In the north, Mussolini, who had been freed by the Germans, took control of the Republic of Salò and fought alongside the Germans. The Kingdom of the South officially declared war on Germany. Badoglio became the main supporter of the Allies, determined to do everything possible to avoid a resurgence of fascism throughout the territory of the new government.

'It is for security reasons, Don Giuseppe…' The mayor of Campi, who had just been removed from his post, stood on the threshold of his house, staring incredulously at the people who had come to arrest him. They gave him the Roman salute. And addressed him with respect. 'Please forgive us, *ssignuria*, but we have received definite orders.'

On the evening of 13 October 1943, the four carabinieri who arrested the mayor were almost imploring his indulgence. 'It's because of the Anglo-Americans, Don Giuseppe; we have nothing to do with it; please forgive us.'

I pictured the scene as I read the memoirs of Tonino, the son of Giuseppe Guarino, who complained about the people of Campi. In a few weeks, he maintained, everyone had switched sides. After the British landing in Taranto in early September 1943, and the sudden retreat of the Germans, who were not about to let themselves be trapped in the heel of Italy's boot, all the inhabitants of Campi, he complained, had turned their backs on his family. From that point on, Don Guarino's ties with Achille Starace were suddenly a source of shame rather than pride. 'They were all ingrates,' writes Tonino. Except apparently my grandfather, whom Tonino mentions several times as, 'the prosecutor Marzano, a loyal friend of my family'.

Again? Exasperated, I sighed. Then I paused to think it over. On the one hand, I was infuriated by the help my grandfather gave to Starace's son-in-law, who ended up joining the Republic of Salò (in April 1945, after a summary trial, Starace would be executed in Piazzale Loreto). But on the other hand, I was happy that, despite the danger, Arturo remained faithful to his friend. A few days after the arrest of the former mayor, my grandfather got moving and put to work his contacts for the Guarino family. As a magistrate, having pledged his allegiance to the king, he continued his activity without hindrance.

'*Sursum corda*, Tonino!' Arturo tried to reassure Don Guarino's son. He asked his driver to take him to the former mayor, climbed out of the car, and headed to the front door. But before he had time to knock, Tonino tiptoed out and closed the door quietly behind him, not wanting to wake up his mother.

'I didn't want to say anything. Mama is very worried ever since they came to arrest Papa.' Tonino tried to remain calm and composed, but when Arturo embraced him, he could not hold back his tears anymore. 'Thank you, Signor Marzano,' he said, moved.

'*Sciamune*, Tonino! Come, get into the car; hurry, we're already late. And anyway, what's with this

Signor Marzano business? How many times must I tell you not to call me that?' He gave him a pat on the shoulder, ushered him into the car, and sat down by his side.

The streets of Campi were empty. No one dared break the curfew and very few windows were still lit. Every night, the village seemed deserted. On the small roads leading to Taranto, the darkness was so dense that you could not see the vineyards or the olive trees. The air seemed to stand still. All you could hear was the isolated echo of a distant gunshot from time to time.

'Stay calm, Tonino! I'll take care of it,' said Arturo when the vehicle hit the army checkpoint and a British soldier, a rifle pointed in their direction, asked where they were going at that time of night. 'To the command of the IXth Corps,' my grandfather replied. 'Everything is in order, soldier!' He showed him his papers and his pass. 'I am the crown prosecutor,' he exclaimed in an imperious tone, emphasising each word. 'In the service of the Navy of His Majesty the King of Italy.'

That my grandfather was an influential man in the region, I already knew. That he was also a generous man, I had understood from what his relatives and his friends said of him. In March 1944, he did not hesitate to acquit a sailor accused of insubordination against the captain of his ship – the MAS 433 – who had supported the Republic of Salò and wanted to join the Duce in the north. This I learned from reading an excerpt of this famous sentence on the internet. But now I found myself learning about another facet of my grandfather: his loyalty in friendship.

In spite of the embarrassment I felt, given that the friend in question was the son-in-law of Achille Starace, I also had a feeling of relief. He was a fascist, no doubt about it, but at least he was faithful. In the end, nothing is worse than the duplicity of traitors.

While the war continued to rage in the north, on 27 July 1944, the king signed a decree launching the process of purging Italy of fascists and he put a high commissioner in charge of the task of cleaning up the public administration. Was my grandfather caught up in all of this?

After consulting the recent bibliography devoted to the purges in the judiciary, I came to understand the complexity of these affairs. From the outset, the effort was undermined by extreme caution. All the more so since the magistrates were in the position of judging not only each other, but also themselves. And that the criteria for judging, sanctioning or acquitting were not clearly defined. What exactly were the charges? Enrolment in the Fascist Party? In which cases were the laws to be applied? In cases of membership in a particularly toxic body such as the Tribunal of Race?

The main criterion chosen was activism, which was evaluated on the basis of the articles that the magistrates had published in fascist journals. It was decided that a judge could not be judged and punished simply for enforcing the law. But isn't there always a continuity between what a magistrate writes in an article and the reasoning used to build a legal argument or to justify a sentence? Applying laws to given facts necessarily involves subjective interpretation. A sentence is always also a confession.

One of the first things I teach my students is the difference between legal and moral norms. I explain to them that it is always necessary to distinguish between law and ethics. 'How else can you evaluate the morality of a norm?' Sometimes I can see their eyes glazing over. But as soon as I talk to them about the death penalty, their eyes light up again. Italy was the first country in the world where the death penalty was abolished, but it was restored during the fascist period. France was one of the last countries in Europe to abolish it.

Usually, I continue my argument with a discussion of the issue of racial laws. I ask them if they think these are acceptable norms from a moral point of view.

'No!' they reply in unison.

'So, there are situations when disobeying is a moral duty. Take Antigone. Who has read Sophocles's tragedy?'

Almost no one has read Sophocles, few know who Antigone is, and even those who have heard of her cannot quite remember why this woman stood up to the king and disobeyed his orders.

Nor did I deem that you, a mortal man,
Could by a breath annul and override
The immutable unwritten laws of Heaven.

I read the excerpt from the tragedy, pausing to see whether the students are listening, and then I continue.

They were not born to-day nor yesterday;
They die not; and none knows whence they sprang.
I was not like, who feared no mortal's frown,
To disobey these laws and so provoke
The wrath of Heaven.

I explain to them that this is why Antigone defies Creon's decree and decides to bury her brother. She believes that all human beings have the right to receive a proper burial. And although the king sentences her to death for this, she remains defiant.

For death is gain to him whose life, like mine,
Is full of misery.

There is total silence in the class at that point. The students are often very attentive. Occasionally, one of them will speak up and protest: 'But we can't all be heroes!'

I thought of the exchange between Attorney General Hausner and Eichmann at the trial in Jerusalem: Hausner asked, 'Were these Jews destined for the extermination camps? Yes or no?' 'I do not deny it,' Eichmann replied. 'I have never denied it. I received orders and I had to carry them out by virtue of my oath. I could not shirk my responsibility and I never tried to. But I never acted on my own volition.' 'Does that mean you were totally passive?' asked Hausner. 'I wouldn't say that I was passive. I was doing what I just said: obeying and carrying out the orders I received [...] I was not an imbecile, but I was taking orders.'

Can carrying out orders be a legitimate defence? When orders are unjust, should they be enforced anyway?

In Hannah Arendt's essay on the trial, she argues that Eichmann shows how any human can banally do evil if they stop thinking with their own mind, obey without reserve the orders they are given, and no longer make the effort to perceive and feel the presence of others. 'The longer one listened to him, the more obvious it became that his inability to speak was closely connected with an inability to think; namely, to think from the standpoint of somebody else. No communication was possible with him, not because he lied, but because he was surrounded by the most reliable of all safeguards against the words and the presence of others, and hence against reality as such.' But is this really something that can happen to anyone?

Suddenly, it occurred to me that everything I had been teaching my students was of little use to me now in trying to understand the history of the purges in the Italian judiciary after the fall of fascism. Deep down, I am convinced that the only moral attitude of a judge is to resign from his post. But does that mean that anyone who did not do so should be punished when all they did was apply the law?

I was losing my sense of direction. I did not know what exactly to prioritise anymore. Of course, I was as convinced as always that disobedience to an unjust authority is not only a right, but also a duty; and that, therefore, certain immoral orders should never be obeyed. I believe that what Thomas Aquinas wrote about unjust laws – *lex iniusta non est lex* – is still today the best justification for civil disobedience. I am reminded too of the words of the German theologian Dietrich Bonhoeffer, a figure of the Resistance to Nazism, who asked himself in a 1944 letter where the boundary was between 'necessary resistance', as embodied by Don Quixote, and the equally necessary 'acceptance of destiny', as embodied by Sancho Pancha.

Then, leaving aside such fine ideas, I asked myself more simply how a magistrate can oppose a regime supported by a king to whom he has pledged allegiance?

On 23 July 2020, my brother went to the Central State Archives.

He was the one in the end to help me out. Arturo is always there when I need him.

'Envelope no. 619: Fascicle no. 84 021; thickness: 15 cm,' Arturo texted me on WhatsApp, followed by the first photos of the file itself, a front view, then a side view. The ochre cardboard cover bears the surname and the given name of my grandfather written by hand in blue pencil. Inside are hundreds of documents: letters, notices of appointments, promotions appeals, recommendations, commendations, honours, records of proceedings. There is also a 'reserved section', which my brother began to leaf through, and which enabled him to quickly locate two other envelopes, no. 5 and no. 9, entirely devoted to the purge proceedings to which my grandfather was subjected between October and December 1944.

To get to Rome by 9.30 am when the archives opened, and thus take advantage of the few hours during which the reading room was open in that period of relaxed COVID measures, my brother had to leave Pisa at 6 in the morning. He immediately began taking pictures of all the documents that seemed important to him. From time to time, he would text me or give me a call. My brother is an historian. He studied fascism and teaches at the University of Pisa but, having been immersed for months in our grandfather's history, I alone can help him contextualise a document.

That very evening, he sent me all the material he had collected and which, applying his skills as a historian, were already organised in files and sub-files: 'matricular status'; 'reserved section'; 'defensive deductions'; 'annex 1 and annex 2'; 'rulings and documents from the purge committee'.

A wave of discouragement swept over me when I received all these documents. I felt overwhelmed and did not know where to start. First, I opened the photos at random. I went from one to the other, and then I closed them all. There were too many things, too much shame, too much pain.

Little by little, I realised that I already knew many of the facts. Some of them I had reconstructed from the online archives of the Official Journal of the Italian Government. Others I had surmised based on the few elements already in my possession. Then I opened envelopes no. 5 and no. 9 and I realised that the reality was beyond anything I could have imagined. It was all much more tragic and painful. I knew that there was also a private truth, which was totally absent from the dossier. And, at bottom, this was the truth that interested me most, beyond what was written in the pages of the purge trial and in the official documents.

What exactly happened to Judge Marzano at the end of 1944? My father was eight years old at the time. Was that when he lost faith in the possibility of 'joie de vivre'?

On 16 October 1944, Arturo Marzano was summoned to the office of the Lecce Crown Prosecutor. It was a Monday morning, and his appointment was at 10 o'clock, but by 9.30 am, he was standing in front of the door to the prosecutor's office. He had an idea of what was coming his way, but deep down inside he still had a little hope. De Mitri, the prosecutor, invited him to sit down. Then he told him that he was sorry, and handed him note no. 472, in which the commission set up to purge fascists informed Deputy Prosecutor Marzano that charges were being brought against him, under the direction of the High Commissioner.

Arturo skimmed through the note. He was accused of having actively participated in and supported fascist politics. He was accused of having taught the history and doctrine of fascism in his capacity as professor and of having been a member of the Disciplinary Council of the Fascist Federation of Lecce. He was charged with having earned the credentials of *squadrista, March on Rome, ante-marche, sciarpa littorio* and having been an officer of the Voluntary Militia for National Security (MVSN). The words blurred before his eyes as he read. Suddenly, he felt his strength, his certainty, his optimism, his willpower, his vanity, and his pride tottering, the very ground giving way beneath him, and the world around him collapsing.

The prosecutor advised him not to waste time, to prepare a solid defence argument, and not to hesitate to seek support from anti-fascist colleagues and friends who could serve as character witnesses. Arturo nodded, thanked the prosecutor for his courtesy. But he was distraught. And when he left the prosecutor's office, his legs were shaking. For several hours he wandered the streets of Lecce, thinking back to the day when he took part in the birth of the Rome section. He thought back to the trial of August 1924 against the subversives who sang *Bandiera rossa*, to his meeting with the Duce in 1926 and to all the hopes he had put in Fascist Italy. He changed direction when he noticed a familiar face from afar, fearing that someone might want to stop and talk, perhaps invite him for a coffee or a drink. Then he tried to get a hold of himself. He thought back to the last few years when, as a deputy public prosecutor, all he did was fight to maintain order and discipline, and he felt at peace with his conscience. But when he returned to Campi in the afternoon, he felt drained and unmoored.

At home, Arturo locked himself in his office. He did not want his wife to worry, but he needed time to gather his thoughts. The first thing to do was to look for a way to challenge the accusations, to dispute them one by one. Obviously, there was no denying that he had earned the credentials of *squadrista, March on Rome, ante-marche, sciarpa littorio*. These were objective facts and appeared as such in all his files. But what did that have to do with the accusation of sectarianism and the support and defence of fascism? There was no denying his membership in the Fascist Party from the outset, but was his youthful exuberance in any way related to the excesses of the regime?

He took a sheet of paper and began to write. 'I must insist on the objectivity and honesty that I have always demonstrated in the exercise of my duty,' he said to himself. He put his pen down on the desk, stood up and went over to his bookcase. He looked for the file where he classified in chronological order all the commendations he received from his superiors. He found it, flipped through the documents, and picked out some letters. Then he looked for the file containing documents from some of the trials that might help him build his defence. There it was, the big black file. He pulled it off the shelf, went through the folders, selected a couple of them and placed them on the desk. Then he sat down and began to write.

'I hereby affirm, on my honour as a man, a magistrate and an officer, that I was neither sectarian, nor partisan, nor fascist. The guiding principles of my professional work and my judicial activities have always been objectivity, equanimity in judgement, utmost balance, the humanisation of positive law, an understanding of human miseries, a kind (not a weak) heart and refined feelings. And for these I have been appreciated and praised by my superiors, as it is abundantly documented in their reports.'

Arturo read over the first sentence; he had the feeling that something was missing, but he did not know exactly what. He read it again and added the expression 'most categorically' after 'I affirm'. 'Now that's better,' he said to himself after rereading the whole paragraph for the umpteenth time. 'Now what I need are concrete examples; otherwise, I risk being misunderstood.' He had to concentrate on factual elements; after all, wasn't that what he always did when he was drafting a verdict or preparing an indictment?

He opened the black file. This one contained documents from several trials in 1929 implicating certain Blackshirts, leaders of the Voluntary Militia for National Security.

'In some of the trials that were entrusted to me against officers of the MVSN, I took a very clear stand and called for their condemnation,' he wrote, adding that this was not easy for him insofar as he was 'pressured by some high-profile people in the party.' But he disregarded them and succeeded in having the *capomanipolo* Raffaele Mauro and the Blackshirt Salvatore Mannucci condemned. 'Guided only by a sense of justice, I carried out my duty with objectivity and equanimity.'

Arturo glanced at his watch. It was getting late. Soon his wife would come to tell him that dinner was ready and that Rosaria and Ferruccio were waiting for him. He had said nothing to her yet about what happened in Lecce.

He ran his hand over his forehead, took off his glasses, pressed his fingers lightly on his eyelids. He was very concerned. What could he do not to worry his family? Should he say nothing? But how could he possibly hide such a serious matter? Sooner or later, rumours risked reaching Rosetta's ear. And with the sensitivity that one could expect from some people: 'Your husband is the disgrace of Campi; he deserves to be purged.' As concerned with appearances as she had always been, how would she react?

He was still thinking about how best to explain the situation to his wife when she walked in without knocking: 'Dinner is ready, Arturo! Are you coming? Come on! The children are waiting for you.'

'Start without me,' he replied. 'I'll explain everything to you tomorrow.'

Rosetta insisted. Apparently, she had no idea what was afoot. Arturo remained silent, staring at her for a few moments. Then, he lowered his eyes and took his head into his hands. Rosetta finally understood that something serious was happening.

'What's going on, Arturo?'

'I've just been notified that I am being submitted to an official judicial review as part of the purification of the judiciary. All my attempts to avoid it have been in vain. They want to remove me from the judiciary and even to take my retirement benefits away from me.'

Rosetta turned pale and sank into a chair. Then, after a few moments of silence, she regained her composure. 'Is this how they thank a servant of the Fatherland? How shameful! But you are going to fight, aren't you? And you're going to show them whom they are dealing with.'

Arturo sighed. Rosetta continued: 'Get a hold of yourself, Arturo, I beg you. You've always managed to work things out, why not this time? Do you remember when you were sent to Vico del Gargano? And how about the time when that complaint was lodged against you by that attorney from Campi! You always came out ahead, Arturo, and you'll do so this time too!'

'Go back to the children, Rosetta,' Arturo begged her, thinking to himself that she doesn't understand these things, she doesn't realise what I'm facing. How could she? It's even too much for me.

When his wife left the office, Arturo resumed the writing of his defence argument. There was an important point that he absolutely wanted to clarify. He was accused of having been a *squadrista*, of having participated in the March on Rome, of being a fascist of the very first hour (*ante-marche*), and of having accumulated medals and functions within the fascist apparatus. 'However, it should be noted,' he wrote, 'that I was declared *squadrista* in October 1940 and not in March 1939, when the title was established; that the certification of March on Rome was granted to me on 10 October 1940, while many others received it in 1922, the month after the March on

Rome; that the *sciarpa littorio* was granted to me as a direct consequence of the two other titles, and not because of a decade of political activity in support of the regime. Finally, although it is true that I was named Officer of the National Militia in February 1924, with the rank of *capomanipolo*, I resigned in May 1925.'

Arturo calmly reread what he had written so far. He added some explanations and denied having engaged in any propaganda activities. He admitted to having given courses on political preparation organised by the Provincial Federation of Lecce, but he specified that they were all courses on public law and not, as he was accused, on the history and doctrine of fascism. He was not entirely convinced that his denials would suffice. So, he decided to attach one last document, which he considered his secret weapon.

'In support of all that I have said, I enclose a letter from a few attorneys in Lecce and in the province of Lecce who, being well-known for their anti-fascist positions, cannot be suspected of favouritism towards me.'

When did Arturo understand that he would need these character witnesses? He must have prepared for this well before he received notification of the accusations against him. He had to recall the favours he received, the friends who were not always backers of the regime. It would need more; he would need people in the Resistance or people regarded as great moral authorities. But who would have the courage to help him? Who would agree to sign this letter?

He searched his memory to recall the names of anti-fascist attorneys with whom he had dealt at one time or another in his career, thinking back to dinners held at his home and every time that someone had promised him to be forever grateful for services he had rendered. He picked up a sheet of paper and began to write a list of names.

On 25 October, Arturo sent his defence argument to Rome. Fifteen typed pages in which, retracing the various stages of his professional life, he tried to show that the accusations against him were groundless, and asked to be subjected to low-level disciplinary measures, such as a warning or censure, and concluded with the following: 'If the honourable committee does not believe that the explanations provided are sufficiently substantiated, I remain at the committee's disposal for further clarification.'

Attached to the argument was a letter signed by eleven attorneys from Lecce and from the province of Lecce who expressed regret at the suspension of Judge Marzano due to the accusations against him and declared their willingness to testify about his activities before the authorities concerned.

'Dearest good friend,' the lawyers write, 'in the period during which you served as substitute for the Crown Prosecutor in Lecce (September 1934 – September 1942), you distinguished yourself and were appreciated for your integrity, your professional value, your balance, your independence, your nobility of manner and kindness of heart, and your deep understanding of the deeds and woes of human beings. No one ever thought of you as a sectarian magistrate [...] We never heard that you were an officer of the MVSN [...] We never saw you in uniform on the streets of the city or anywhere else.'

Absurd phone call with my mother today. I told her everything I discovered about my grandfather from the documents in his personal file in the Central Archives of Rome. I told her that not only had I read his purification files, but also that I had come to perceive many of the minor and major events of his life. I told her that now, I was beginning to have the impression that I really knew him through and through.

'I can picture him talking to people, writing a verdict or preparing an indictment, I can picture him arguing with his wife, who adamantly opposes his accepting a position in Oristano or Catania, even though she knows that not leaving Campi will be detrimental to his career.'

I found, among other things, a report by the Public Prosecutor of Bari from 1940, which explicitly states that Arturo Marzano is a great worker and an excellent magistrate who deserves to be promoted and to be given more important positions, and that his refusal to leave his home town is incomprehensible.

'I'm pretty sure that was because of grandmother,' I told my mother. 'There must be a reason and I will discover it sooner or later, maybe when I can finally get back to Campi. Listen to what the Public

Prosecutor of Bari writes; it seems so obvious to me that there was something strange going on!' I read a passage from the document to her: 'Marzano is trying to get around the obligation of residence, which clearly shows his attachment to Salento for family and patrimonial reasons [...] Although I have not received any specific complaint about Marzano, I am of the opinion that his activity in our administration would be much better if he were to discharge his duties outside his province.'

But my mother did not seem to be very interested in what I was saying and she abruptly interrupted me: 'The next time you come to Rome, you have to sort through the things you left here. There are two boxes, firmly closed with string and tape. You see which ones I'm talking about?'

'The ones with tapes of my recordings of my therapy sessions? But why are you bringing this up now?'

'You should throw them away. Imagine if they fell into someone's hands one day, and everything would be disclosed!'

'What are you talking about, Mama?'

'Everything you've been through! It could be used against you.'

'Mama, do you realise what you're saying?'

Absurd phone call. It brought home the extent to which my mother too did not understand what I was doing in writing this book. And I felt hurt, because I was convinced that there was at least one person who understood how important it was to confront one's own past. Wasn't she the one who, just a few weeks earlier, had said to me: 'You are right to be doing what you're doing, my daughter; it's so useful.' But apparently my mother too did not feel the need to really confront an uncomfortable past. She would still rather hide things. But isn't the past uncomfortable for everyone, not just our family?

'And what exactly do I really have to hide, Mama?'

The story of my anorexia had been known for years, as was the fact that it took me twenty years of psychoanalysis to overcome it. But I am not ashamed of what I've been through. Yes, I always felt a lot of shame when I was a child. Even today, I am sometimes ashamed, like when I think that I did not realise that my grandfather had been a fascist of the very first hour until I was fifty years old, or when I think that I will never be a mother. But I am not ashamed of my anorexia. What have I to blame myself for?

On 28 November 1944, at 10 am, Arturo Marzano appeared before the purification committee. The summons arrived by telegram at the office of the Public Prosecutor of Lecce. He first phoned my grandfather to give him advance notice and then sent a telegram of confirmation.

In the personal file of my grandfather, from the Central Archives in Rome, in addition to the presentation of charges and Arturo's defence brief, I found the original copy of all the official telegrams that the president of the purification committee exchanged with the prosecutor of Lecce. Arturo Marzano's file contains everything, except for what my grandfather said to his wife and children before he left for Rome. It contains everything, except what he said that Wednesday morning to the committee. It contains everything, except what the members of the committee responded to his attempts to contextualise, to explain away or qualify the scope of the accusations against him.

I pictured my grandfather kissing his son before going to Rome, explaining to him that he'll be back soon and that there's no reason to cry or be sad.

I pictured my grandmother devastated, adjusting

the collar of her husband's coat and telling him not to catch a cold, to eat well and not to stay up too late.

I pictured my grandfather the next morning, standing in front of the door to the chamber of the Ministry of Justice, his hands clammy, his breathing shallow. I pictured him, embarrassed and tense, thanking the commission for giving him the opportunity to express himself personally and to better clarify what he wrote in his defence brief, which was undoubtedly written too hastily, and may be confusing at times.

I pictured the stern look on the face of the committee chairman, Giuseppe Pagano, one of the magistrates who had disobeyed the Minister of Justice in 1938 and was purged because he refused to present a declaration affirming that he was not a Jew. By an irony of history, he is now the one who holds the fate of my grandfather in his hands. How can he even bear to look straight into the eyes of this *squadrista* who, now that his back is against the wall, is trying to minimise his intense and active participation in the political life of fascism?

I pictured President Pagano barely listening to the words spoken by my grandfather in a low voice, convinced that it is now time for Deputy Public Prosecutor Arturo Marzano to take responsibility for his deeds and his choices, which is something that Pagano had clearly done during the years of fascism!

On 2 December 1944, Pagano asked the secretary to send a copy of the verdict concerning my grandfather, first to the High Commissioner, and then to the Public Prosecutor of Lecce:

'In view of the fact that Marzano's participation in the political life of fascism was so active and so intense, that his support for the regime was manifest, and that his unworthiness to serve the state is obvious, Deputy Prosecutor Arturo Marzano is removed from service, with the provision that he is eligible for a pension.'

I felt outraged. Without a doubt, my grandfather deserved to be purged. That was not what outraged me. But when I read his file, something happened that I could not quite describe, and for a few days I found myself writing and deleting and hating myself for my manifest inability to find the right words.

What happened was that time first stopped, then went backward.

What happened is that I found myself by my grandfather's side, feeling his distress, his inability to realise what was really happening to him. And the certainty that so many people would celebrate his downfall: So, Signor the Judge, how do you feel now that you find yourself dragged through the mud?

And then, instead of my grandfather, I saw my father and felt the despair of an eight-year-old who sees everything abruptly change, and no one telling him why. When you grow up, I'll explain it to you. But he grew up and no one ever did. But that was not what made me feel outrage.

What outraged me when I dove into the recent bibliography devoted to the purges in the administration and the judiciary was the fact that in Italy the measures for the defascisation were applied in a fragmentary and contradictory manner, and often impacted people of lesser importance.

What outraged me was that those most implicated in the regime were not purged. The most visible ones, that is to say, the most exposed high-ranking officials like Starace, obviously suffered the same fate as the Duce. But all the people who were truly responsible for the administrative machinery of fascism, remained in their posts, and in liberated Italy, they were even promoted, often at the request of our liberators, in the name of pacification and the 'cold war' on the horizon.

What outraged me was that my grandfather was one of the few magistrates to pay for what he did, when he was nothing but a small provincial judge who had not hesitated to put forward his early adherence to fascism. To be sure, Arturo was a vain fascist who instrumentalised politics to further his career, but he did not really give himself the means to do so in the end, due to his attachment to Campi, where he was a highly respected man. His provincialism was stronger than his ambition. In Campi, he was called 'commander' and people took off their hats when they crossed paths with him. Was it his wife who stood in his way and would not let him leave the region, or was he secretly enjoying his life as a magistrate in Lecce? Why throw himself into the fray and compete in the big league in Rome? Amongst those major league players who never paid for what they did. The ones who are always changing sides, who never believe in anything and who are ready to do anything to hold onto their privileges. The ones who were counsellors in the Court of Cassation or members of the Council of State, and then remained at their posts, and continued to further their careers as if nothing had happened.

I felt outraged and even disgusted.

Was I overreacting? Was I losing my sense of proportion? Had I lost my ability to be objective?

One of the names that comes up most often in recent research on the defascisation of the judiciary is that of Antonio Azara. I have already mentioned Azara when I listed some of the members of the scientific committee of that horrible journal *Il Diritto razzista*. I did not know that I would be brought to refer to him again, nor that I would come across his name in reading one of the speeches my grandfather made in the National Assembly after he was elected deputy in 1953.

It must be another person with the same name, I said to myself the first time I saw his name on the first page of an amnesty bill that he was presenting to Parliament as Minister of Justice. I skimmed through the entry on him in *Le Dizionario biografico degli Italiani* and there were no two ways about it: It was indeed him! But where does it say that in September 1944, Azara was prosecuted for defending and supporting fascism and that the charges against him were dropped when he produced some fifteen declarations signed by counsellors of the Court of Cassation and more than 180 letters signed by foreign jurists?

Nothing. Not a word anywhere.

But it gets worse. Azara was not alone, not by a long shot, among the major players to come out unscathed quickly and easily. I could mention so many other names, but there is one that deserves more attention than the others: Gaetano Azzariti.

In 1938, Azzariti adhered to the Manifesto of Race and was appointed president of the Tribunal for Race. Was such a fascist purged in 1944? Removed from his functions? Forced into retirement? Not at all. The proceedings against him started in 1944 and were quickly dropped. Azzariti minimised his role in the Tribunal of Race, even though it was he who declared, in 1942, in a speech to the Milanese Legal Circle: 'Racial diversity is an insuperable obstacle to the establishment of personal relationships, from which biological or psychic alterations to the purity of our people may arise.'

After the liberation, Azzariti worked in the legislative office of the Ministry of Justice under the presidency of Palmiro Togliatti, the first secretary of the Communist Party. In 1957, he became president of the Constitutional Court.

The numbers of purged from the judiciary are telling: In March 1946, out of 11,400 employees of the Ministry of Justice, 4,052 were subjected to a purge procedure; 589 trials were initiated; 575 were brought to completion; only 56 people were suspended. Some experts maintain that it would have been hard to enable the judiciary machine to function smoothly if there had been a more extensive purge. Others explain that, at some point, the decision was made to move forward and not remain stuck in the past. But why did those who were most implicated get away with it?

'There is something rotten in the state of Denmark,' Hamlet says, when he realises the extent of the intrigues and betrayals that hung over the Danish throne. But isn't this, in the end, what we could say about Italy? No house cleaning has ever been done. And the bust of Gaetano Azzariti is in place in the palace of the Constitutional Court, the guardian of our fundamental freedoms and of our Republic.

I reread some pages from *The March on Rome and Its Surroundings*. Emilio Lussu had understood everything already at the beginning of the 1920s: The problem in Italy has always been a lack of consistency. Saying one thing and doing the opposite. Or saying exactly the opposite of what was said before. Who is going to remember today what was said yesterday? A lack of memory. Amnesia. But also a lack of courage. Maybe that is why in Italy, we have never made the effort that it takes to reckon with our history.

'And where's the consistency?' Emilio Lussu asked his colleague Lissia when he discovered, in November 1922, that Lissia had accepted the position of Secretary of State for Finance in the Mussolini government. And this was the very same Lissia who, after the March on Rome, had spoken of the need to fight to the last drop of blood for freedom in his country. 'Consistency? Reality is always consistent,' Lissia replied. His argument stands as a short treatise of pure cynicism: 'Politics is not an abstraction, it is an art. And anyway, do you really think it was easy to accept this position? Do you think the decision was taken lightly? Is it possible that you really don't understand that this is how we can be useful to our country? It is as fascists that we can best serve our Fatherland!'

I was confronted in politics with the same type of arguments, in fortunately less tragic times. 'Wake up, Michela!' my parliamentary colleagues would say to me. 'You're not in university anymore. We are dealing with serious business here. This is politics. Don't be so rigid!' I am ready to admit that there is sometimes a fine line between consistency and rigidity. And that in the name of consistency, there is sometimes a risk of never putting oneself in question.

Sometimes, being true to oneself requires changing one's opinion. But when people change their minds all the time, aren't they betraying themselves?

When I decided in 2016 to leave the Democratic Party, Italy was so fascinated by Matteo Renzi that anyone who voiced objections to the President of the Council was accused of defeatism, and even obscurantism. Renzi had decided to toss out the old-fashioned views of the left. He said that right and left were outdated notions, that there were, on the one hand, people who move forward, and those, on the other, who stand still. And, of course, the people who move forward were supporters of the anti-social reforms that Renzi wanted to impose on the country. All you had to do at the time was raise such issues as social justice or equal rights to be labelled antiquated, a loser, or a failure: in short, someone who absolutely could not understand that the times had changed.

For months, I had been voting in disagreement with my parliamentary group and had been proposing amendments that were systematically rejected. I couldn't see where my place was in the Democratic Party, especially after Renzi proposed a bill on labour that exacerbated the precarity of workers. And this was followed by the question of civil unions. To avoid antagonising certain right-wing Catholics, Renzi proposed a watered-down reform, which provided no rights to children for same-sex couples. When the former secretary of the Democratic Party proposed the position of deputy to me, he knew exactly how I felt about marriage for all and the rights to children for same-sex couples. How could I stay on in a party that had compromised to the point of, in the end, reversing its positions?

The same day that the civil unions law was passed, I decided to leave the Democratic Party. It was a difficult decision, but I believed in the importance of consistency, of being true to yourself, and I did not want to be consumed by shame when I thought of the promises I had made to gay people.

The next day, a famous editorialist from *La Repubblica* wrote a short piece on me: 'Michela Marzano's departure from the Democratic Party, after the approval of the bill on civil unions (which she considers very important, but very incomplete), is undoubtedly a serious, and carefully considered move [...] She explains that she wants to remain true to herself [...] I wonder, however, if the purpose of political activity is to be true to oneself, or if the very nature of politics, which is a collective activity, entails contravening this principle, even when doing so is very difficult and even painful, notably because politics is not about the self; it is about this catch-all category that we call society.'

I read the editorial several times. I did not know what to do. I felt torn between a desire to let it go and the need to explain what I had done. I finally decided to reply. 'Yes, you are right that I spoke of consistency, but I was not referring to consistency toward myself. "I am not that special," a friend of mine told me once, and I think that this is true of each and every one of us. The consistency that interests me has to do with the moral values that justify, or should justify, one's engagement in politics. [...] Politics, as you rightly point out, is not about the self, but about society. And society is precisely what was on my mind when I made my decision. My gesture, at bottom, is but a testimony: It is not worth engaging in politics if all you do thereafter is follow the way of the world, and then use your mind to justify this attitude.'

I had forgotten this incident. But suddenly it came back to me when I reread the exchange between Lussu and his friend who had agreed to be part of a 'fascist government' for 'the benefit of society'. 'Reality is always consistent.' Cynics in all times repeat this. I think back to all the times I sat in Parliament and witnessed a reversal or a sudden change of convictions. I saw some members of

Parliament turn around and do the opposite of what they had said they would defend 'at all costs' only days and even hours before. I saw elected representatives go from having total confidence in leader no. 1 to having total confidence in leader no. 2, who had just politically assassinated leader no. 1. And don't get me started on the turncoat journalists who are capable of writing, within a few weeks, just about anything and its opposite. In Italy, this is a well-known strategy, and the person who flipflops like this is called a *voltagabbana*!

Voltagabbana, a renegade, a turncoat, literally, 'one who turns on one's cloth', is commonly used to designate someone who is always turncoating for their own self-interests. In politics, they call such people 'transformists'. I call them 'traitors'.

'So, to your mind, we aren't entitled to change our minds? Is that what you're saying?' Jacques looked at me, wide-eyed and baffled. 'I think you're overstating things. There is a need for party discipline. And, even more importantly, isn't there room for doubt? Isn't doubt the basis of philosophy?'

'I'm always ready and willing to change my mind when I realise that I'm wrong, and you know that! Never questioning yourself is synonymous with stupidity. But that's not what I'm saying!'

'Oh really? And yet that's what you seem to be saying.'

'Not at all! The problem is not about doubting or changing one's mind, but about doing so for purposes of convenience; the key word is 'convenience'. That's where the betrayal lies. Traitors change their minds for their own personal interests, and therefore for convenience's sake!'

When traitors change, it is not because they have been listening to others, questioning themselves, accepting that they may have been wrong, and apologising when appropriate. It is not because they see their interlocutor's point. It is not as if they have come to a new realisation. The only new understanding that traitors have when they change their minds is that they will profit from doing so. For traitors, the issue of the other's otherness does not even arise.

When I left the Democratic Party, my father did not speak to me for several days. And when I tried to find out why, his answer was that when you are part of a group, you adapt to their decisions and you don't go about grandstanding!

'Excuse me, Papa, I'm not sure I'm following you. What exactly do you mean? What about all the things you taught Arturo and me when we were young? Haven't you always said that the most important thing in life is to be true to oneself and to one's own values?'

'Yes, of course! But the Democratic Party is the only group that defends your values, Michela! And sometimes in life you have to learn to cut your losses and hang in there.'

Salvare il salvabile, literally save what can be saved, meaning cut your losses. I had forgotten that one. My father used to say it all the time. And when I was little, I used to get angry. What the hell does that mean? That there are times when you have to renounce your ideas? That there are days when you have to accept making certain compromises? Where does it end? When does compromising become compromising oneself?

Once again, with my father, something was off. Like this group business. Who decides where the group is? Who in the group makes the decisions?

The scene was more or less as follows: We're on vacation, my father is walking ahead of us, and he's walking fast; when he realises that my mother, my brother and I have lagged behind, he berates us, saying that when you're out with a group, you have to stay 'in the group'. 'C'mon, get a move on it,' he says. 'And I don't want to hear any arguments.' My mother and I get moving immediately without a word. My brother on the other hand does not budge. My father yells: 'Arturo, that goes for you too.' My brother says, 'Sorry, but who decides where the group is when three out of the four people do not want to follow the fourth?' My father flares up: 'I'm the group!' he snaps back, enraged.

On 22 June 1946, a few days after the birth of the Republic, the Council of Ministers unanimously approved the amnesty decree of the communist minister Palmiro Togliatti. 'It was important, on the one hand, to let the masses of former fascists know that we were not out to banish them,' he explained a few months later. 'And, on the other hand, to let the middle class know that we are a reasonable party, capable when necessary to say a pacifying word.'

PACIFYING. The purpose of this amnesty was clear: to calm people's fears by wiping the slate clean after years of civil war that had torn the country apart between 1944 and 1945. Unfortunately, the first to benefit, as the Italian historian Mimmo Franzinelli has recently shown, were above all the highest-ranking fascists, all those who had large sums of money at their disposal to hire the best lawyers and exploit the intricacies of the judicial machine. That was how some of the Blackshirts who had been at the head of execution squads came to be acquitted of the charge of murder: After all, they did not actually pull the trigger. As for those who participated in gang rapes of the *stafette*, the partisan couriers, they were merely found guilty of 'indecent behaviour'.

Some people maintain that all this was a consequence of the Cold War. They say that defascisation soon came to be seen as secondary and even embarrassing. Sometimes, they even justify this amnesty by arguing that caring about the future of a country necessarily involves trying to move on.

But how can one move on without a reckoning with one's past? How can amnesia be extolled, when it is only by cultivating memory that there is any hope that certain things will not happen again?

'*Cosa fatta, capo ha,*' 'what is done is done,' my father always used to say, and it could not be undone. It was the way he always had of not engaging in, or cutting short, what he considered useless discussions about the past. *Cosa fatta, capo ha.* What's the point of dwelling on the past? 'You must look forward to the change.' This too my father used to say all the time.

I was fourteen the first time I heard it. I had just come back to Italy from England, leaving behind me a French friend I had met in Cambridge. Florence and I had become inseparable. It was perhaps the first time I understood what friendship was. And the first time I lost someone dear to me. Florence was not dead, but that day I knew I would never see her again. And it was unbearable for me to hear my father telling me to move on. *Cosa fatta, capo ha.* I tried to hold on to my memories, replaying them over and over again in my mind. The hours that Florence and I had spent together, the butter cookies and bergamot tea that afternoon in Florence's room; the pint of beer that had sent my head spinning that night. Wasn't that Swedish guy cute? I didn't care about anything else.

Cosa fatta, capo ha. I thought about my desire to have a child. The die was cast now. I watched the latest video of my nephew and felt a pang in my heart. There is no other way to describe the mixture of tenderness and pain, the regret for all that I would never experience, but also a certain sense of relief. Would I have been able to love my child? I mean to really love the child and make her feel that she exists for my love? Or would I have driven her crazy by turning her into the object that I lack?

My heart sank.

It contracted and nearly stopped beating. Then picked up again faster than before. Always excessive! Even when I was simply watching images of my little nephew who was starting to explore the world. No doubt I did the right thing in not having children. I would not have been able to be a good mother. But is that really the case? Or was I just afraid? But afraid of what? Of becoming like my father? Did I want to protect this child from me?

What was my father thinking that afternoon in 1974? I was three and a half years old and had been having trouble breathing for a few months. The ear, nose and throat doctor explained to my parents that my tonsils were causing the trouble and they would have to be removed. 'It's a commonplace operation,' he said, adding, 'given your daughter's age, it would be better to give her general anaesthesia.' My father took me to the clinic and waited there for the operation to be completed. When I woke up from the anaesthesia, I asked him what was that red thing on my leg that was hurting me. He told me it was nothing.

'It will go away soon. Don't touch it! Think about something else.'

My father looked but did not see.

The wound escaped him; it went unnoticed. Now, in thinking about it, a Greek word appeared before my eyes, the verb *lathein*, meaning 'to escape from sight', which forms, with the alpha privative, the term *alètheia*, meaning 'truth'. Truth would be that which does not escape from sight. What my father cannot see. As if it were submerged by the tiny *alpha* privative. The same one that erases all memory in *amnesia*.

Without memory and without truth.

That must be it. Or was it I who was losing my way?

My father did not see the wound and let the nurses apply the kind of ointment that they used in those days for insect bites, allergies and rashes. And he let it go at that. But as it turns out, it was not a bite or an allergy or a rash.

'What have they done to my daughter?' my mother asked as soon as I came home and she took a look at my leg. She couldn't believe her eyes. Neither could she understand how my father could have neglected such a wound. 'It's deep,' she said. 'Looks like a burn. What did they do to my little girl?'

It was, in fact, a serious burn caused by drops of nitrogen, and, in a few days, it became infected. By the time I was taken to the paediatrician, the wound was already full of pus, and had to be cleaned. 'How could they have let drops of nitrogen fall on her calf?' Even the paediatrician couldn't believe his eyes. Only my father remained unfazed.

The lesion was so deep that it left a permanent scar. The liquid nitrogen did not only burn my skin, but it also burnt the subcutaneous fatty and muscular tissues. As a result, I stopped wearing skirts when I was in secondary school because I was ashamed of the scar. And still today, I find myself blushing when someone stares at my calf and asks me what's on my leg.

No point in dwelling on the surgeon's irresponsible attitude: The renowned professor had first minimised the incident, before blaming it all on the nurses. No point in dwelling on the pain either: I have no memory of it, either because I was too small, or because it was so painful that the memory was shut down, leaving no trace. But what I still could not understand was my father's reaction. How was it possible that he did not realise I had been burned? Where was his head? Where were his eyes? Was I invisible?

My grandfather wanted to be active in politics. After his rehabilitation, history caught up with him. Now he wanted to get his revenge on life. He had been thinking about it since he was reinstated in his position in the judiciary. Although his work as public prosecutor in Taranto brought him great satisfaction, his head was elsewhere. He was worried about the turn of events; he did not appreciate the fact that the Christian Democrats were gaining so much ground in the south. And, above all, he wanted, as in 1919, to defeat the communists and the socialists.

In 1949, Arturo ran during the municipal elections in Campi on the list of the Italian Social Movement (MSI), the newly formed neo-fascist party. He was convinced of the need to hold onto the sacred ideals of 'God, King and Fatherland'. But the results of the elections were not good for his list. So, in 1953, for the administrative elections, he threw his support behind a joint list of the MSI and the Monarchist National Party (PNM), on which both his brother-in-law, Nino, and Tonino Guarino, Starace's nephew, were running. Then he ran again, this time to become a member of the National Assembly in the PNM ranks. 'You can't stay with those MSI people,' a friend of the family told him. 'They are too overtly linked to fascism. Some of them were even officers of the Republic of Salò, and people don't forget those kinds of things.'

On 7 June 1953, in the district of Lecce-Brindisi-Tarente, the PNM won 14.41% of the votes and came in third after the Christian Democrats and the Communist Party. Arturo was elected with 15,806 votes. During the entire election campaign, my grandfather held high his monarchist convictions. But once he was in Parliament, he fought many political battles on the side of his colleagues from the MSI.

26 November 1953 was a very important day for Arturo. Since he was elected, it was the first time he was to take the floor in Parliament and he was very moved. The matter at hand was close to his heart. It was a discussion and vote on the Amnesty and Remission of Sentence Bill introduced by Azara. The minister was convinced of the need to adopt additional measures of clemency, in order to continue the process of pacification initiated in 1946. But he thought that it was best to avoid amnesty for crimes punishable by a prison sentence of more than three years and apply a simple remission of sentence instead.

In previous sessions, only Deputy Degli Occhi took the floor on behalf of the PNM. 'But Degli Occhi has absolutely no charisma,' Arturo told his son the day before. 'He's a good person, but the party needs more than just him to speak out on such a touchy subject!'

Since my father moved to Rome in 1954 to study at the Faculty of Law, he and Arturo got into the habit of meeting for lunch every Wednesday. When he was in Rome, Arturo would stay in a hotel, while my father was living with a couple of friends who had an apartment right near his university. But on Wednesdays, during the hour dedicated in the Chamber of Deputies to the questions to the government, Arturo and Ferruccio would get together in a trattoria right by Montecitorio, where the deputies meet.

'Degli Occhi's presentation last Thursday was quite pointed. He's a member of the Justice Commission and he knows what he is talking about, but his speech lacked vehemence and conviction.' Arturo told his son that, in his opinion, the only one who really grasped all the implications of this bill was Giambattista Madia, a deputy of the neo-fascist party MSI. 'Titta Madia has experience; he was already a deputy in the 1930s. He is a master in the art of public speaking, and the only one who has really understood the situation in which we find ourselves today. Do you realise that all of Italy has been on trial for years and years? This litigation madness has got to stop. There's no point in rehashing the past over and over again!'

Ferruccio listened to his father in silence. He hadn't the courage to contradict him, despite the fact that he could not understand what fascinated him so. He had looked into Titta Madia and nothing about him inspired confidence.

It was exactly 4.30 pm when the President of the National Assembly entered the chamber, accompanied by the Secretary General. He slowly climbed the steps to his seat and waited for the officials and clerks to take theirs before sitting down. After a quick scan of the room, he concentrated his attention on the agenda, turned on the microphone, cleared his throat and read the minutes of the previous session.

My grandfather was the second on the list of deputies who were to take the floor. The first one was Mario Berlinguer, the father of Enrico, the famous communist leader of my youth.

While Berlinguer spoke, Arturo reread his notes, altered a sentence and deleted some words here and there. From time to time, he checked his watch with a worried look on his face. He did not even react when his neighbour pointed to a colleague's tie, laughing, and said: 'These communists dress without any taste!'

Arturo was used to speaking in public. He had done so in court for years, but now his mouth felt pasty and his throat dry. The amnesty discussion was complex, and he hoped that he would not let himself be rattled by the noise that is often made in the chamber. Above all, he wanted to keep calm, and he knew that someone may very well interrupt or boo him at some point during his speech.

'How deliberately misleading,' Arturo thought when he heard the socialist colleague explain that the amnesty concerned only partisans. 'Why wouldn't it concern fascists as well? As if the communists were choirboys, when we have all seen in the USSR what they are capable of doing. By contrast, the fascist revolution was a romp in the countryside. Then he turned his attention back to his notes. About ten minutes were allotted to his speech. He had to try to stick to that time frame. He could still cut a few sentences. He cast a glance at the ceiling of the chamber but without due appreciation this time of the canopy by Beltrami. 'When you're in here, you never know what the weather is like outside!' he mused. 'From here, you'd think it's always lovely weather in Rome and yet today the weather when I left my hotel was horrendous: It was raining cats and dogs. But why am I thinking about the weather? What does that have to do with my speech?'

'*Onorevole* Marzano now has the floor.'

It was 5:23 pm. Arturo glanced at the clock right near the seat of the president, stood up, adjusted his microphone, and, with a nod of his head, he thanked the clerk who had come to bring him a glass of water, took a sip and launched into his speech.

'Some colleagues have been complaining about there being too many measures of clemency in recent years.'

Arturo had been undecided until the last moment about whether he should read his text or speak without looking at his notes. In the end, out of fear of speaking too long or, worse still, not saying everything he meant to say, he opted to stick to his notes.

'Yet one would be hard-pressed not to see that a very broad measure of clemency, aimed at healing the wounds of a tormented recent past, represents today a historical and political necessity that cannot be disregarded.'

Disturbed by the noise, my grandfather took another sip of water, then went back to reading.

'Reconciliation is needed, if we are to inaugurate an era of national solidarity by erasing the vestiges of civil war and the consequences of the aberrant emergency laws against fascism.'

Arturo paused for a moment. He raised his tone when he said, 'aberrant emergency laws against fascism,' pronouncing each word distinctly, but he could not hide his emotion and his voice cracked. Although years had passed, the memory of his purge from the judiciary was still with him; the wound had not yet healed.

'Signor Ministro, Ladies and Gentlemen, at this point, eight years after the end of the civil war, we have to have the courage to adopt measures that apply without distinction to both partisans and fascists. They are all children of Italy. And they all fought for the supreme good of the Fatherland.'

A murmur rose from the left side of the chamber. Some shouted, 'Shame on you!' Arturo fell silent. Then, encouraged by his neighbour, he went on.

'The clemency, which should be broad and far-reaching, must wrap in a dense cloud of oblivion the sad memory of a recent past of blood, mistreatment, suffering, brutal and horrific vengeance, unparalleled atrocities and humiliations. It must sink into the deepest depths of amnesia the memories which have tormented and undermined our national conscience, leaving traces so indelible that they can only be erased by a measure that really reckons with the need for true pacification…'

My grandfather's speech went on for quite some time. But now I found it hard to continue reading the minutes of the session. There is not a thing that Arturo said with which I agreed. All I wanted to do was shout 'shame on you', like his opponents, even though I always hated being interrupted when I spoke in the chamber by shouts from the Lega, Forza Italia and Fratelli d'Italia. They made my blood run cold.

But I hated even more what my grandfather said. Right at that moment, all I wanted was to be there, to stop him in the corridors of the National Assembly and tell him that he was wrong. 'Grandfather, forgetting never brings peace; on the contrary! And how can you still be saying that the laws against fascism were aberrant? Those laws were not what was aberrant; it was fascism itself. And even more, the racial laws of your precious Duce, and the Social Republic. Those were the things, Grandfather, that were aberrant, not the laws against fascism! And we must never forget those horrible things. We must remember them, because we have to make sure that it never happens again!'

I needed to calm down. I needed to find some peace of mind and reread my grandfather's speech with a cool head from beginning to end. I needed to analyse it rigorously. If I let myself get angry and stopped trying to understand exactly what Arturo meant, I would ruin everything.

I decided to go out for a walk. I went to the Luxembourg Gardens. 12,000 steps and 9 kilometres. When I came back, I was exhausted, but calm. Calm enough to go back to reading the minutes of the parliamentary session of 26 November 1953 and go over some of the passages of my grandfather's speech. I underlined some of the words and took notes in a notebook:

- without distinction (partisans and fascists)
- oblivion, cloud, abyss, amnesia
- indelible or erasable traces

Gradually, I came to understand that the issue for Arturo was the remission of sentences. My grandfather wanted amnesty for all: 'Ten years after the dark days of the national disaster, we are at it again: collusion with the enemy, sabotage, indiscriminate surrender, militia, mistakes by Mussolini, mistakes by the general staff, partisans, Black Brigades, shootings, cruelty, atrocities, massacres of fascists by partisans and vice versa, etc.'

Arturo wanted to erase history. And he was wrong on all counts. Even though I had to admit at least that he acted in good faith. During the remainder of the speech, he cited the reopening not only of trials against *squadristi* amnestied in 1922, but also of trials against partisans.

Looking into it, I discovered that 1953 was a critical year in the history of Italy. It was a year when people sought to silence anyone who wanted to turn a critical eye on the wartime and post-war past, to the paradoxical point of not celebrating the liberation. On 25 April, the *Corriere della Sera* did not even mention the anniversary. But the trials grew in number, not only against those who tried to shine a light on the horrors of the war, but also against those who, at the end of the conflict, and in the name of 'partisan justice' had conducted summary executions. My grandfather cited many facts, and then concentrated on the *Corriera della morte*, the 'Death Bus' massacre, on which the Court of Assizes of Rome had just pronounced judgement on an appeal. On 14 May 1945, about forty people – including some prisoners from the camps in Germany, but also some militia from the Republic of Salò – were returning to their homes in the south in a bus provided by the Vatican. Departing from Brescia, they crossed the centre of the country but were stopped, near Modena, by partisans who made the passengers get off and proceeded to check their identities. They discovered sixteen militia, took them to Villa Medici and brutally murdered them.

Arturo wanted to erase history with an amnesty. The entire history. To his mind, the only way to create a climate of national harmony was to forget about the atrocities of the civil war. To wipe the slate clean and to start afresh. *Cosa fatta, capo ha*. To avoid the spectacle of a country that spends its time in courtrooms 'going over for the umpteenth time the horrible stories of its prolonged war, and of how Italians killed each other for pleasure and for the benefit of the foreigner'.

My grandfather preached amnesia: 'The term amnesty, which is derived from the Greek and resonates acoustically with "amnesia", implies forgetting the past.' But what reconciliation can be born out of repression? Isn't it precisely because the country has not come to terms with the past that it has never really freed itself from its violence?

The fire under the ashes. Which suddenly flares up.

Like the terrible violence that tore Italy apart in the 1970s, the red terrorism and the black terrorism, the kidnappings and massacres, a hatred that never subsided, maybe because whenever the opportunity arose, this nation never had the courage to question itself thoroughly.

I thought of the resonance between the words 'amnesty' and 'amnesia', which is not merely acoustic. In Greek, both words, besides sharing the alpha privative, are constructed from the root of the verb *mimnêskô*, 'to remember'. Forgetting and loss of memory go hand in hand.

I repeated the words amnesia and amnesty. Then, by a bizarre association of ideas, the word 'anamnesis,' came to mind. It also derives from the Greek *anmimnêskô*, 'to remember', although this time the alpha is not privative at all; on the contrary, anamnesis is a remembering. When we go to the doctor, we give an account of ourselves. We tell the doctor about our sick body, but it is never only about our body that we complain.

I needed a new doctor. The one I had been seeing for more than twenty years, whom I had chosen by chance when I arrived in Paris, had retired. But the mere idea of looking for a new doctor made me anxious. I would have to go over the list of everything that had happened to me since I was a child – my anamnesis – and the doctor would think that she was dealing with an unbearable, delusional hypochondriac.

'Just stick to the facts,' Jacques told me. 'You'll see. It'll be fine.' Because he is a good hypochondriac, he always manages to get doctors to take him seriously.

'But my problem is precisely the facts!'

The facts: when I was three years old, I fell off a slide and broke my collarbone; at three and a half, I had trouble breathing through my nose and my tonsils were removed; at six, I slipped on a banana peel and fractured my malleolus; at seven, I tore a tendon in my knee while playing; at eight, I was rushed to the hospital for an emergency appendix operation; at fourteen, I fractured a bone between the index and the middle finger on my left hand when I fell off my scooter; at nineteen, I had mononucleosis; at twenty-three, I had pulmonary tuberculosis; at twenty-six, I tore the lateral and the cruciate ligaments of my right knee; at twenty-eight, I tore the cruciate ligament of the left knee; at thirty, I had whooping cough.

More facts, this time with regards to the attitude of the members of my family and my doctors.

When my tonsils were removed, I left the clinic with a burn on my calf (but I've told that story already, so there's no need to dwell again on the attitude of my father and the doctor).

I was at school when I fractured my malleolus, and I went that afternoon to my figure skating class despite the pain. When my mother came to pick me up, the teacher told her that it was probably nothing, that I wasn't walking well but that I'd taken my skating lessons. 'Children can be capricious,' she said. 'You'll see. Everything will be fine tomorrow.' The next day, I was put in a cast. The doctor asked my mother why she waited a whole day before bringing me to the clinic.

When I fractured the little bone between my index and middle fingers on my left hand, they took me to the emergency room for an X-ray and told my father that there was no fracture. I kept saying that I was in a lot of pain, but no one listened to me. I was still complaining after several days of being in terrible pain. This irritated my father, but my mother convinced him to take me to an orthopaedist. During the examination, he touched a spot that made me scream. His diagnosis? 'Internal fracture, she needs a cast.' 'But we were told in the emergency room that there was no fracture,' my father protested. 'The X-rays must have been taken poorly,' was the orthopaedist's reply.

When I got tuberculosis, for months, the doctors kept saying that it was the flu or laryngitis or bronchitis. One day, on the suspicion that I might have pneumonia, I was sent for a scan. By the time I was finally hospitalised, the medical quacks had taken so long to diagnose the illness that I was spitting blood.

When I had the scooter accident, they again concluded from the X-rays taken in the emergency room that nothing was broken. I was screaming in pain but, as usual, they thought I was having a panic attack. Only hours later did they agree to take me to an orthopaedist, only to find the lateral ligament and anterior cruciate ligament tears.

I had been living and working in Paris for several years when I developed whooping cough. Nearly everyone in France had been vaccinated against it, so the possibility that I had caught it seemed inconceivable to the doctors. And it was only after a month of fever and coughing fits that they finally decided to run biological tests. Jacques said it was because I did not explain what was going on well. No doubt, I was the one to blame!

One night, at a friend's dinner party, someone told a joke. A guy goes to the psychiatrist. He says he's in despair. 'Doctor, I have a problem, nobody notices me, I feel transparent. Please help me!' And the doctor looks right through him and says, 'Next!' I burst out laughing, one of those irrepressible laughs, before the laughter turned to sobbing.

Why didn't anyone listen to me? Why did I always feel transparent, like the poor guy in the joke?

My mother told me that my father had been acting strange of late. She heard him talking in his sleep, conversing with someone, saying, 'I'm the one who's right! You'll see. You'll have to admit that I'm right in the end!'

My brother said that this was nothing new. 'Papa has always been like that! He has always lived in his own world disconnected from reality.'

I didn't know what to think of my father anymore.

I knew that he didn't listen to anyone.

He didn't listen and he never answered questions that were put to him. He would just continue his own monologue, unfazed. If you said something that didn't fit into what he was thinking at a given moment, there wasn't a chance in the world of getting through to him. In his world, there was only him. When I was a child, I would scream to try to get him to listen to me. Screaming was the only way of shutting him up and making it into his world. But it only lasted a few moments, after which he too would start yelling. 'That's enough!'

I knew there were some things that he obsessed about.

He was like that about food, he was like that

about water, he was like that about studies at school. Now at least his obsessions concerned him alone. He would stick to a number of rituals: In the morning, he would prepare a caffé mocha, and drink a third of it at breakfast, another third during his 11 o'clock break, and the last third after lunch. Instead of drinking his coffee in a cup, like everyone else, he would always use the same glass jar, which he would rinse under the tap every day. Just like his small plastic bottle of mineral water, always the same one, which he would fill and empty every day, without ever replacing it. No point in telling him that it was unsanitary!

He took it into his head at some point that he had a perforated eardrum and explained to us years ago that it came from an ear infection that he had had when he was a child. He would wrap a wire in cotton, slip it into his ear, and move it around inside his ear for a few minutes, then he would throw the cotton away, and cover the wire in paper tissue, and do the same thing the next day. By now, my father wasn't hearing well anymore. When he watched TV, he would turn up the sound so high that one day my exasperated mother forced him, screaming, to go see a hearing specialist. The day of the visit, my father rehashed the story about his perforated eardrum.

'Your eardrum is not perforated,' the doctor replied. 'But if you continue to insert implements like that into your ear, sooner or later, you'll end up perforating it. Instead, a hearing aid could help you hear better.'

My father nodded his head and went right back to

using his wire device. 'I know exactly what I need to do for my perforated eardrum.'

He would transform reality to suit himself.

'I could have been a successful singer. An impresario wanted to organise a tour for me of America,' my father would claim, as he sang an aria from *Rigoletto* or from *La Forza del Destino*. 'I could have become a great tenor. I was the one who didn't want to,' he'd insist.

The facts: My father was in the United States. He had arrived in August 1961 with a Bank of Italy scholarship for young graduates. Before his classes started at Harvard, he had worked as a waiter in an Italian restaurant. When the academic year began, he flirted with a young Ecuadorian girl and participated in university life with the other foreign students. At the end of year party, a singing, dancing and cooking competition was organised by the students. My father went on stage, sang *O sole mio*, and won first prize.

To my father, what mattered more than the facts was the story he built around these facts, always turning them into something epic or out of the ordinary: the restaurant where he worked became a place full of cooks and waitresses of Italian origin who adored him and treated him like a son; the Ecuadorian became a very beautiful girl who was crazy about him; the student contest became an international competition where he was recognised for his gifts as a singer.

When my brother's voice began changing, and like all teenagers, the sounds that came out were more guttural, my father insisted that he speak in a higher pitch.

'C'mon, make an effort!' he said to Arturo in a high-pitched voice. 'Do as I do, ahhh! And stop with those low sounds. They're unbearable!'

My brother tried his best, but to no avail.

'Don't use your pharynx; try bringing your voice from your throat! Why can't you do it?' My brother tried again, but still to no avail. My father grew frustrated.

'Why are you so clumsy?'

And the exchange would be repeated for hours on end. My father took the matter very seriously. Locked in his office with my brother, he forced him to speak and sing in high notes.

I had tried all my life to understand my father. But despite my efforts, I simply couldn't. For years, I wondered how he functioned, what he was trying to achieve? Now I was not sure that there was really something to understand, or if I just needed to resign myself to the idea that he had lost touch with reality so long ago that there was no point in trying to throw it in his face.

I was looking for a definition, a label, a term. Once again, I needed to create order. Like when I would ask my analyst, 'But what am I exactly? Bipolar? Borderline?' And she would tell me that it was pointless to lock myself into a diagnosis.

'Those are constantly changing categories, whereas

every person has their own specificities. Why do you have to have a label?'

But how can you justify yourself to others, when you don't know what's wrong with you? Why would I suddenly find myself overpowered with anger or the weight of guilt?

Everyone understands, when you have a specific illness. You say, 'I've got pneumonia,' and everyone feels sorry for you. 'Get some rest; take care of yourself.' You say, 'I have a torn anterior cruciate ligament.' And everyone understands that you'll need surgery, then physical therapy, medication for the pain and anti-inflammatories. But what can others possibly understand when you say 'I feel lost and transparent'?

I just wanted to be able to put a name on what was ailing me.

I thought back to discussions that my brother and I had had a few years ago. Both of us would have been sent to the camps, I because I'm insane and he because he's gay. Homosexuals, Sinti, Roma, the mentally ill. Who in Italy now evokes their memory in sorrow? Who is aware of what happened to them even before the racial laws of 1938 were promulgated? Who has heard of the *confino*?

Confino. Starting in 1926, one did not have to have committed a crime or a misdemeanour to be 'sent to *confino*', that is into internal exile. It was enough to have been accused of disturbing the order established by the regime. 'The danger of being sent away hangs over one and all,' wrote Emilio Lussu. 'The punishment was applied only to some, but the threat existed for all.'

For Mussolini, sending someone to *confino* was a smart way of cracking down, at least that's what he said in 1927, before a very silent Assembly: 'It is a measure of social hygiene, a national prophylaxis, to remove such individuals from circulation, as a doctor removes from circulation someone who is contaminated.' And homosexuals, of course, counted among the 'contaminated'.

Vice, disease, infection.

In Italy, where the new man and manliness were attributed mythical proportions, the goal was to stop the spread of homosexuality. Better therefore not to talk too much about it, even if it meant backtracking on plans to introduce into the Penal Code article 528, which provided for imprisonment for people found guilty of homosexual relations. 'Fortunately, this abominable vice is not so widespread in Italy,' the Appiani Commission concluded. 'The intervention of the legislator is not justified,' the commission unanimously decided, and expunged article 528. It was better to make these 'fagots', 'deviants', 'sub-species of humanity' disappear. To cure them when possible or to hide them and make them forever invisible.

The same was the case for the Sinti and the Roma, who were also dispatched to remote isolated villages in the Mezzogiorno or to some of the small islands. They had to be grouped together and banished from society in order to erase their existence and avoid contagion.

I thought about some of the passages in the curriculum vitae that my grandfather drafted in August 1941 for the competition to become councillor of the Court of Appeals. Arturo wrote that he participated in the meetings of the committee for the *confino* of Lecce in 1938 and 1939. And then I thought about the debates in Parliament over the bill against homophobia in which I participated when I was a deputy and wondered what my grandfather would have said had he been there.

Would he have denied the existence of homophobic physical and verbal violence, as did my colleagues from Matteo Salvini's League or Giorgia Meloni's party, a post-modern offshoot of the neo-fascist party born after liberation? Would he have explained that homosexuality is a fact, not a right, and that punishing someone for homophobic speech amounts to a violation of freedom of expression? Would he have challenged or applauded the deputy who, in August 2013, did not hesitate to put this question to the Assembly: 'Are homosexuals and transsexuals really a discriminated minority in Italy, a country where homosexuality was decriminalised a century before such countries as the United Kingdom?'

August 1st. August 1st, August 1st, August 1st… I woke up with the thought that it was an important date, but I did not know why. I got up and had breakfast. What happened on 1 August? Is it a date I read about in my grandfather's file?

'Does August 1st mean anything to you?' I asked Jacques when he pointed out that he was still waiting for me to tell him whether or not I wanted another cup of coffee.

Later, the phone rang. It was a video call from my brother, who was feeding Jacopo. He put his phone on the table so I could see my nephew, who was obediently opening his mouth to receive the small spoon of food. Suddenly, Jacopo refused to open his mouth, turned his head away and cried: 'Ba! Ba! Ba!'

'Do you think that ba ba ba is his way of saying he doesn't want it anymore?'

My brother smiled and shrugged. Then I remembered that when I was little and had eaten enough, I would beg my mother: 'bata, bata, bata!'

The video call stopped suddenly. A few minutes later, Arturo called me back.

'Sorry, I got another call; it hasn't stopped all morning.'

And then it came to me. It was my brother's birthday and it was the first time in my life, I hadn't given it a moment's thought.

I woke up fully aware of the fact that it was 1 August, repeating as I did 'August 1st', again and again and again. What could have happened on August 1st? I had erased my brother's existence.

I did not understand.

I could not forgive myself.

What was happening to me?

Last month, my brother told me he thought I was being unfair.

'Why are you reproaching our father for not coming to terms with his past? What does he have to do with his father's fascism? Do you not see that he has demonstrated a certain amount of courage by taking a political stance in opposition to his father and expressing left-wing convictions? Have you forgotten how he used to scold us whenever he heard us say, "Who cares?" He would tell us that that was the way fascists spoke and that we should follow Don Milani's example and counter the fascist "who cares?" with the humanist "I care!". What more could he have done?'

'And where do you think our father's obsession with manliness, normalcy and deviances come from? You can hardly claim that those are leftist ideas!' I replied, fully aware that I would not have been able to explain to him the conviction that had gradually taken hold of me in recent months.

I was sure that our father's silence about our grandfather's fascism was a problem. I was sure that a reality does not cease to exist simply by not talking about it. I was even convinced that the opposite was true, that the less we talk about something, the greater the effect of that thing on us and in us and the more it poisons our existence. To our father, fascism was always the ultimate evil. There was no doubt about that. But every time he spoke to us about it, he talked as if it was something outside our family, as if it did not concern us at all.

I knew I wasn't being clear. And my brother may well have had a point when he said to me, 'Well, hurray for the left! Have you forgotten the resistance you faced from the Democratic Party when you were in Parliament and you voted in favour of the bill on marriage for all?'

But nonetheless, I remained convinced that not talking of certain things amounts to repressing them. And that if you repress something, it is because you're ashamed of it.

I thought that my father never wanted to feel this shame, and that was what led him little by little to cut himself off from reality, and never accept not only his own weaknesses, but also those of others.

My brother argued that my father was mentally ill.

'What you reproach him for is that he never underwent psychoanalysis. But what does that have to do with his father's fascism?'

But I was still convinced that everything leaves a trace. And that if the past is not re-examined, it suffocates us. And ends up dominating us secretly.

Just as I thought that the unconscious inhabits and moves us. And one need not have undergone psychoanalysis to know this, but not facing one's past creates crypts filled with family secrets.

I thought that dirty laundry should not always be washed in private, and that forgetting can never bring peace to a country. At the same time, I was fully aware of the fact that the communists too were among the advocates of amnesia, after the fall of fascism and the birth of the Republic. And that repression was common among partisans too, and that their children and grandchildren should also have the courage to face the facts.

I thought that saying, '*cosa fatta, capo ha*,' is at the origin of our sense of impotence and despair. I knew that our family was not the only one to have to carry the cross. But I refused to absolve anyone for the violence that was still rampant in Italy.

I woke up in a sweat last night again.

I dreamt that I was in Rome, at the National Assembly. I was in the middle of the *Transatlantico*, the long lounge where the deputies go for the breaks between sessions. I was heading towards the small room at the end where monitors display the schedule of the committees. I was trying to figure out what time the second committee meeting was scheduled. But I could not read the display, the image on the screen was blurry. I stopped one of the employees. 'Can you tell me what time the Justice Committee is meeting?' The employee stared at me for a few seconds. 'Excuse me, but who are you? Who let you in?' he asked. I tried to tell him I had received an email invitation from the Chamber, and that I was a former member of Parliament. But the employee refused to listen and kept on repeating, 'Who are you? Who let you in?'

Then I saw another employee, who was at the entrance of the Chamber every week when I came to the National Assembly, and with whom I had often exchanged a few words. 'You recognise me, don't you?' I asked. But she didn't know who I was either. She didn't remember me. And when I tried to tell her that all I wanted was to find out the exact time of the Justice Committee meeting, she replied curtly: 'If you received an email invitation to come, it must be marked somewhere!'

Puzzled, I decided to leave. 'What happened? Why doesn't anyone recognise me?' I said to myself as I quickened my pace and headed for the exit. 'Could I have made it all up? Maybe I was never a member of Parliament?'

I walked out of the building and walked over to the small newsstand at the centre of Montecitorio Square to buy a bus ticket. 'Would you like a bus ticket, or would you rather get a train ticket?' the vendor asked me. 'Do you know that there is now a direct Montecitorio-Balduina shuttle?' Surprised that the man knew where I lived, I replied that I didn't know. 'Here's your ticket! That'll be 11 euros,' he said before I had time to make up my mind. 'No, thank you, that's too expensive. I'd rather take the bus.' 'The ticket is already printed Signora! I'm waiting for my money. If you don't give it to me, I'll call the police.'

That was when I woke up.

A few hours later, I was sitting on the couch, my leg restlessly jerking, and I lit a cigarette. I tried to write, without success. I was distracted by the sounds of the construction work in the building opposite mine. But maybe these noises had nothing to do with my difficulties writing. I told myself, it must be due to last night's nightmare. Once again, I felt transparent, like I used to feel I was to my father when I was a child.

But how exactly could I describe this feeling of invisibility?

I thought about Monet, when he was on a trip to London, looking at the Thames and the Parliament from the terrace of Saint Thomas's Hospital. But what he wanted to paint was neither the river nor the Parliament. He wanted to paint the air and the fog, brushstroke after brushstroke, his eyes on his palette of colours: ash grey and platinum grey, slate grey and powder grey. What colours should I use to describe my invisibility to my father?

Who are you, Papa? What is it that I still cannot comprehend?

Are you the man who reads, pencil in hand to underline a sentence in a book, indifferent to my presence? Look at me! Listen to me! Please! Or are you the other man, the one who approaches me and awkwardly caresses my face, his hand stiff from arthritis?

I stared at pictures of you looking for answers. I looked at your eyes, your mouth, your hands. But my questions found no answers. I could not figure out who you were.

Do you know that sometimes I too curse my life? Do you know that you have transmitted to me all your anger and your fear of failing? Do you know that even Jacques is scared of me when I lose my temper?

PART FOUR

Redemption

One thing is sure: We must help to increase the reserves of love on this earth. Every little bit of hatred that is added to the hatreds that are already far too many makes this world even more inhospitable and unbearable.

Etty Hillesum

My dear uncle,

This is a terrible time for me and for us. The concerns and the unexpected turn of events are such that I don't know what to do anymore. Each day brings a new problem, and I don't know what to do or whom to turn to.

Now, even your brother, Nino, is trying to profit (unfortunately, that's the right term) from the situation. First, he presented me with an old invoice, and told me that it was now time to settle the accounts. It was an acknowledgement of a debt in favour of Papa that amounted to four million lire. Then he told me that he was the creditor of the four million because he had given up his share of the house and of the estate of Don Francesco, and that thus his debt and our credit balanced each other out. Not knowing how that happened, I didn't know what to say to him. He is the one who, for the past few months, has all the documents for our affairs. Not satisfied with having gambled everything away, he is now about to get us into trouble in our own house.

[…]

You know the condition my father is in; my mother, understanding nothing of all these matters, gets upset, says things she shouldn't say, and then regrets what she said; Rosaria is completely absorbed by her marriage to Pierino;

and I don't know who to turn to anymore or what to do. You are the only one who can help, the only one who knows how things really happened and what agreements were made.

So, dear uncle, the situation is very complex, very tricky.

Everybody wants to profit from the fact that Papa is not talking, that he cannot talk (I say everyone because even strangers have brought up old business matters and made claims).

[...]

As for the most important matter, namely our trip to Genoa, we received a telegram informing us that a room was ready for Papa. Fearing that we will be taken advantage of in Genoa, where no one knows us, I turned to Pierino for advice, since he is a doctor, and he wanted me to write to Dr Francesco, Rector of the University of Milan and former monarchist deputy, so that he could let us know if he had spoken with his neurologist friend. Pierino thinks it would be better for us to wait for him to examine my father and tell us sincerely if it is worth our while to take him to Genoa. He is afraid that the neurologist in Genoa may not give us a disinterested opinion. I'm not sure I agree. I would still like to go to Genoa, but I didn't want to contradict Pierino. What do you think about all this?

Campi, 13 January 1959

Finally! Jacques and I arrived in Campi.

Nothing went as planned. It was now mid-August and terribly hot and humid. It was probably the worst time of the year to go to Salento. I was so afraid that our flight would be cancelled at the last minute, as it had been repeatedly over the last few months, that I only managed to calm down after take-off. And when I got off the plane in Brindisi, I was so moved, I knelt down to touch the ground. I stayed like that with the palm of my hand on the tarmac for a few moments.

Jacques, with a frightened look on his face, burst out with a, 'What the hell are you doing?' while an airport employee screamed, 'Lady, get up! You're not allowed to stop on the runway; go to the exit right away!'

We were in Campi. In front of the big porch.

I touched the brass handle, just like my grandmother used to do when I was little as we were leaving at the end of August: my brother and I going back to Rome with our parents, and my grandparents to Taranto. She would stand there holding the handle and murmuring, 'My house... my beautiful house...'

I put the key in the lock, switched off the alarm, and looked at the big staircase and the jasmines in the terracotta pots. I contemplated the high vaulted ceilings, and my heart opened: I was in Italy; I was in Campi; I was home; I was happy.

A few moments later, Jacques was already rushing out to the garden.

'Wait before you take out the deck chairs!' I shouted after him. 'We should clean up first; there's too much dirt. Let's do things in order!'

But it was no use. Jacques had already opened the door to the shed and grabbed the first chair he could get his hands on. So, I decided to ignore the dirt and the housework too, and I phoned my father's cousins to ask if I could come by for the keys to their cellar, telling them not to worry, that I would wear a mask and, yes, of course, we would see each other at leisure after the quarantine!

At the end of January, I had spent barely an hour in this cellar and had promised myself I would come back quickly. I didn't think, at the time, that I would have to wait so long. But, at last, here I was. I could finally start sorting through my grandfather's papers.

I opened the cellar door. The dust and the mould made my nose start to run. 'It's better that Jacques doesn't come here,' I said to myself. 'With his asthma, he's sure to feel terrible.' The humidity had continued to eat away at everything over the months. I moved a box so damp that it fell apart between my legs. Loads of envelopes scattered onto the floor. I hastened to pick everything up before the letters got soaked with water, and I put them on the shelves of an old bookcase in the adjacent room.

Then, among the papers and documents, I glimpsed a bundle of letters and recognised my father's handwriting. I opened the packet and found a letter sent by my father to his uncle, his mother's brother, who lived in Bologna. I started to read it to see what it was about, and suddenly my eyes filled with tears. My father wrote: 'Papa is not talking; he cannot talk.'

I went back home. I drank a glass of water, lit a cigarette and, sitting in an armchair, I started to reread the letter a little more calmly. My father wrote to his uncle on the letterhead of the National Assembly. He crossed out the heading with a stroke of his pen. And, on six very densely packed pages, he gave in to his discouragement. Overwhelmed by what was happening, my father asked for help. This was my father, fragile and in a panic.

I did not immediately understand the meaning of the letter. I had to return several times to the cellar to look for other files and read other documents. And I had to face certain secrets that I, perhaps, would have preferred never to discover. But what did I imagine when I embarked on this work? Did I not know that at some point I would have to confront the misfortunes that befell a family hounded by destiny? Knowing that my grandfather had lived for eighteen years in a wheelchair, and that one of my grandmother's two brothers squandered away his fortune, could I have expected there to be no pettiness, no backstabbing?

Never once, when talking about *Zio* Nino, had my father mentioned those days of despair when 'everyone', as he wrote in his letter, profited from Arturo's misfortunes, including this somewhat depraved uncle, to whom my father was nevertheless very attached. This son, whom Donna Giuseppina cajoled and spoiled more than the other, would go out every evening to play cards or visit one of his many mistresses, and come home late at night. Angelo Campo, known as Nino, borrowed several million lire from my grandfather, and agreed to surrender to Rosetta, his sister, a part of his mother's inheritance. And then, when his brother-in-law fell ill, he profited from the naivety of my father, his nephew, to try to turn the situation to his advantage.

Money, land, property. Betrayals and deceit. Shattered confidence in life. Leaving nothing but meanness and lies, and everyone taking advantage of the situation.

'That's how it is, my little one!' my father would often say to me when I was a child. Now I understood, or at least I was beginning to understand, my father's mistrust of others. All the more since his world had already fallen apart once before, in 1944, when he was only eight years old and his father was purged from the judiciary.

This was not something my father realised or remembered. I was the one who was thinking in those terms. But I was convinced that what happened in 1958 was experienced as a repetition of the previous trauma. And that it was likely the source of my father's lifelong fear of being happy. If after happiness comes suffering, it is better never to be happy and eliminate this cursed happiness from the outset!

My father denied all this. Perhaps he repressed it.

But isn't the origin of it all to be found in the midst of this wreckage?

And what was this Genoa business all about?

'Pierino is afraid that the neurologist in Genoa may not give us a disinterested opinion.'

I called up my father. I asked him if there was ever a question of bringing his father to Genoa. If Pierino, his sister's fiancé at the time who married her in April 1959, had given him any advice in this regard. If there had been money problems, something that had impacted the decisions and choices that were made after Arturo's accident.

'Why are you asking me about Genoa?'

'I heard something about an excellent neurology department in Genoa at the time.'

'I don't know; that doesn't ring a bell. We took my father to Milan. A colleague of his, a monarchist deputy, helped us find an opening in a very good hospital, although after a few weeks the head of the neurology department told me that there was nothing more they could do. He called me into his office and said, "Young man, I'm really sorry about your father. I think you'd best take him home!"'

I didn't insist. I didn't want to put my father through more suffering.

'And what will happen when he reads your book?' Jacques asked me when I told him about the letter and the conversation I had with my father. 'Are you sure it's really worthwhile to reopen these old wounds?'

Freud spoke of the healing power of truth.

But how far can one go when looking for truth? What price was I willing to pay, or to impose on my family?

Botrugno, Thursday 22 May 1958

It was 10.30 pm, and this was the third meeting of the day for my grandfather. A fourth was scheduled for later that night. Arturo was tired. He felt his strength waning. But he was not about to give up. It was always like that during the final days of an election campaign. 'The vote is on Sunday,' Arturo thought, setting his jaw with determination. 'Chin up,' he said to himself as he climbed onto the platform. 'We're almost there!'

Barely a week had gone by since my grandfather, on that very same stage, had had a difficult spell. He had stammered, had needed to stop for a few moments. '*Nun me sta piaci*, I don't like how you look, Don Arturo,' the doctor said to him that day, at the end of the meeting. He was the son of a childhood friend, a doctor in Botrugno. He advised him to stop campaigning and get some much-needed rest. But it was inconceivable to my grandfather even to think of stopping when elections were only seven days away.

It was 10.35 pm, the day of Saint Rita, and my grandmother was offering novena prayers: 'Help him, oh patron saint of lost causes. Cast out this affliction!'

A crowd gathered at the foot of the stage.

Arturo explained that he needed everyone's help in these final crucial hours. How many still-undecided voters could we win over by the next day?

It was 10.45 pm. It had been dark for a while already, and despite the floodlights, it was impossible from the stage to make out people's faces; there was no way of knowing from their expressions what they were feeling. But my grandfather was not concerned: In Botrugno, he was on home ground.

First signatory of bill no. 129, for changing the status of Botrugno from a hamlet to an independent municipality, Arturo had kept his word. He had promised his fellow citizens that he would get them municipal status and he had done so. The bill was approved in the Chamber on 18 July 1956, and on 13 March 1958, it was promulgated by the President of the Republic, Giovanni Gronchi.

The main square of the town was packed, and the crowd continued to grow. My grandfather cleared his throat and began to speak: 'This Sunday's elections will test the political maturity of the Italian people, their democratic life, their problems and their anxieties.' Arturo stopped, drank from a glass of water, and resumed his speech. 'The Christian Democracy must have its votes; it would be delusional and foolish to think that it does not deserve its victory! But let this victory be such that the Christian Democrats will have to govern with us, we who represent the healthiest, most active and noblest part of the nation.'

Someone interrupted with a 'Bravo!' Arturo took the

opportunity to wipe the sweat off his forehead with the cotton handkerchief that Rosetta had put in his pocket before he left the house. Covering his mouth with the handkerchief, he sighed and swallowed forcefully.

'We must garner a large number of votes if we are to have an influence over the Christian Democrat's politics.' My grandfather uttered the words, one by one, slowed down, and stopped again. 'We must present ourselves as representing the noblest part of the nation, as I was saying, and I reiterate that we are the part of the nation that, armed with our experiences and the glory of our past, looks to the future without ignoring what has been!'

The people were listening attentively. They applauded.

'Let us plant the future in the glorious furrow of the paaa…sst.' The word became garbled.

My father looked at Arturo. What was happening? My father was worried; he would have liked to go up on stage, but he did not want his father to be angry at him. 'Be quiet!' Arturo had shouted just before the start of the rally, when his son had pointed out that he looked pale, and suggested, 'Wouldn't it be more sensible to cancel tonight's rally?' 'I'm perfectly fine!' 'Mama also thinks that you are…' 'Silence!'

Arturo tried to speak again, but all he could do was stammer. 'Gloooo…ri…ous.' He paused once again. The crowd began cheering to encourage him. He tried again, but this time he could not get a sound out. He collapsed and lost consciousness.

Some people immediately rushed onto the stage. My grandfather remained inert. He showed no sign of life when my father drew near him and he remained unresponsive when the doctor tried to revive him.

On Thursday 22 May 1958 at 11 pm, Arturo Marzano had a stroke. No one realised at the time that that was what had happened. He remained unconscious for a week at the doctor's home in Botrugno, before being hospitalised in Lecce.

It was too late.

But maybe nothing could have been done, even if he had been taken immediately to the emergency room.

'What do you think people knew about strokes in those days in Puglia?' my father replied when I asked why Arturo was not hospitalised right away, why so much time was lost, why the doctor hadn't realised straight away how serious my grandfather's state was. But my father didn't understand my insistence, and he kept repeating that nothing could have been done, and that later he took my grandfather to Milan and that Arturo was hospitalised there for several months and it did him no good.

TIA, a transient ischemic attack, is the description today for these early symptoms of a cerebral vascular accident, numbness in an arm or leg, a sudden loss of energy, difficulties in speaking. These may last only a few minutes and then disappear.

A week before his stroke, my grandfather had these

symptoms. He had all of them, but he probably told himself that nothing would happen to him, and that at any rate he would have plenty of time to rest after the elections on 25 May. That is why he continued campaigning in the country and the towns of his electoral district, against the better judgement of his wife and son.

My father had tried several times to reason with him, but my grandfather would not listen to anyone. He always did things his way. All the more since he thought his son didn't know much about politics. Arturo did not understand where Ferruccio had picked up his ideas, or how he could possibly believe in the things the socialists said. 'Communists or socialists, they're all alike,' he maintained. 'Listen to your father. I know those people well!'

When I was born, my grandfather was still alive. He was in a wheelchair and could not speak. When my father asked him to say who he was, he managed with great difficulty to stammer, 'AAA RRR TTT UUU RRR OOO.' I was afraid of him; I did not comprehend what was wrong with him. And no one told me. 'He collapsed and it was all over,' my grandmother would repeat. This 'all' that was over was, of course, meaningless to me. I did not comprehend what was over, what was lost, what had really happened.

When the term stroke began to make sense to me, I was a teenager, and my grandfather had been dead for a long time. I was very tired that day and I was struggling to find my words. My mother stared at me with fear in her eyes. 'Go rest!' she said, in a tone that was more an order than a plea. As if what happened to my grandfather could happen again. 'When will you finally make up your mind to take better care of yourself?' As if my grandfather's stroke had skipped a generation and been passed on to me.

My grandfather came in third in the elections that year. So, he was not re-elected. News of what had happened to him during his speech spread immediately; some people even said that he had died. The attempt to hide his condition and pretend that he'd be back on his feet in no time was in vain. Equally vain were any hopes that the people whom my grandfather helped would demonstrate gratitude and recognition.

'Mama was angry with Saint Rita. She often said that the patron saint of lost causes should never have done such a thing to her,' my father told me. 'The world had collapsed around her and she was talking nonsense.'

'What about Arturo? Did he understand what had happened to him?'

'Alas, no.'

'Of course he understood!' my mother interjected.

'That's not true! After his stroke, Papa didn't understand anything anymore.'

'Then why did he cry the first time he saw me?' my mother insisted.

'Maybe he was emotional,' my father finally conceded. 'But from a rational point of view, he understood nothing anymore.'

Trying to understand what happened to my grandfather on 22 May 1958, I found myself recalling images from Clint Eastwood's 2004 film *Million Dollar Baby.* I thought of the scene of the fight for the world title against Billie 'The Blue Bear'. Frankie, her coach, was against the fight, since Billie was known in the boxing world as a cruel, dirty fighter, but, after so many wins, Maggie managed to convince him to arrange the match. And Maggie indeed dominated the fight, but Billie refused to accept the idea of defeat, and as Maggie was heading to her corner, she made a one-punch attack from behind. Maggie fell to the ground, landing on the corner stool, and fell into a coma. 'I shouldn'ta dropped my hands. I shouldn'ta turned. Always protect yourself; how many times he tell me that?' she says when she wakes up and discovers that she's a quadriplegic. But the problem was not her inability to protect herself. The problem was the injustice of life, which, after having given her everything, took it all away in the space of a few moments. The problem was the loss. The problem was the end of all her dreams and all her hopes, all her joys and all her possibilities.

I knew this movie by heart. I had watched the scene of the fight over and over again. But I couldn't help crying each and every time. Maggie loses everything, and I was inconsolable. Maggie loses everything, and I, who for years couldn't understand why I was so obsessed with loss, found that in recounting that evening in 1958, for the first time I was beginning to understand. This absence that always pursued me was perhaps the same as what my father felt after his own father lost everything. Wasn't it then that my father learnt the sad truth that life is made of nothing but defeats? Notwithstanding all the efforts and the control. Notwithstanding the illusion of having succeeded. Because in the end, no one actually succeeds, and life, sooner or later, takes back all that it has given.

Is that what you thought, Papa, that day in 1997, when you and Mama got that phone call?

Ma mia figlia è impagabil tesor,[1] as Rigoletto sang. That was what you pretended not to understand when you and Mama set out on the road, and arrived in Pisa, and you sat in the waiting room and let Mama go alone into the intensive care unit? *Miei signori, perdono, pietate, al vegliardo la figlia ridate.*[2] Where did you put the note that I wrote you that night, Papa? *Tutto al mondo tal figlia è per me.*[3]

[1] But my daughter is a priceless treasure.

[2] My lords, forgive me, have mercy, give back the old man his daughter.

[3] She is everything in the world to me.

I wanted to die that Friday in 1997. I had been unhappy for so long that I just wanted to stop living. If life was nothing but suffering, what reason was there to hold on to it? All the more since, by then, I had tried everything. The promises to myself, the efforts, the psychotropic drugs, a new partner, a different house, psychoanalysis. Nothing helped. It was all useless. There had been no improvement. On the contrary. Things were only getting worse.

For years, I felt trapped in a tunnel, plunged in darkness, and I could see no way out. Yet every day I would get up and force myself to do what I had to do. I would drag myself through the day until night came and then start all over again the next day. Every day was the same: always that knife planted in my heart. I had passed my exam at the Scuola Normale Superiore in Pisa; I had won a scholarship for my doctorate; I had even been accepted to the National Film Academy to become a screenwriter.

Nothing made any difference.

My condition only got worse.

I would start each day with the best of intentions. I would ride my scooter to Cinecittà; I would attend classes, go to see my analyst. On Friday afternoon, I would leave for Pisa, where the man I loved lived. On Monday, at 6 in the morning, I would take the train back to Rome where I would get on my scooter again, attend classes, go to my analyst. Nothing changed.

On the contrary.

My condition only got worse.

This constant despair, the urge to throw myself on the tracks, the vomiting whenever I ate – I was vomiting all the time, vomiting everything – the pain and the anger, a black hole. Even as there seemed to be no valid reason to be in such a state. What are you lacking? An absurd question. How do you explain that, in spite of everything that one has, there is a lack of joy, a lack of desire, a lack of the simple and obvious certainty that life is beautiful?

That Friday night in 1997, it was not a 'suicidal raptus', as the doctors said it was when I was hospitalised. I had woken after forty-eight hours in a coma and was immediately transferred to the confined ward of the psychiatric hospital in Pisa.

It was not a rash act, a passing impulse. If you had really wanted to die, you would have succeeded, my therapist said to me the first time I saw him after I was discharged from the hospital, as if the violence I had inflicted on myself was not enough, and there was still a need to twist the knife in the wound: If I had really wanted to…

For months, I had been saying that I wanted to die; for months, I could see no other solution.

That Friday, I did not utter a word during my session of psychoanalysis.

I cried for the whole hour, without ever looking my analyst in the face. He let me leave in that state. Did he think I was lying, pretending, playing a part? Did he think I was just trying to get his attention or manipulate him?

I cried the whole way in the car when my father drove me to the station, as he did every Friday afternoon. Why did you let me leave, Papa? Did you not know what to do? Did you feel powerless? Did you think that your daughter was not the same person as before and that life was betraying you once again? But I was still your daughter, wasn't I?

I cried the whole way from Rome to Pisa, despite the young man who tried to console me and that woman who said to me, 'There's always a solution!' I cried, convinced that there was nothing more that could be done, thinking only of the pills that I had managed to accumulate little by little. A simple raptus? What about all the bottles of Lexomil and Laroxyl that I had put aside after going from one pharmacy to another in Pisa and Rome?

I cried until I arrived in Pisa. Life had betrayed me – period.

Then, my eyes swollen, I told the man I loved that everything was fine, that I was just tired. In any case, he too was tired, tired of his work, tired of me, tired of our relationship that was going nowhere: What can I do about it; she's emotionally disturbed and a pain in the arse.

That night, I waited for the man I loved to fall asleep. I went to the kitchen, opened the drawer where I had hidden the bottles of pills, took a glass from the cupboard and put everything down on the dining room table. I opened the bottles and poured their contents into the glass. I added a little water. I took the glass in my hands, after staring at it for a few minutes. I wanted to write a note, but I was afraid of wasting time and not having the courage to follow through. I took a deep breath. Then, still holding my breath, I drank it all. Only then did I begin to write a note.

I apologised to everyone: to my father, because I hadn't been the daughter he would have liked me to be; to my mother, because what I was doing was going to break her heart; to my brother, because I was abandoning him; to my partner, who had nothing to do with it all; to God, despite the fact that he had not been by my side for a long time, but goddamn it, how do you ask for forgiveness when you are about to kill yourself and life has been a curse, and all you want is to stop suffering?

This note is what saved my life.

In planning my suicide, I had thought of everything, except for the fact that, after swallowing the medication, the minutes it would take to say my farewells in writing would be enough for the massive dose of anxiolytics and antidepressants to start having an effect, and that I would begin to feel dizzy, and that I would faint when I got up from the chair, and that my fall would make noise, and that this noise would wake up the man I loved, and that he would take me to the emergency room, and that the doctors would pump my stomach, and that I would end up in a coma, to be sure, but that I would wake up.

'As soon as I get out of here, I'll try again,' I said to myself as soon as I opened my eyes and felt the pangs of pain in my heart again. Why am I still alive?

It was 12 September 1997.

The day of the Feast of the Most Holy Name of the Blessed Virgin Mary.

Even that I had not taken into consideration.

The Most Holy Name of Maria.

My name.

The only one that appears on my identity papers and my diplomas. Officially, Michela Marzano does not exist.

So, it was Maria, the miracle child – for this name was given to me in thanks to Our Lady, who answered the prayers of my mother when she couldn't get pregnant – who was saved on that 12 September 1997. Another miracle. As if life had to compensate my father for the grace that Saint Rita had not granted my grandfather.

For months, I tried to get the few photos I had of my grandparents to talk to me. I tried to draw meaning from a crease in the eye or a piece of clothing, or from the short notes written along the edges or on the back.

Now that I was in Campi, I had hundreds and hundreds of photos. They resurfaced little by little as I went through the cellar in the home of my father's cousins, opening boxes and bags, sinking my hands into a past that had remained alien to me for years. There were so many of these photos now that I spent whole days classifying them and putting them in files, decade by decade, year by year.

For months, I managed to make progress by checking the information I had in my possession against the appointment and promotion decrees published in the Official Journal, and by reading every article or book on the judiciary under fascism and in the early post-war period.

Now I was swamped with documents. And I felt hopelessly lost even though I had sorted through them all and put everything away in folders and files, by topic and sub-topic: 1916-1919: Brigade Novara, Bainsizza, Nagymegyer; 1920-1922: March on Rome, judicial entrance competition; 1923-1927: 'Bandiera rossa', Don Pippi, wedding; 1928-1934: trial, Rome, birth of Rosaria; 1935-1942: birth of my father, *confino*, World War II; 1943-1949: purge, amnesty; 1950-1958: State Prosecutor, electoral campaign, Chamber of Deputies, cerebral vascular accident.

Jacques said that I had succeeded in a short time to assemble an archive that would likely have taken a historian months to do. He said that no one would believe that I managed by myself to create order out of all the material I had collected. He told me to take a picture of the cellar, to photograph the boxes and the bags, and every document I found. Otherwise, he said, no one will believe me when I say that I managed to get a copy of every single one of my grandfather's Fascist Party cards from 1919 on.

I copied whole passages from the documents and private letters. I found thousands of letters. My grandfather wrote all the time; he wrote to everyone; he wrote down everything.

I read and reread the notes I took.

But I was having a hard time making any progress.

I was so terrified at the thought of making a mistake on a date, or of losing a fragment of my family history along the way, that I was not writing anymore.

And I found myself looking forward to the moment when I would finish this book and be able to devote myself again to fiction, free to invent from scratch and play with my characters, exaggerate their traits, shake up their lives, even mistreat them, if I so desired. Who could reproach me for what I wrote about them, if they were only the fruit of my imagination?

Folder no. 35. Electoral campaign of 1958

Facsimiles of ballots for the National Assembly; electoral campaign agendas; handwritten drafts for a good many speeches; ledgers with detailed records of expenses; posters and handouts. I had in my possession all of the materials used by my grandfather during the electoral campaign of 1958. And among the leaflets, one is printed on a green tissue paper of sorts, 15 by 10 centimetres.

Monarchist National Party

Voter,

Apri la scheda
Guarda la STELLA
Fra tutti i Simboli
È la più bella.
Do'una CROCETTA
Con la tua mano
Vota tranquillo
ARTURO MARZANO

The electoral committee

```
To vote for Arturo Marzano, Monar-
chist National Party candidate for
the Chamber of Deputies, put an X on
the 'Star and Crown' and write the
number 3 next to the 'Star and Crown'.
```

I showed the flyer to Jacques, who burst out laughing: 'How *cafonata*!' This *cafonesco* business delighted him; it was a word he had not previously known and there is no real equivalent in French or English to indicate the lack of taste or the vulgarity of those who conflate class with wealth and imagine that being chic means wearing a lot of embroidery, lace, gold jewellery and trinkets.

This time, I was not laughing. I was almost moved, even though the beautiful star image and the rhyme at the end were so trite they verged on the ridiculous. So that was the source of my father's obsession with finding rhymes, which he would then repeat again and again, very pleased with himself, like the lines about the '*raccordo anulare*' and the '*bere da bagordo*', I thought as I returned to my office and began reading one of my grandfather's campaign speeches. But almost immediately, my sympathy evaporated and I felt ashamed again and had to stop.

Grandfather, how could you say that the fascist regime was not a dictatorial regime? How could you even have entertained the belief that the Fatherland had been betrayed in the name of freedom and democracy? But I guess you never stopped being a fascist, Grandfather, did you? How could you have still

felt attached to the Duce in 1958?
We claim the label 'right-wing' solely when it comes to asserting and exalting national dignity. We are the guarantors of all the traditional and national values which are often ignored or forgotten.

I set aside my grandfather's speech. I needed to clear my mind. Beyond his hatred of communists, Arturo also had an obsession with nationalist rhetoric, with the binary opposition between them and us, with traditional values and moral order. How would he have reacted had he known that his grandson, Ferruccio's son, the one who bears his name, is gay?

If he hadn't had his cerebral vascular accident, if I had been born before, if I had had the opportunity of talking to him… If, if, if… I couldn't stop thinking that way, even though it made no sense. What would I have done if…? Would I have argued with him? Would I have tried to show him the folly of some of his ideas?

It's absurd, I told myself. And then I realised that that was precisely what I did when I was elected to Parliament, when I took the floor in the Chamber and looked the far-right colleagues right in the eye. Wasn't that my way of making amends for my family's past?

I set aside my grandfather's speech, telling myself there was no point in staying focused on this. It would be better for me to turn my attention to some of the other documents I had found.

I flipped through the schedule of the increasing number of meetings and rallies in my grandfather's agenda starting on Sunday 13 April, the day of the official opening of his electoral campaign, and I recognised my father's handwriting. He must have been the one who wrote down Arturo's schedule every day and went with him to all corners of his electoral district. But how could he follow my grandfather around and listen to him saying all those absurd things? Didn't my father always tell me that he was already a socialist at the time? In that case, what was he thinking when my grandfather attacked the socialists and communists? And how about when he spoke of moral order and the traditional values that the right had helped to preserve? Didn't it bother him?

I flipped through my grandfather's agenda and saw that he travelled every day from one end of the region to the other. On 13 April, at 4 pm, he was in Calimera, in the Grecia Salentina; at 6 pm, he was in Martano; at 8 pm, in Zollino. On 14 April, he was in Lecce in the morning, and in the afternoon he went first to San Pancrazio, then to Maglie, and then to Nardò. 15 April he spent travelling across the southern tip of Salento. He went down to Castrignano del Capo, which is only a few kilometres from the Santa Maria di Leuca lighthouse and the Santuario di Santa Maria de *Finibus Terrae*, at the southernmost tip of the Italian peninsula, where the Adriatic Sea embraces the Ionian Sea, before stopping on his way back to

Lecce in Presicce, Acquarica, Taurisano and Scorrano. On clear bright days, you can see the exact spot where the waters meet, a chromatic demarcation line due to the difference in the salinity of the water, where the ultramarine blue fades into sapphire blue, the sapphire blue into turquoise, the turquoise into azure. When I was little, my mother taught me all the differences in the shades of blue and green: Caerulean blue is different from sky blue; sky blue from turquoise; turquoise from cyan, and so on.

The rallies began on Sunday 4 May. At 6 pm, he was in Maglie; at 8 pm, he was in Martano. That week, my grandfather held two rallies a day. Then there were three a day. Sometimes even four.

I flipped through his campaign schedule, and I felt the anxiety mounting. I recalled telling my father about my hectic schedule of conferences, seminars and presentations when I would come to Italy, and he exclaimed, 'Don't forget to rest from time to time!' all the while knowing that there was no point in telling me to, but he felt he had to insist. Otherwise, I would wear myself out and then something could happen to me!

But the material I found in the cellar of my father's cousins' home did not only concern his last electoral campaign. There were also a great many boxes filled with files dating from 1953 to 1958, five years during which my grandfather worked day-in and day-out without a break.

When I started opening the boxes, I found hundreds and hundreds of files. I began counting them at first, not realising how many there were. But I soon reckoned with the impossibility of the task and began shoving whole piles of files directly into the canvas bags I had brought from Paris.

I did so pell-mell, thinking that I would look through them unhurriedly when I got home. I did, however, separate the photos, letters, newspaper articles and court documents, which had sometimes slipped in between the files. I filled up six bags with these files alone. From time to time, I would open one of them, intrigued by a name. Guerrieri? That rang a bell… maybe that's someone from Campi; I was sure I had heard that name somewhere before…

My grandfather was extremely, even compulsively, organised. Every file was inside a small cardboard case; on each cardboard case figured the first name, the last name and the address of the person who had contacted him or had come to ask for a favour or assistance in obtaining an exemption from payment of a fee, or their disability pension, or a transfer, or a military pension, or a life annuity, or a job possibility, and so on. Inside each folder were dozens of typewritten or handwritten pages, minutes of the National Assembly and pages from notebooks held together with a paper clip. Many of the clips were rusty, and I would have to be careful not to damage the paper. What was he doing writing on tissue paper? Why didn't he write on something stronger and more resistant?

My grandfather answered everyone: He wrote to secretaries of state and ministers, to the Court of Audit and to the National Union of the Blind, to the Inspector General of Credit and to commanders of military districts; he sent a copy of these letters and the replies he received to the people who had asked him for help; he would write again if the matter was not resolved or if it seemed to have been put on the back burner.

I now understood a little better what my father's cousins meant when they spoke about the long lines that would form on Saturdays and Sundays in front of the porch of the house in Campi. They all came there to beg, to ask, to plead. I also understood much better why all those who knew Arturo told me that he was an infinitely good man, generous and loved by all. I even understood the panic and anger my father felt whenever someone asked him for a recommendation. I don't do that kind of thing, he'd say; whom do they take me for?

A whole box was filled with files dating from 1958. Between May 3 and 5, smack in the middle of his electoral campaign, my grandfather wrote 136 letters. I not only counted them and arranged them in order, but I also read them so as to gain a better understanding of him.

'Dear Imperiale, I assure you that I am doing everything in my power to see that you get your military pension [...].'

'Dear Latino, I have strongly insisted to the Minister

of Justice that that you be promptly enrolled in the corps of prison guards [...].'

'Dear Manieri, I am doing everything in my power so that you can regain your position [...].'

'Dear Scardino, I assure you that I take the utmost interest in your being promptly granted a pension after the death of your son [...]'

After reading like this for some time, I felt exhausted and did not want to think about the health of my grandfather, who answered everyone, regardless of whether the person was a monarchist, a liberal, a socialist or a communist. 'Papa was there for everyone,' my father said. 'Arturo never forgot anyone,' his cousins confirmed.

'He worked himself to death,' I told Jacques with a pang in my heart. 'It doesn't surprise me that he had a stroke in the end.'

I said this. Then I thought of all the evenings that I too spent answering emails, to the point of upsetting Jacques, who would tell me, 'Enough already! You're burning yourself out!' But I kept at it. How could I not answer someone who writes me that her daughter has been suffering from anorexia for ten years and that she doesn't know where to turn anymore?

Among the stacks of things in the cellar of my father's cousins, there was a photo taken on 14 September 1958. The date is written on the back; once again, I recognise my father's handwriting.

It was the birthday of Rosaria, my father's sister, but also the day of her official engagement to Pierino. In the photo, Lala, as my father called her, stands opposite her fiancé, looking at him while he puts the ring on her ring finger. She is wearing a velvet dress with a square neckline. Is it brown? Green? Blue? Hard to tell from the black and white photo, but clearly it isn't black, like his mother's dress, nor is it as light in colour as Pierino's suit. She wears a string of pearls, too long to be a choker, but too short to stay on the dress when she tilts her head slightly.

The couple are smiling, even though they are not looking at the camera. In fact, no one in the photo is looking in the direction of the photographer, and that may be what makes the picture especially beautiful: No one is posing; no one seems to have noticed that someone, at that particular moment in time, is trying to immortalise the event.

The engagement party was held in the house in Campi. I could not immediately recognise the room where the big table had been set with *rustici*, pies and marzipan pastries. I walked around the house from room to room with the photo in my hand trying to figure out where it could possibly have been taken. And after some time, I recognised my grandfather's old office, a room that is separated from the rest of the house and is now my parents' bedroom when they come to visit me here.

Satisfied with my discovery, I went back to my desk and began examining the picture closely again. There was something about the scene, about the people, their expressions and their gestures that made it look like a painting. The scene called to mind Caravaggio's *The Calling of Saint Matthew*, where the painter, through his play with chiaroscuro, brings the gaze of the viewer to bear on the face of the saint, who is sitting at the end of the table and is about to get up. In this photo too, the viewer's gaze is directed straight at one person, who finds himself willy-nilly in the centre of the scene.

In the foreground, my grandmother, Rosetta, stands next to the couple, with a glass of champagne in her hand, looking at her daughter, who is looking at her wedding ring. Arturo, who is next to his wife, is seated; he too is holding a glass of champagne and looking at his daughter; his mouth is slightly open and his expression is one of stupefaction. My father is behind Rosetta, Arturo and the betrothed couple. Unlike the others, he is looking neither at his sister nor at her ring.

Yet his face is the one that draws my attention. My father's gaze is concentrated on his father, whose eyes are wide open in amazement.

The more I contemplated the photo, the more convinced I became that he is the subject of the photograph, not Lala's engagement.

When my brother came with Jacopo to spend a few days at my place, I showed him the photo, saying, 'Look at the look of despair on Papa's face!' And he said, 'That's his usual expression!'

It was true. My brother was right. That was my father's usual expression. A mix of sadness and helplessness. But only now was I becoming aware of what I may have always known but chose to ignore. And if not ignore, at any rate push aside and even repress. That was it, my father's despair was something I had always repressed.

I, who prided myself on understanding people, I had understood nothing about my father. I, who had always believed that I was capable of grasping the contradictions and failings of others, with my father, I had been unable to do so.

For years, I told myself that my world revolves around human vulnerability, that the rest is only '*appiccicaticcio*', 'bogus', as my father used to say referring to the students who would learn his lessons by heart and would cough it all up on his exams without understanding a thing. That my world is composed of people, their uncertainty around a word, their gaze that clouds over, their uncertain smile and suddenly their silence, that these are things that I notice, interpret, understand...

But when it came to my father, what happened to my constant, nearly obsessive, attention to human frailties and contradictions?

My grandfather died on 31 August 1976, after spending eighteen years in a wheelchair.

I had just turned six, and I remember absolutely nothing about that day.

I have a photograph of the funeral procession that went from the house to the Capuchin convent. I am next to my mother, and we are holding hands. Her tear-filled eyes and swollen face do not detract from her extraordinary beauty. When she was young, she was even more beautiful than the most beautiful actresses. I know I have said it before, but every time I see her in a photo, I marvel at her beauty.

Among the hundreds of things heaped up in the cellar of my father's cousins, I found a photo album dedicated to my grandfather's funeral. On the first pages, there is a copy of some funeral notices that were posted on the streets of Campi. The death of Arturo was announced by Angiulino Cassone, the manager of my grandmother's estate, on the evening of 31 August. This was right in the middle of the patronal festival when the streets and squares of Campi were decked with illuminations and adorned with thousands of lights of all colours, in the form of fountains, clouds of flowers, stands overflowing with the culinary specialties of Salento, *cupete, mustazzoli, scapece* and *pupiddhri*, and the procession carrying the statue of Saint Oronzo through the city centre.

The photos shot on the day of the funeral begin after pictures of the funeral postings. There is one taken in the living room: My grandfather's coffin has just been closed; on top of it is his black magistrate's robe with a gold trim; my grandmother is seated on a chair, dressed in black, her eyes half closed, one hand on the coffin, as if she wanted to caress her husband one last time. I recognised the living room window on the street side, the closed shutters, the yellow curtains in the same fabric as the sofas and chairs. I recognised the Luigi Filippo console in mahogany, with a cream marble top and a large mirror, and on it a clock in gilt bronze full of scrolls and curls. This console has been in the living room of the house in Rome for years. Who knows when it was moved there, along with the yellow room's sofas and armchairs.

A few photos were taken on the veranda. You could see men walking down the stairs to the courtyard, with the coffin on the men's shoulders. I recognised Totò, a farmer from the Tresca estate, and Lucio and Rapanà from the Don Francisco and Ochineri estates.

I stared at the photos of the funeral procession. I looked at my father advancing arm-in-arm with Pierino, pale, a closed expression on his face, his eyes fixed on the ground. I looked at my mother, who is holding my hand and telling me something. I seem distracted, maybe annoyed. I have a grimace on my face and the wind is blowing my hair, despite my blue headband, which is the same colour as the little flowers on the dress I am wearing, which my mother made for me a short time before. Behind us, in no particular order, relatives, friends, a few farmers.

At my grandfather's funeral on 2 September 1976 at 5 pm, there were barely a hundred people, very few considering the thousands of files with names on them that I found in the cellar of my father's cousins' home and the thousands of people whom Arturo had helped, listened to, done favours for and protected when he was a deputy.

'He collapsed and it was all over,' my grandmother had repeated to me so many times when I was little. Even though this 'all' had no meaning to me at the time. And only now was I perhaps beginning to really understand.

That morning, I decided to swing by the cemetery and pay a visit to the family mausoleum. I asked my cousins for the keys, told Jacques that I would rather go alone, and picked up a bouquet of sunflowers at the florist's by town hall. I crossed the main square framed by an impossibly blue sky and then walked through the streets of the centre, paved in the old-fashioned way, the cobblestones all crooked. I shot a glance at the small white houses that had been hastily restored in the 1960s in irritatingly poor taste. Then I hurried on, not wanting to dwell on the extravagant paint jobs, the incongruous windows bigger in width than in height, the walls ruined by drab ceramics, and the oversized gates.

The cemetery is small. I had not gone there for many years, but I knew exactly where the Malvani mausoleum was located. I just wanted to pay my respects to my grandparents, pause for a few moments in thought, and fill a vase with water to place the sunflowers by Arturo and Rosetta's graves. If I had a little time left, maybe I would also see if I could find the graves of the Schiavones and the Leuzzis, the Parlangelis and the Perrones, the Palazzos and the Macis. I had committed to my memory the names of the people who had come to pay their respects after my grandfather died; now it would be my turn to visit their deceased kin. For days, I had the words gratitude and ingratitude, fidelity and betrayal running through my mind. These were no longer only concepts with which one was confronted when working on ethical issues; they were now flesh and blood.

As soon as I crossed the threshold of the cemetery, I found myself disoriented. Everything had changed since the last time I was there. I was sure that I had to turn right, but was it at the first lane or the second? Wasn't there a big monument right at the corner of the square and the central lane? Where did that big obelisk-type structure in sandstone from Lecce go? I walked past the first lane. There were too many cypresses there; that was not where I should turn, I thought. But after a few minutes, I had lost my bearings entirely. New mausoleums had gone up. Some in marble and glass. Others in reinforced concrete. Still others were under construction, surrounded with scaffolding and with the tuff bricks still visible. It looked more like a small village inside the town than a cemetery.

I saw a big building that looked like a church, climbed the steps and went inside where I found dozens and dozens of niches surrounded by flowers, tea lights and votive candles. I started to read the names engraved in the marble, wondering how many of them figure among my grandfather's files? I glanced at my watch and hurried out. I had taken the wrong path and time was passing. If I didn't move quickly, I would never have time to find the family mausoleum.

I headed back in the direction I came from, but that wasn't right either: After a few minutes of walking, instead of arriving at the central esplanade, I found myself at the cemetery's outer wall. At that very moment, I heard the sound of a siren, as if an alarm had just gone off.

I looked at the time. It was 6.30 pm. The siren was certainly a warning to visitors that the cemetery would be closing soon. What if I couldn't find my way out? I broke into a sweat. What if I got stuck inside? I started to panic. What would happen to me if they didn't know I was still inside and they locked the gate?

I dropped the sunflowers by the grave of someone named Teresa Lucia Tricarico and started running. But the more I ran, the more agitated I got, and the more agitated I got, the more lost I felt. Three times, I passed an iron door with a skull and crossbones on it. I was running in circles. By now I was drenched in sweat. How could I find my way out of this labyrinth?

After about fifteen minutes, with the alarm now sounding relentlessly, I finally found the exit. As I was leaving the cemetery, soaked and panting, a young man approached the exit gate.

'Did you get lost, Signora?' he asked me, mixing the familiar form of address with the polite Signora in the same breath as almost everyone does in Salento.

'My God, yes!' I replied, all red and coughing. 'Forgive me if I delayed you, but I couldn't find my way out.'

'Not a problem, Signora! I wasn't going to lock you in!'

'How could that happen to you? That cemetery is so small!" Jacques burst into laughter when I got home and told him that I had lost my sense of direction.

'You have to understand, everything has changed since the last time we went there together.'

'If you say so… There may be a few more mausoleums or some additional cypress trees, but to say that everything has changed… Aren't you exaggerating a bit?' As I was about to protest, the image of my father's family grave sprang into my mind. The rose window on the façade. The inscription: *Malvani Family, 1926*. The gothic style pointed arch. The wrought iron gate with its mauve leaves. I realised that I had passed it several times. Even the name Malvani, read and reread when I was trying to gain my bearings in the cemetery, made absolutely no impression on me, as if it were a foreign name.

Genoa, 13 August 1961

My dearest Mama and Papa, when I left last night, I had a fever and I felt very tired. But I stayed in bed from 7 pm until noon today and I feel much better now. But I must say that I'm having great difficulty with the language. I'm on an American ship, and most of the people speak only English.

On the evening of 12 August 1961, my father left Naples on the *SS Constitution*, an American Export Lines cruise ship, famous at the time not only for being the ship on which Grace Kelly travelled from New York in 1956 when she went to Europe to marry Prince Rainier, but also because it was featured in the poignant 1957 movie *An Affair to Remember*, with Cary Grant and Deborah Kerr. On this ship, Nickie and Terry fall madly in love and promise each other to meet six months later but on that day, Terry has an accident on her way to their meeting and loses the use of both legs.

My father did not travel in first class – his was a third-class ticket – and he did not board the ship to go on a cruise or to join the woman of his life. He had interrupted his studies for a while after Arturo's stroke. He had just graduated, had won a scholarship and been accepted in Harvard University. He would have rather travelled there by plane, but his mother was against it. She was afraid, and she had been so insistent that Ferruccio finally gave in, knowing that when his mother had an idea in her head, it was well-nigh impossible to get her to change her mind! And, because her husband was so very much diminished and she was so unhappy, my father was intent on doing everything he could not to vex her.

Ferruccio arrived in Naples early in the afternoon. He waited patiently for the boarding to begin at the end of the day. His papers were all in order, with the visa stamped on his passport. The only problem was that he contracted a fever immediately after he had had the smallpox vaccine; the vaccine was required for the medical certificate, which was required for the United States visa. 'How fussy these Americans are!' he had written to his mother a few days before embarking

'Everything's ok, I'm fine!' my father replied to the navy officer who had noticed, while checking his ticket and documents, that the young man was shivering. He had rehearsed this sentence at least a hundred times in front of the mirror, since he did not speak English, and had a hard time understanding it. The officer could barely restrain his laughter at Ferruccio's catastrophic pronunciation, which made it as clear as can be that the young man did not speak English, and he let him through without asking or saying anything else.

Ferruccio strode quickly to his berth, even though his head was spinning. And only when the boat had finally left the dock and he had heard the noise of the engines and looked through the porthole and saw that the port was far away, did he go to the infirmary and tell them that he had a fever and was sick.

My father would tell us this story about his fever again and again, each time boasting about having managed to pull it off. He used the same proud tone to tell us how one day on deck he met a man travelling in first class; they exchanged a few words and he told him about the scholarship he got from the Bank of Italy to study in America ('the Stringhen Scholarship! You never heard of it?'). And impressed by the young man's panache, the traveller invited him one evening to a party organised for first-class travellers, and he went, although he had nothing decent to wear for the occasion, and the waiters stared at him in disbelief wondering what the hell he was doing there.

My father now had to be careful not to spend too much money. Between the medical expenses for Arturo, his uncle's gambling debts, and the fact that there was no one to take care of the family business anymore, things had changed quite a bit.

In the stacks of boxes in my father's cousins' cellar, I found dozens and dozens of documents written or received by my father: a letter of resignation on behalf of my grandfather from his position as municipal councillor in Campi; a notification of resignation from the Monarchist Party of Campi ('I hereby advise you of the cessation of all my father's political activities, as well as all family ties with the PNM,' Ferruccio wrote to the secretary of the Campi section on 8 July 1958); registered letters to an attorney in Lecce requesting that he handle the collection the debts owed to Arturo; letters to the Chancellery of the Court of Cassation; forms for fiscal medical examinations; an application for early retirement; a ledger of accounts from the Tresca, Don Francisco, Occhineri and Fusaro estates.

My father, who had never taken care of anything until 1958, suddenly found himself over his head in files. He tried his best, but his heart wasn't in it and his head even less. On the first pages of the accounts ledger for the year 1959, he methodically wrote down the details, estate by estate, the number of hectares, the municipality of registration, and the number of land plots. But he soon began crossing out and erasing entries, as the expenses and the income didn't coincide; something was always off. My father was not very attached to the lands and estates of his family. To be sure, he loved the centuries-old olive trees. I clearly remember the day he explained to me how to tell the age of an olive tree: 'Look at the trunks. Don't they look like statues? They are almost three metres in diameter. You can read their age from the spirals and the hollows, the cavities and the way they stand.' He also loved the vineyards and I will never forget our walks through them when I was a child. But he had absolutely no desire to manage them. My father was eager for one thing only: to leave Italy and resume his studies.

'I'm gradually adapting to my new life,' Ferruccio wrote in a letter to his parents on 31 August 1961. He had just arrived in Cambridge and was trying to find his bearings.

'The food is very expensive, like everything else here, but I'm managing and I don't lack a thing. I want to be in good shape to be able to work well. The sadness I felt during the first few days is passing. Now months of sacrifices await me, but I have to look at the bright side of things and try to live normally [...] As far as family affairs are concerned, follow my instructions well, I noted everything on the sheet that I left with Mama. If there is something that you don't understand about the accounts or anything else, write me, and I'll explain it to you.'

The crossing took ten days. When the boat docked in New York, Ferruccio was out of his element. He had to go through the visa control procedures and customs; he had to pick up his luggage and find a train ticket from New York to Cambridge. The city appeared huge, frenzied and confusing to him and he found himself in the throes of nostalgia: He missed his home; he missed his friends; he missed his language.

'The greatest difficulty is the language,' he wrote his parents. 'It makes it extremely difficult for me to communicate with other people.'

In Cambridge, my father was living in William James Hall. He shared his room, number 108, with an American from Colorado and they soon began exchanging language lessons, Italian for English. But his concerns about food persisted: 'How poorly people eat here!' he commented several times. And the fact is he put on weight, so much so that I could scarcely recognise him in a photo taken in February 1962; he must have gained at least ten kilos!

'Here, there is not so much as a trace of anything resembling a good Italian coffee!'

His mother wrote him every day. She carefully copied on the envelope the address her son had sent her: Mr Ferruccio Marzano, William James Hall no. 108, Harvard University, Cambridge, Mass. (USA). She even paid close attention to copying the capital and lower-case letters correctly, and followed all the instructions her son had given her. Ferruccio had explained to her that 'Mr' is the way of writing 'Signor' and that she should never add 'Doctor', as she had been accustomed to doing when he was in Rome. She told him in her letters that nothing new was happening at home, but she nonetheless always filled them with complaints: 'A letter from the Court of Appeal arrived, but I can't understand a thing and I have no idea what to do.' 'I want to hear from you twice a week, I already told you! We can't go so many days without getting a letter from you. A week is much too long; it's painful for us; it's painful for me.' Or recommendations: 'Don't overdo it! Make sure you rest and eat well! Buy a hat to protect yourself from the wind! Remember your ear is so fragile!'

On 1 January 1962, the day of Arturo's birthday, my father sent him a long message: 'Best wishes, my dearest Papa! I wish you a long life, even in the state you are in. I know that everything was different before, when you were not sick. But what can we do? How nice it would be to continue receiving letters from you, full of advice! From now on, I'll have to content myself with your signature. I think of you and of everything that you have done for me over time. Sometimes I think about how happy you would have been to keep abreast of my life, my decisions and my choices from afar. But everything has changed, and everything you built up little by little has become distant and insignificant.'

When I saw my grandfather's signature alongside my grandmother's, my heart skipped a beat. The shaky handwriting, the muddled lines… Arturo, who had always written so much – in his notebooks, letters, judgements, indictments, even some poems – could no longer write Papa. And this attempt to leave a trace of himself on the letters that his wife wrote to his son, struck me as the umpteenth blow of fate. Why force him to sign? I wondered. Or was he the one who wanted to? How did he feel about his own impotence? Was he aware of it?

'Everything was different before, when you were not sick,' my father wrote to him. 'Everything has changed.'

Those were exactly the words he used to say to me when I wasn't doing well. I, who without realising it, was making him relive the trauma of his loss.

When I was a child and we all spent the summer together in Campi, my father would spend hours on end in his office. The peasant farmers who worked his lands would knock on the door, enter, sit down, talk with him, plead, get irritated, stand up and leave. At the time, I did not understand much of what was going on. All I knew was that when my father was in his office with the farmers, he was not to be disturbed, no matter what.

The only one who was allowed to enter his office was Angiulino Cassone, the manager of his properties. He was basically the one in charge of overseeing the work of the farmers and who would push my father to think about installing an artesian well to resolve drought-related problems or about planting new grape varieties.

The memories I have of Angiulino are vague. He is there on a photo of me taken when I was three and a half years old. My hair is short and I'm wearing a red dress. Dark-skinned and wrinkled, he is standing there, squinting because of the sun; he is wearing brown cotton pants and holding his hat in his hands. I remembered my mother asked him to stop calling me 'Donna Michelina'.

'Why do you address the little one like that? Her name's Michela! Not Donna or Michelina.'

'Very well, Donna Paola,' he had answered, insisting on the 'donna' for he was in the habit of putting don or donna in front of all the names of everyone in my father's family: Donna Rosetta, Don Arturo, Don Ferruccio, Donna Rosaria.

One day, I was with my grandmother and I wanted to play, but Angiulino had yelled at me.

'Your grandmother is old and tired,' he shouted. 'Don't make things difficult for her.' He was always on my grandmother's side. Or my father's. My mother claims that he was a good man, and that with her he was always welcoming, protective, and paternal.

'But call her Michela, Angiulino, please! How many times do I have to ask you?'

My fondest memories of the vineyards and the olive fields are connected with Totò, a farmer on the Tresca estate. Often, in the late afternoon, my mother, my brother and I would accompany my father there. And while he was visiting the vineyards with Totò ('How does Totò walk barefoot on the ground, Mama? Doesn't it hurt?'), we would wait by the big fig tree planted right next to Totò's house. Arturo would climb up and make the figs drop, and Mama and I would eat them. Inevitably, I would have a stomachache that evening, but I loved stuffing myself with freshly picked figs so much that I didn't mind that they gave me diarrhea. Sometimes, I too walked with my father and Totò among the rows of *alberelli*, the 'saplings' of primitivo grapes. I loved the smell of the earth mixed with that of the grapes, the goblet-trained vines and the olive trees planted all around. From time to time, Totò would pull a grape off the vine and give it to me: 'It's very sweet already, isn't it?'

The last time I saw Totò was three years ago. I was with Jacques, we were both on our bikes, and as we rode across the main square of Campi, I recognised Totò sitting on a bench with the other old-timers. I got off my bike and approached him. From the look on his face, I realised that he didn't know who I was.

'Totò?' I smiled. He stared at me in silence.

'I'm Michela; do you remember me?' Stunned, he examined me.

'Ferruccio Marzano's daughter, Rosetta's granddaughter.' He then jumped up and cried out, 'Donna Michela!'

Totò had not recognised me in 1993 either. I was suffering from anorexia at the time, and my father took it into his head to imagine that I would get better if I spent more time with him, that I would become the 'Michela from before'.

'Anorexics have issues with their mother,' he said.

He had read that somewhere or other and was convinced that it was true of me too. So, he took me to Campi, despite the fact that the house had been abandoned for years. That time too, Totò had stared at me at considerable length.

'You look so wan,' he exclaimed.

'Yes, everything has changed,' my father commented, adjusting his straw hat on his head and looking away.

When my grandparents died and we stopped going to Campi, my father also stopped taking care of the vineyards and olive groves. Slowly but surely, the various estates were all sold.

There were the debts. There were the inheritance taxes. There was the meagre income. And there was my father's desire to leave the past behind, perhaps also his need to erase his history.

Above all, there was the cursed spell of loss cast on his family.

Losing his chance or losing his father; losing face or losing his daughter; always losing, no matter what.

It was a Sunday morning, and I was live streaming the mass. At the beginning of the celebration, I was distracted. I kept thinking about one of the sentences written about my grandfather after he died: 'After many long years of suffering with exemplary resignation, he passed away peacefully at the age of eighty.' Resignation. That is something I am incapable of. Maybe that's why every time I hear people talking about resilience, I get annoyed: Resilience in what respect? Why and for whom?

But when Don Andrea started his sermon, his words compelled me to stop this line of questioning myself.

'The spirit comes to our aide,' he declared. 'We are all good clods of earth where seeds can grow.' Don Andrea said that the Lord is not looking for faults and failings in us, that He is encouraging us to have trust and to love.

'Even if good makes less noise than evil, and works in silence, it is like leaven: It has no taste and no colour, but it is the very substance that makes the bread rise. But are we capable of being the leaven of growth and love?'

Don Andrea said that there was no point in being intransigent with oneself. And that engaging in true scrutiny of one's conscience does not involve a litany of complaints: 'It is forbidden to complain! Just as it is forbidden to criticise, to allow oneself to feel defeated. Above all, it is forbidden to feel inadequate: We cannot permit ourselves do so!'

I looked for a sheet of paper and a pencil, and I took notes, jotting down some of the terms: complain, criticise, feel discouraged, inadequate. I had the impression that Don Andrea was speaking directly to me, for I complain and feel discouraged so often. He was, at any rate, speaking about me. And didn't the source of my discouragement reside precisely in my feelings of inadequacy?

Don Andrea spoke of a mother who came to complain about her son. Seeing that the woman was not so young, he asked her the age of the disobedient son.

'Thirty-seven,' she told him.

'Then he is a man,' Don Andrea replied. 'You must trust your children. They are not eternally children. They have the right to make mistakes and what they need most of all is your trust in them.'

For ten years, I refused even to think about becoming a mother. I considered myself incapable. I could not have managed. How could I possibly imagine taking care of a child when I was incapable of taking care of myself? What would I have passed onto him or her? Pain and despair? Would I have poured all my anxiety and anguish onto my progeny? Used them to fill the voids inside me? And then, what would I have done the day my child came to me and held me to account for the life that they had not chosen?

That is what always happens. One day or another, your child will ask you why you brought them into the world. What would I have said? That he or she was his mother's little darling? Her only joy, and the most important thing in her life?

That was what my mother used to tell me all the time. And it did not do me a bit of good. How could being her joy help when I did not even know what joy was?

For years, I was always the one who was leaving the men I lived with, even after I moved to France. As soon as they brought up the question of children, I would fall in love with someone else, or I would start thinking about suicide again.

I was running away.

I had a house, a job, a man. Sometimes even more than one. There was a time when I accumulated them, like you accumulate trophies. They were all alike to me. I did not trust them.

I had everything except the desire to live. How could I give a moment's thought to bringing a child into the world?

I even wanted to die in 2004, after I had met Jacques. He was the one who came to pick me up from Sainte-Anne hospital in Paris, where my friend had brought me when I'd broken down crying and asked her to help me die. Jacques and I had been together for only a few months. He could have left me and disappeared.

'She'd be better off hospitalised,' the psychiatrist at Sainte-Anne's told Jacques. 'She is not well and she could do something irreparable.'

Jacques had come to the hospital immediately when they called him.

'If you decide to take her out of the hospital anyway, you'll have to sign this release.'

I don't think Jacques really understood what it meant to sign this document in which he took responsibility for taking an insane woman who wanted to die out of the hospital. But he signed it. Rash, reckless, and generous. Jacques is like that, at heart. He is like a child. Maybe that was why he signed without hesitation when I begged him to. And then later, the first time we talked about children, he asked me, 'Do you really think you are capable of taking care of them?'

One day my mother told me that when she met my father, he would faint at the very sight of blood.

'So how did you manage,' I asked my father, since he was the one who would disinfect our wounds when my brother and I were little. He would soak a compress in alcohol and clean off the blood without paying any attention to our screams and cries. He looked at the blood and cleaned it without batting an eye.

'Well, I went to see a psychologist who told me that I had to stop taking care of everyone around me and start thinking of myself a bit more. And when I left him, I was cured.'

My mother claimed that the psychologist had also advised my father to go into therapy, but that he, of course, had followed his own judgement and never gone back to see him again.

'Why would I have gone back? I never fainted again.'

This story always seemed very odd, not to say absurd, to me. What had happened that day? Had my father been hypnotised?

This business about the blood and the psychologist came to mind as I read through the hundreds of letters that my father wrote to his mother or received from her between 1962 and 1968, when he was in England studying at Churchill College in Cambridge. Many young economists at the time went to America or to England to study Keynesian and neo-Keynesian theories. My father was always very proud of the bachelor's degree and the Master's in Economics he got in Cambridge, which allowed him, once he returned to Italy, to have a university career.

Reading and rereading the correspondence from those years, I thought back to the story of my father's fainting at the sight of blood. Despite his departure abroad, my father continued to take care of everything. He desperately sought to *salvare il salvabile*, save what could be saved. And even though what truly interested him was his studies, he came back to Campi regularly for the harvests and to settle accounts with the estate farmers. He filled out the tax returns of his parents and his sister, he paid the employer's charges, he oversaw the work of Angiulino Cassone and followed through on Arturo's affairs: After four years of sick leave, Arturo had retired and obtained the honorary title of magistrate of the Court of Cassation.

'Six o'clock, sir! It's time to wake up.'

'That's how it was every time I left the country,' my father used to tell me when I was a child. 'I would sleep at the airport and at 6 on the dot a policeman would appear and tell me that it was time to get up. No ifs, ands or buts. It was 6 o'clock, and at 6 o'clock, in England, you get up.'

As a little girl, I looked at him wide-eyed, thinking, my poor Papa, having to sleep at the airport.

'I was travelling all the time,' he told me, 'back and forth between Campi, Rome and Cambridge. What a life! It was dreadful. I'd get up at 5 in the morning and Angiulino would drive me to the airport in Brindisi. From Brindisi I would fly to Rome where I'd make a connecting flight to London. Then I took a bus from Heathrow to Victoria Station, from Victoria Station I took the underground to Liverpool Street Station, where I caught a train to Cambridge. Thank goodness for Angiulino. He did everything I told him to do; he loved me like his own son.'

When I grew up and started to travel a great deal myself, I began doubting certain things my father had said. I realised that he was exaggerating, amplifying, dramatising. And when he told me this story again during the period when I was flying every single Tuesday morning from Paris to the National Assembly in Rome, and then going back to France Friday afternoon, and cramming all eight hours of my classes at university on Mondays, I said, 'Enough!'

'You would come back to Italy during Christmas, Easter and in August. You can hardly call that a dreadful life! And enough with this story about Angiulino! Very well, so he was a good man. But he worked for you as your manager; he called you Don Ferruccio and never dared to contradict you.'

My father was always exaggerating. That much was true. But it was also true that his responsibilities towards his family weighed on him, all the more because his mother never missed an opportunity to reproach him for something or other. Having read the hundreds of letters that my father wrote and received between 1962 and 1968, I was beginning to understand a lot of things, including his phobia of blood and his desire to free himself from the burden of others, even though after having perhaps too quickly rid himself of his symptom, my father proceeded to retreat into his own crazy, paranoid world.

Things got worse at the end of 1967, when my father fell in love with my mother, a young woman from Taranto, who came from a family Rosetta described as 'much too humble'.

'Don't worry,' my father wrote in a letter to his mother in April 1968, after having received a long list of reproaches and accusations. 'I am still the same person, and my affection and love for you are unchanged.'

A few weeks later, my father had to defend himself again. Apparently, his mother had complained about the fact that my mother had no dowry.

'Such things do not interest me,' he wrote. 'I am a modern person, an intellectual, and I am in love with Paola [...] but if you want to get something, you can always talk with Paola's mother. But please, I beg you, make sure that Paola doesn't know anything about it, because it would cause her pain, and I don't want her to suffer.'

I read the letter and I could not believe my eyes. This business of a dowry made no sense! It was the end of the 1960s and there was my grandmother protesting to her son because her future daughter-in-law didn't have a dowry? I reread it, torn between anger towards my father's family – which was probably at the origin of many of the tensions and arguments between my parents – and a new feeling of tenderness towards my father, who truly loved his fiancée and who tried perhaps to rebel against his family. But then what made him completely withdraw into his own world afterward? Why, as time went by, did everything at home go wrong? Why did my father, who had studied in America and England with the most brilliant Italian economists of his time, gradually end up isolated and withdrawn into his own small world?

On 20 August 2020, we were all together in Campi: my parents, Arturo, Matteo, Jacopo, Jacques and me. It was my fiftieth birthday and my lower back was hurting. I was probably as fed up as Jacques was with having all those people around. Between my father's mood swings, the little one who needed attention twenty-four hours a day, my mother who wanted to continue to do a thousand things but who was now too old to manage, and me, who wanted to get some work done but also to be a good aunt and a perfect daughter, the atmosphere was utterly suffocating.

Little Jacopo, however, was a universe opening up. He looked at everything, touched everything, tasted everything. He loved the water and loved nothing more than bath time. Yesterday, for the first time, I was the one to give him his bath. The bathroom was flooded and I was soaked from head to toe, but it's marvellous to play with a child, isn't it, Jacques?

When I looked at the way Jacopo looked at his two fathers, my heart sank. I told myself that no one would ever look at me that way. Only a child can look at his parents like that. But is that any reason to bring a child into the world? Do you do so to give or to receive? And anyway, what can one really give?

What the child needs, or what we might have needed as children?

I would be going back to Paris at the beginning of September and had no idea when I would be able to see my little nephew again. No doubt he would forget his aunt. I would be just another one of the many faces that he sees on the computer screen or on the iPhone, one voice among so many, an unfamiliar person who says 'my treasure' to him, but who remains a stranger. Without contact, there can be no attachment; without attachment, no affection: Little children forget you and all traces of you are gone.

I blew out the birthday candles but did not make a wish. Actually, I did. I wished that someone would look at me the way Jacopo looked at my brother and Matteo. But was that why my brother wanted to have a child? And why hadn't I had one?

I was thinking that if I had a child, I would suffer less; that if I had a child, I wouldn't suffer at all; that I suffered because I did not have children.

Then I realised that my reasoning did not hold up. It was sophistic. Everything was fallacious: the syntax, but also and especially the logic, which was non-existent. I should have been ashamed of myself for imagining that there was even a minimum of coherence in these muddled thoughts.

'Meaningless words,' as my father used to say: 'Why don't you try to translate yourself into English? If the translation makes sense, then what you're saying in Italian does too. If it doesn't, that's proof of the fallacy of your words and the confusion in your head.'

I thought: *Ho bisogno di un bambino.* I need a baby. So far, so good: There is no contradiction, no incoherence. The sentence makes sense in Italian and in English. But is it really true? Do I really need a child? Is it a child that I was missing, or would I be missing something even if I had a child?

Jacques said that I would be dissatisfied and unhappy even if I had a child.

'It would be even worse,' he added. 'You'd feel guilty all the time! Either because you're working and you're not with the child or because you are and you're not working. It would be a real nightmare!'

'Are you absolutely sure?' Jacques asked me about ten years ago, when I had convinced myself that I wanted a child.

'Do you really think one can be absolutely sure of anything?'

'But we're talking about a child here! It's not something you can regret afterwards!'

'So, according to you, anyone who becomes a mother or a father is one hundred percent sure of never regretting their decision or of doing the right thing at the right time? Or am I the only one that has to be absolutely sure? Were you absolutely sure when you had Alice or Rodolphe?'

Are you absolutely sure you can succeed?
Are you absolutely sure you're up to it?
Are you absolutely sure you'll be happy afterwards?

I thought: If I had a child, I would never stop looking at her, I would never look through her, I would not judge her, I would love her as she is, end of story. I would love her with unbound love because she is my child and nothing could ever separate us.

I thought: If I had a child, I would drive him crazy.

I thought: I would have to protect the child from myself and from my insanity.

I thought: I would never be a good enough mother.

I didn't know if the reasoning held up this time, but it didn't really matter. In spite of the severity with which I continued to judge myself; wasn't it precisely because of how terrified I was of hurting my child that this child did not exist today? The fear of reproducing what I lived through or of doing exactly the opposite and being wrong, even so.

'I don't deserve this,' my father used to say when I poured out my anger on him.

'I don't deserve this,' I sometimes said to Jacques when he ignored me.

But is love something that has to be earned? Is that what I would have taught my child?

The fear of seeking revenge on life, all the while knowing that a child is not a tool of vengeance, although a child can be a debt that one contracts with the future. And what if I were unable to settle that debt in the future? What if it were up to my child to settle it? And what if the debt were, on the contrary, infinite?

I looked at Arturo looking at Jacopo.

And I saw all the love that Arturo may have wanted to receive from his own father and never did. But was this really what Jacopo needed? Was this what my nephew wanted?

Or, in loving a child as we would have liked to be loved ourselves, are we giving what we don't have to someone who doesn't want it, as is abundantly clear from the seminars of Jacques Lacan, who crucifies love. He is probably right. It is inevitable, especially when it comes to love for a child, which is always selfish and serves to repair our past and our woes. Would it be better to give up once and for all on becoming fathers and mothers?

'Who is Bice Serafini, Papa?'

'I don't know; why are you asking?'

'I found her name in my notes on Arturo and I thought it was you who mentioned her to me.'

I'm lying. I know he didn't say anything to me about Bice; I discovered her existence when I was digging through family papers. But I want to see how my father reacts to hearing me pronounce that name.

'I think you can forget about it; it can't be anyone important.'

Unlike me, my father seems sincere. He does not seem to know who this Bice is. And even though I cannot look him in the eye, since we are on the phone, his tone of voice makes me think that he is not lying.

Folder no. 45: Bice-Arturo correspondence

When I discovered the exchange of letters between my grandfather and Beatrice Serafini – who at the time that my grandfather was in Rome was working in a pharmacy on Piazza della Lucina – it took me a while to understand what it was all about.

At first, I could not figure it out. I was looking for a detail, a word, a sign, something that could explain the existence of this yellow envelope filled with letters, which was simply marked *correspondence.*

I had to reread these letters several times before I could bring myself to accept the fact that Arturo, between 1933 and August 1934 – the year he worked in the capital, after having been transferred there at the request of the Minister of Justice – was cheating on his wife.

> *Campi, 5 September 1934: […] I beg you, please make sure to keep this letter and those that will follow at home, and not leave it lying around in your bag. We have to be very careful because people are curious and often mean-spirited. I already told you when we spoke in person, but I'm repeating it in writing: Be discreet; don't say anything to anyone. A great deal of caution, even hypocrisy, is needed when it comes to very sensitive and serious matters. And, as I have always said to you, if speech is silver, then silence is golden […] Think of me as I think of you and write to me often, my dear and beautiful Bice. Tell me everything. I send you thousands of kisses, just like the ones I have given you in the past and that you know so well.*

This was the first letter my grandfather wrote to Bice. He had recently returned to Campi and his wife was about to give birth. Although he was happy in Rome and had excellent career prospects there, Arturo gave in. He listened to Rosetta, who had written, 'There's no reason for you to stay in Rome, now that you're going to be a father. Your place is here we me, in our home, in Campi.' But he also listened to the voice of his own conscience. He missed Bice very much. But what mattered most of all was that the whole affair should not come to light just as he was about to become a father. Speech is silver; silence is golden. I smiled as I read this sentence. I couldn't count the number of times I heard it from my father. He, on the other hand, used it to silence my mother, whom he felt talked for no good reason and would have been better off keeping her mouth shut at times! I smiled with bitterness. For I too sometimes told Jacques that silence is golden. And now that I had read these words written by my grandfather to his mistress, I felt very guilty.

> *Rome, 7 September 1934: [...] You can't imagine how much pain I'm in since you left and how lonely I feel now. It's as if I no longer know where to go or what to do. I see myself doing one thing after another mechanically and detached. I thought that life had made me impervious to love, but the truth is that no one really knows his own heart [...] I don't know if it will be possible for you to write to me; but if you can, I'll be most grateful. It's very hard for me to bear this great emptiness that you've left behind.*

Inside an envelope that has turned yellow with age, the letters were arranged in chronological order and numbered. How was it that he had not only the letters he received from his mistress, but also the ones he wrote her? How did Arturo get them back? Did Bice return them to him one day? Or did he himself go to regain possession of them?

I asked Jacques what he thought. But he was not very interested in this correspondence. 'It's of no importance, just another one of the countless stories of mistresses,' he said, adding: 'Are you sure you want to talk about it in your book?'

Campi, 11 September 1934: [...] I too, my dearest Bice, feel that I'm with you from afar, and when the clock strikes 12.35 or 9.20 pm, I wish I were in Rome. The memory of your warm and affectionate company makes my heart ache with pain and sadness. I received your photo and I thank you for it. I looked at it again and again, a million times, until my eyes filled with affection and love, and there you sprang up before me. What memories, how sweet [...] I will always write to you, and you too must do so, my beloved Bice! I will come to join you in October, as I promised, and you and I will spend four or five days together. The handkerchief that touched your lipstick and with which you wiped your tears is with me. I have kept it in a sealed envelope, which I will show you when I come to Rome [...] I embrace you with great affection and with all the voluptuousness of love.

At first, even the handkerchief wrapped in a sheet of silk paper, carefully folded and kept in the middle of the letters, was not enough to convince me that Bice was my grandfather's lover. On the contrary, I had taken out the piece of cloth, opened it to see if there was anything in it and dropped it on the floor, almost irritated by this insignificant object that had slipped into my grandfather's papers.

Now I did not have a doubt about it. The affair with Beatrice was not a mere adventure. But, in that case, how was it that no one knew about the existence of this woman?

> *Rome, 12 September 1934: [...] Thank you, my darling, for all your thoughtful attention! I thank you most of all for bringing me the immense joy of loving you. I love you so much that you are my one and only thought every hour and every moment of every hour; I live in agonising anticipation of the moment when I will see you again [...] I beg you to believe that I will do whatever you want so as not to lose you; you can trust me! [...] Mother sends her regards and I embrace you with long loving kisses.*

I looked for my grandfather's reply to this letter, but I could not find it. Then it came to me that 14 September 1934 was the day my aunt, my father's sister, was born. Bice must have known that the little one would soon be born. Arturo must have told her that that was why he had asked to be transferred to Lecce. They must have talked about it several times and Bice must have been understanding. But what did she actually feel?

Was she jealous? Or was she concerned? What did she think of this little girl who arrived after almost seven years of marriage, just when she and Arturo were so happy together?

> *Rome, 14 September 1934: […] Your letters fill my soul with sweetness and joy and sometimes I have the impression of being back in those days when everything looked rosy and we could look forward to tomorrow with joy. As for you, and this handkerchief story, you seem to have reverted to the days of knickers and books under your arm, to being a little boy and not the 'big shot' you now are and who made me tremble so many times; a good little boy whom I will never be able to forget and whom I wish were here by my side so I could tell him between a kiss and a caress how much I loved him!*

I had the same reaction as Beatrice: What got into my grandfather?

If I had invented Arturo as a character, I'm sure people would have told me that he lacked coherence, that he wasn't credible, and that this handkerchief business did not fit the picture they had of a man who was a *squadrista* and who participated in the March on Rome. But Arturo is not a fictional character and, as often happens in real life, he does not need to be consistent. Like most of us, he too has his contradictions and inconsistencies. *Je est un autre*, 'I is another,' as Rimbaud wrote. This is true even though sometimes it is precisely with this 'other' that we have difficulty living.

Campi, 17 September 1934: My dear beautiful Bice, you made me laugh when you reminded me of those 'knickers' days gone by. Even if the handkerchief story, as you call it, is not a story at all. As I have often told you, my beloved Bice, the heart does not grow old as long as you are capable of loving. Bice... your name alone resonates in me with an explosion of strong, ardent kisses full of mad love and passion. And from now on, your name is even closer and dearer to me, for I have given it to my daughter, as her fifth name! The hours of labour were intense and filled with trepidation. But my trepidation was rewarded by the birth of a little girl who is a real bundle of love. My little Rosaria Giulia Giuseppina Rosetta Beatrice brings to my life hours of sublime and immeasurable tenderness. If only you knew how beautiful she is! Did you see? I kept my promise: The fifth part of her name is dedicated to you. [...] I reiterate what I have already told you. I haven't changed, I am still the man I was in Rome. [...] If you need anything at all, write to me [...] All I have to do now is confirm my visit to you in October. There is a good chance that very soon I will be appointed federal secretary of the party. If that's the case, as I hope it will be, we will see each other very often: I will be able to come to Rome every other week. I hope so, because I know that you hope so too.

For hours I had been totally absorbed in reading these letters, to the point of forgetting the time, even forgetting my husband. But when I reached the end of this letter, I stopped and ran to Jacques.

'Arturo named his daughter after his mistress. Can you believe it?'

'What do you mean? Wasn't your aunt's name Rosaria?'

'Yes, but that wasn't her only name. Like my father, who was named not only Ferruccio, but Ferruccio Michele Arturo Vittorio Benito, my aunt was named Rosaria Giulia Giuseppina Rosetta Beatrice. Rosaria for the vow made by her mother to the Madonna of the Rosary; Giulia for Arturo's mother; Giuseppina for her mother's mother; Rosetta for her mother; and Beatrice for Bice Serafini. How do you think Arturo justified this name to his wife? What did he tell her? Did he lie? I know it's only the fifth name given to his daughter, but when you think my father's fifth was Benito… Do you think my aunt ever knew the truth?'

Rome, 21 September 1934: […] A week has gone by since the birth of your daughter, and I can just imagine your feelings of pride and joy. I am very touched at the thought that your daughter also bears my name, and I hope with all my heart that it will be a sign of good things for her. I am so grateful to you! You have made me feel that your little one belongs to me a little bit too; and with sweet tenderness filling my soul, I hope that her pretty eyes will know nothing but joy throughout her life [...] I have been offered a position in a pharmacy outside Rome, but I have not yet decided what I'll do. No doubt, we'll make that decision together, when we can talk about it in person, because I so hope to be able to embrace you very soon and relive those hours that fill me with deep nostalgia, especially at night, when I see from my window, in a tiny square of sky, that beautiful, smiling moon that followed us on our sweet peregrinations [...] Kisses to little Rosaria and lots and lots of kisses for you.

I copied these letters word for word. When a word was illegible, I sometimes got stuck on it for a quarter of an hour; bogged down, the minutes passed, and sometimes I felt like I was wasting my time, which made me anxious. But was it really the passage of time that was giving me anxiety?

Here I was entering the private life of my grandfather and revealing secrets and lies that he may have thought he would take to his grave with him. But then why did Arturo keep these letters? If he hadn't had a stroke, would he have got rid of them? Or did he start seeing Bice again when he became a member of Parliament and was back in Rome?

Campi, 25 September 1934: [...] Thank you for your wishes for my beautiful, precious Rosaria, who's a model of indescribable tranquillity [...]

Just try to imagine, Bice – you who know my soul so well – the joy, the happiness and the tenderness that have taken hold of me since the birth of this little being, who for the past twelve days now has been making sounds that are not so much cries as invitations to paternal love. I am totally absorbed by her, always attentive to the needs of my little girl, a fifth of whom carries the everlasting memory of what was never a 'mere adventure' but rather a second, and still open, parenthesis of my life. I rock her in my arms and softly sing the most beautiful of songs in our dialect, those memories of times gone by that hold the expression of love, affection, tenderness and hope. And when she falls asleep, I lay her down with great care beside her mother – who has given me the chance to experience new delights in life – and as I watch my little girl, I find her ever more precious, ever more beautiful, ever more adorable […] I will surely be able to be in Rome around October 10; like you, I too feel the need to see you, to talk to you, to embrace you, to hold you close to me, as I did during our nights of love that gave us so much strength and life and a real frenzy of voluptuousness and caresses […] I send you lots and lots of very, very ardent kisses.

I continued to ask myself a great many questions. But this time I did not have answers. A book by Pierre Drieu La Rochelle that I read some years back came to mind. I thought it was an outstanding book, even though I detest everything that this far-right intellectual stands for. I thought of 'Nelly's very busy days', that he described so well in *Journal d'un homme trompé*, 'divided between me, Jacques and the other one'. I recalled how tormented the man was, and incapable of comprehending that his mistress could 'leave the other one at noon, have lunch with James, and then make love to me'. Whom does Nelly really love? When I read this novel, I had wondered about that. Who is betrayed and deceived throughout the story?

I came to the conclusion that the very complexity of complementary relationships can sometimes give you the feeling of being whole and of having everything, and that having two parallel relationships can sometimes make you feel at peace with yourself and ready to accept what another person cannot give you, not because they aren't the right person, but simply because they are 'other' in relation to your needs and desires. And then you convince yourself that this is the only way, with him, her and yet another person, that the void inside you can be filled. Even if, subsequently, you realise that what you give to one person, you necessarily take away from the other.

Was this what it was like for Arturo? Did he need the passionate relationship he was having with Bice and, at the same time, the day-to-day life he had with Rosetta, or was he primarily lying to himself?

Campi, 4 October 1934: [...] My dear beloved Bice, I'm impatiently looking forward to the day

> *when I will have the possibility of leaving for Rome and being with you. A month has gone by since our bitter parting, but you are still as precious and present in my mind; my passion for you remains unchanged. Write to me, do not hold back the news that I await with impatience and fondness [...] I send you lots and lots of kisses full of love and blazing passion.*

I read these letters and they moved me, like when I watch a movie and, try as I might not to make comments or cry, at some point or another I break down in tears, which irritates Jacques: 'C'mon, it's just a film; stop bawling!'

But this time it was not a film; it was the story of my grandfather. And what I was feeling reading these letters was so intense that at some point Arturo's nostalgia becomes mine. Then, little by little, I found myself taking Beatrice's side. When are you going to go see her in Rome, Grandfather? Knowing as you do that Beatrice is waiting for you, how can you write to her all the time that you're coming to see her soon and not go! Besides, weren't you going to be appointed federal secretary of the Party and go to Rome every other week?

> *Rome, 5 October 1934: [...] I'm flooded with emotions when I think of the tenderness with which you speak about your daughter and I'd like to find the right words to say to you, but somehow I can't. The mystery of this reincarnation is too*

great and too impenetrable for me to understand; but you, knowing the sincerity of my soul and the deep affection that binds me to you, must be able to imagine the extent to which I share your joy and happiness. The news of your upcoming trip to Rome has given me such great pleasure. I can hardly wait to see you and talk to you and feel your presence again and spend hours in your company like those whose memory is so dear to my heart. But won't you feel remorse, my treasure? Won't it be too painful for you to leave your daughter even for a few days? I speak to you from the bottom of my heart. I want you to know that! And I want you too to be sincere with me, because there can be no deep affection that is not based on mutual sincerity [...] write back quickly and... love me.

Who gave me the right to divulge and reveal? Who is the repository of memory and who, on the contrary, has no right to it? Who is betrayed and who betrays? My grandfather, who had a great love affair without ever telling anyone about it and kept absolutely everything related to it, including this cotton handkerchief folded inside a sealed envelope, or me? For I knew perfectly well that Arturo was a fervent proponent of forgetting and yet I continued, nonetheless, to dig up his past in search of a truth that may not exist?

Campi, 10 October 1934: [...] The waiting to be in my company will soon be over. It's a matter of days now. I'll send you a telegram beforehand and I will wait for your confirmation in return. Is that all right? And then there will be nothing but kisses, kisses and more kisses. It will take thousands of them to make up for all the time without them in the past and make huge reserves for the future […] I will not hide from you, my darling, that I'll be hearing my little Rosaria's voice calling me to her, but in your company I'm sure I can withstand a separation of a few days […] Get ready to receive, in a few days, so many of my kisses that you can hardly even imagine.

I thought of Tomáš's constant betrayals in *The Unbearable Lightness of Being*. I thought of Tereza's intense pain. For Tomáš, Tereza was unique: She was the only one to occupy his poetic memory, thereby obliterating the trace of all the other women. Tereza was *unique*, because she was the only woman with whom Tomáš wanted to sleep: 'Love is not manifested through the desire to make love (this can be the desire for countless women), but through the desire to sleep with her (this is just the desire to find one woman).' And you, Grandfather? With whom did you want to share your sleep? With the mother of your daughter or with Bice? Or is it possible that neither Bice nor Rosetta was 'unique' in your eyes?

Rome, 20 October 1934: You haven't come and you haven't written. What's happening? I beg you, please don't leave me so long without news. You can't imagine the extent to which your silence is a source of immense anxiety for me.

I knew it! I said to myself as I searched in vain for a letter or a card from my grandfather. It isn't true that time and distance do not have an impact on our feelings. Now that Arturo had become a father, he had forsaken poor Bice! Does that mean that paternal love is stronger than the love one can feel toward a woman or a man? Or are they incomparable feelings? And what happens if you have to choose?

Then I thought of the unresolved question of his appointment to the position of federal secretary of the Fascist Party of Lecce, and it occurred to me that something was amiss.

'Completely out of the question,' said my father when I tried to ask him if he thought his father could have cheated on his mother.

This is, incidentally, exactly what I would say if someone asked me if my father had ever cheated on my mother. It's inconceivable. But my father is nothing like Arturo. My father takes after his mother more, especially when it comes to feelings. As long as I have known him, my father has never been able to go with his feelings.

Rome, 27 October 1934: I finally received your letter and I am thrilled. I was so worried and pained by your long silence that I was ready to move heaven and earth to have news of you. I love you so much and I've become so attached to you that the mere thought of ever losing you brings tears to my eyes! But I want to tell you just one little thing, to whisper it in your ear. You know that I'm frank and that it's impossible for me not to say what I think. Well, I think, my dear, that you invented this whole business of being sick in order not to come to Rome. That it's a lie. A little white lie that will leave no trace, but a plain and simple lie, nevertheless.

I continued to react as if I were watching a film. And like Nanni Moretti, watching the final scene in *Doctor Zhivago*, screaming 'It's her! Turn around! Get her off the tram!' I find myself crying out, 'No, Bice! You shouldn't write that to him!' But only for a moment. Because after a few minutes, I changed my mind and told myself that she had done the right thing. I too thought this business of his being ill didn't hold water. What exactly did happen? Why didn't Arturo tell the truth? Why was he starting to lie to Bice too?

Campi, 6 November 1934: […] What I wrote was not a lie: I really was sick […] Next Monday, I'll be in Rome, as I promised. And then we will finally be able to let ourselves go to our passion. I'll be staying in Rome for four days, and we'll be together the whole time. How does that sound? But please send me your confirmation by telegram. I won't say anything else right now, since the time separating us is now practically nil.

Bice replied, asking Arturo to set the place and time for their meeting.

> *8 November: I'll leave you to imagine the immense joy that envelopes me at the thought of seeing you again, of spending a few days with you, of telling you so many things, of saying to you face-to-face what my pen cannot say, even when the heart speaks and the mind does not forget. [...] I have the impression that your coming is but a dream and I'd rather not harbour any delusions. I won't really believe it until I see you here before me. [...] We'll have to be extremely careful, because there are very ill-meaning people who are trying to hurt me by any means they can.*

So, she was the one this time to advise caution. I looked for my grandfather's answer, but I couldn't find any. There was only one other letter from Beatrice, dated 11 December 1934.

> *I thank you again for all your kindness and for all the small, thoughtful gestures toward me during your brief stay in Rome, and I am infinitely grateful to you. You are so good; I will remember forever everything you have done and continue to do for me. It is very rare in life to meet people like you. Only in difficult circumstances do you discover a person's heart and character.*

And then there were two postcards: 'I think of you all the time' (10 January 1935); 'I, too, send you my fondest regards' (13 February 1935).

What happened exactly? Apparently, Arturo did go to Rome. But what did he say to Bice? Did he tell her that their relationship was over? Or that they would see each other again from time to time? What happened then? Did Rosetta find out about it, or did Bice decide that it couldn't go on like that? Or was it my grandfather who lost interest in the end? Supposing that was true, what came of his appointment as federal secretary of the Fascist Party? Was it his wife who didn't allow him to accept the position in order to keep him by her side, or did she have nothing to do with it?

Even though this film stopped abruptly, I couldn't stop thinking about the love affair between my grandfather and Beatrice. I kept thinking that something did not add up. It couldn't have ended like that, I found myself repeating again and again. If Beatrice was just a mistress, why did Arturo name his eldest daughter after her?

There was one last postcard in the envelope yellowed with age. It dates to 27 August 1935. From Tivoli, Beatrice sent Arturo a picture of the Temple of the Sibyl: 'Fond regards, Bice (Riccardi Pharmacy, Piazza Veroli).'

Bice chose the Temple of the Sibyl rather than the much more famous Temple of Vesta. Which actually makes sense. After all, Vesta is the symbol of the home and hearth, everything that Bice could never have with my grandfather. So, it's up to Sibyl to shed light on her future: Will he ever come back to me? Will I ever be a mother?

I identified with Bice and I hated my grandfather, the family home, Rosaria and Ferruccio. Even though Ferruccio is my father, and even though I knew that if Arturo had chosen to live with Bice, I would not have been here today digging into his past like a grave robber. Coward. Traitor.

I imagined the monotony of Arturo's life in Campi with Rosetta. I imagined that this was the reason he accepted the job in Rome in 1933, perhaps thinking that it was the only way to further his career and not to find himself buried in the Salento. I imagined his passion and his desire to start from scratch. I imagined how tormented he must have felt when Rosetta announced that she was finally pregnant and asked him to come back home, but also his joy the day Rosaria Giulia Giuseppina Rosetta Beatrice was born. And then?

'And then?' I asked Jacques.

'How should I know?' he replied, shrugging his shoulders.

I showed him a postcard that I found among my grandfather's papers, a drawing depicting Sibyl gazing up at the starry sky. But it's not just a drawing. Inside two sheets of paper glued together, there is a wheel that turns; by the picture of Sibyl, there is a list of instructions for playing the game.

'Choose a question and then, at random, one of the numbers: Turn the wheel of chance and you will get your answer.

Does he love me? 1-4-8-12-16

Do I have rivals? 20-24-28-32

[...]

Is he faithful to me? 22-26-30-34-38'

I tried my hand at the game. I chose the first question and number 4, and 'madly' came up. I chose number 28 for the second question, and I got, 'No, you needn't worry'. I burst into laughter. Then I chose number 30 for the question about faithfulness and got, 'He is more faithful than you'. I smiled, and then I turned back to question Jacques again.

'Why do you think their love affair ended?'

'The rule of law must prevail.' Jacques was mocking me in quoting this old proverb. But then he added, 'I'm sorry, but how would you have wanted it to end? Your grandfather returned to Campi, his daughter was born and they lived happily ever after, right?'

My dear grandparents, did you really live happily ever after? Or was there a snag someplace, a veil, something left unsaid, that later became an avalanche that swept everything away? And how about that little girl born seven years after you were married? Why did she come just when Arturo had fallen in love with another woman? Grandfather, did you ever confess to your daughter that her fifth name was that of your mistress? Grandmother, what did you say when your husband suggested the name Beatrice? Did you know about the existence of Bice Serafini? Did you suspect anything at all? Is that why you became pregnant at that point? Or was it really Our Lady of the Rosary who performed a miracle? If Rosaria had not been born, would Arturo have returned to Lecce, or would he have remained in Rome?

'Did you know that your sister was named Rosaria Giulia Giuseppina Rosetta Beatrice?' I asked my father.

'What?'

'Rosaria like the Madonna of the Rosary, Giulia like your grandmothers, Rosetta like your mother. And then Beatrice.'

I watched him carefully as I said this. But he remained impassive. He didn't say, 'Beatrice?' He didn't even say, 'Who is Beatrice?' He simply dropped the subject.

I knew him too well not to suspect that the fifth name was not unfamiliar to him, but I did not insist. I did not want to picture when or how he might have heard mention of it...

My grandfather kept everything.

I found the documents of my father's enrolment starting in 1937 in the fascist youth organisations *Gioventù Italiana del Littorio* (GIL, Italian Youth of the Lictor) and the *Opera Nazionale Balilla.* I found Ferruccio's and Rosaria's school reports. I even found a small notebook in which Arturo had noted his son's weight: At birth, he weighed 3.95 kg; at one month, 5.05 kg; at three months, 7 kg; at six months, 9.15 kg; at one year, 11.25 kg. He noted that Ferruccio was weaned on 15 May 1938, that his first tooth came in on 26 August 1937 and that he stood without help for the first time on 15 June 1937. There is also a detailed account of an ear infection that my father had in 1938, then again in 1939, and in 1940 and in 1941, until they took him to Rome to see a renowned doctor.

My grandfather kept everything.

This man, who was in favour of amnesia for Italy, forgot nothing. Although there seem to have been many things about which he spoke to no one, perhaps because what mattered most to him in the end was his children. In a letter dated 25 December 1943, signed

Father Christmas, and addressed to his eldest daughter, he writes:

> *This year, because of the war, I was not able to bring you a lot of things. I was not able to bring little Ferruccio much either. I brought both of you exactly the same thing: album recordings with songs of the adventures of Pinocchio. I had very few copies, but I managed to reserve one for each of you, since my informant, Ching, told me that you have both been very, very good.*

My grandfather loved his children with the same heartwarming tenderness that I see in my brother today when he takes care of Jacopo. My brother is so much like my grandfather.

Does our given name condition us?

When I told my brother that the more I learnt about our grandfather, the more he made me think of him: The orderliness, the obsession, at times the anxiety, and then this very profound love for his children.

'You know I don't believe in genetics at all!' he replied simply.

But genetics has nothing to do with it. Neither do education or habits: Neither my brother nor I really actually knew our grandfather.

This time, it's really a matter of the unconscious, of unlikely and yet very powerful identifications. This time, it's a matter of a 'historical object', as some psychoanalysts say, that we carry inside us even in the absence of any memory whatsoever, and that drives us to turn what has preceded us into an event.

My grandfather kept everything.

He wanted amnesia for Italy, but he forgot nothing.

I thought of this again in seeing a photo of the Italian President Mattarella and the Slovenian President Borut Pahor. There they were on 13 July 2020, holding hands before the *foiba* of Basovizza, the sinkhole where Yugoslav partisans killed 2,000 Italians in 1945 and threw them into the abyss. A few minutes later, they did the same thing at the monument in memory of the four young anti-fascist Slovenes sentenced by the Special Tribunal for the Defence of the State created by Mussolini: 'History cannot be obliterated,' Sergio Mattarella told journalists. 'We can nurture it with resentment, or we can make it a shared heritage through remembrance and respect.'

Since Mattarella was elected President of the Republic, Italy has begun to better understand the importance of memory work and the need to come to terms with past. Mattarella was the first president to speak of the racial laws as a 'dark chapter', an 'indelible stain' and an 'infamous page' in our history.

'Conceived and written by Mussolini himself, they were met on all levels of Italian institutions, politics, culture and society with willingness, complicity or indifference,' he said in January 2018, on the occasion of the Day of Remembrance. 'With the cynical pen of propaganda Mussolini pretended to distance himself from Nazi anti-Semitism and created a slogan to reassure Italians and the rest of the world: "Discrimination does not mean persecution". But driving children out of schools, expelling Jews from the administration, forbidding them to engage in intellectual work, erasing Jewish names from books, plaques and even telephone directories and obituaries in newspapers constituted persecution of the worst kind.'

Only by coming to terms with its own history can Italy extricate itself from the deep-seated contradictions that characterise it. This is exactly the opposite of what my grandfather advocated for the nation but did not apply to his own life. For he may have wanted amnesia for Italy, but he cultivated memory with regard to his family.

He kept everything close to him. And so, despite the fire in the house in Campi, the boxes forgotten in the cellar of my father's cousins and the years that passed, nothing was lost.

This was a heritage of memory just waiting for me. Or at least, that is what I like to think.

Because not forgetting is the only way for me too to extricate myself from the contradictions that characterise my own existence.

I came back to Paris and resumed my life as before, even though my university courses were still being held online and I had no idea when I would be able to return to Campi, see my nephew again or visit my parents in Rome.

I came back to Paris and got to thinking about everything that had prevented me for years from undertaking this journey into the past of my family and my country.

I came back to Paris and continued reading and rereading everything I had written, telling myself that I was far from having discovered and understood everything.

Then I stopped tormenting myself.

Life is not a puzzle. I have to resign myself to that. I have to accept the fact that some pieces are gone and will never be found. I have to be content with the chapters or the fleeting moments that I have managed to reconstruct.

I went over everything I had written one last time. Then I went outside and called my father. I was walking in the Luxembourg Gardens while talking to him. I had my earphones on and I moved my hands as I talked.

At one point I may even have raised my voice because I saw someone turn around and stare at me. But maybe that was simply because I was speaking in Italian, plus I had walked around the same area of the garden six times already, passing by the same statues and the same people again and again.

I said to him: 'Do you remember when we read the short story by Oscar Wilde together, *The Selfish Giant*? Do you remember that my English teacher asked us to memorise some passages from it and I wasn't able to?

'*The Selfish Giant*, yes! But remind me what it was about. I can't quite remember.'

'It's about a giant who decides one day not to allow children to play in his beautiful garden. From that moment on it stayed winter in his garden, even when spring came. One day, because of a very small child, he came to understand that his selfishness was the cause of this never-ending winter. So, the giant allowed the children to play in his garden again, and spring returned, as if by miracle. Time went by, and the giant never saw that one little boy again. He grew weaker. Do you remember how many times we repeated this passage together? "Years went by, and the giant grew old and feeble"?'

My father said he remembered this. And he repeated the sentence, as he used to do, with an emphasis on the long 'ee' of 'feeble' – 'watch my mouth, Michela, and make a long 'ee' sound' – as if I were a child again and needed his help to speak English without an accent.

'Now I understand why this sentence touched you so much, Papa.'

Even though understanding does not mean forgiving. But this I didn't say. For even if I don't forgive him, I still love him.

My father remained silent for quite a while.

Then, 'You can talk all this over with your mother. She understands those things better than I do.'